Richard J. Hinton

Rebel Invasion of Missouri and Kansas,

and the campaign of the army of the border against General Sterling Price, in

October and November, 1864

Richard J. Hinton

Rebel Invasion of Missouri and Kansas,
and the campaign of the army of the border against General Sterling Price, in October and November, 1864

ISBN/EAN: 9783337385927

Printed in Europe, USA, Canada, Australia, Japan

Cover: Foto ©ninafisch / pixelio.de

More available books at **www.hansebooks.com**

REBEL INVASION

OF

MISSOURI AND KANSAS,

AND THE

CAMPAIGN

OF

THE ARMY OF THE BORDER,

AGAINST GENERAL STERLING PRICE,

IN OCTOBER AND NOVEMBER, 1864.

By RICHARD J. HINTON,
LATE CAPTAIN 2D KANSAS COL'D VOLS.

SECOND EDITION.

CHICAGO:
CHURCH & GOODMAN, 53 LASALLE STREET,
LEAVENWORTH, KANSAS:
F. W. MARSHALL,
1865.

Entered according to Act of Congress, in the year 1865,
BY CHURCH, GOODMAN & DONNELLEY,
In the Clerk's Office of the District Court of the United States,
For the Northern District of Illinois.

PRINTED BY
CHURCH, GOODMAN & DONNELLEY,
LA SALLE ST., CHICAGO.

CHICAGO TYPE FOUNDRY:
J. CONAHAN,
STEREOTYPER.

COX & DONOHUE,
BOOKBINDERS.

PREFACE.

The work, of which these words are introductory, is designed to be a full and impartial narrative of the stirring events which occurred in the campaign whose progress and results it tells. The author has not aimed at criticism, except those obvious remarks which naturally grow out of the body of works of this character. It has been his desire to do justice where it was due; not to give fulsome panegyric. Having participated in the operations recorded, with every opportunity of knowing all necessary details, as well as the reasons which actuated the policy and movements of those in command, the author hopes he has succeeded in his main purpose—that of telling plainly the history of an important campaign, and thereby adding a valuable contribution to the great work which shall one day tell the story of the Great Rebellion.

His secondary object—that of recording the services and sacrifices of our volunteers, and especially of the Militia of Kansas—he is hopeful of having properly accomplished.

CONTENTS.

CHAPTER I.
Introductory 3

CHAPTER II.
General Price crosses the Arkansas — Organization of the Rebel Army. 11

CHAPTER III.
Invasion of Missouri — Battle of Pilot Knob 15

CHAPTER IV.
Movements in the Department of Kansas — Proclamation of Martial Law 29

CHAPTER V.
Grand uprising of the People of Kansas 41

CHAPTER VI.
Affairs in the City and at Fort Leavenworth 49

CHAPTER VII.
Generals Curtis and Blunt take the field — Organization of Troops 56

CHAPTER VIII.
March to Lexington — Preparations at the Big Blue — Movements of Militia 73

CHAPTER IX.
Battle of Lexington 84

CHAPTER X.
Battle of the Little Blue 92

CHAPTER XI.
March of Rosecrans' Cavalry from Jefferson City to Independence 106

CHAPTER XII.
Battles on the Big Blue and State Line 122

CHAPTER XIII.
Battle of Westport 149

CHAPTER XIV.
General Pleasanton's Operations on the twenty-third 168

CHAPTER XV.
Pursuit of Price down the State Line 183

CONTENTS.

CHAPTER XVI.
Attack on the Mound — Battles of Marias des Cygnes and Mine Creek.. 197

CHAPTER XVII.
Engagements at the Little Osage and Charlot — March of Moonlight — Engagements at Mound City and Fort Lincoln — Rebel Camp on Drywood Creek — Ours at Fort Scott and Marmaton............ 220

CHAPTER XVIII.
Fort Scott during the Invasion and the Battles of the 25th — Martial law abolished, and Militia disbanded — Proclamations of the Governor. 240

CHAPTER XIX.
Pursuit from Fort Scott — Battle of Newtonia — General Rosecrans' Orders — Consequent abandonment of the Pursuit.............. 259

CHAPTER XX.
Resumption of Pursuit — Route of the Rebels — The Pea Ridge Battle-Field — Attack on Fayetteville — Gallant defense.............. 279

CHAPTER XXI.
From Fayetteville to the Arkansas River — Termination of the Pursuit — Storm on the Arkansas — General Orders................... 289

CHAPTER XXII.
The Homeward March — Incidents — Results of Campaign.......... 304

CHAPTER XXIII.
General Orders and Congratulations 313

APPENDIX.
In Memoriam... 322
Horatio Knowles 323
Daniel M. Brown — Dr. L. M. Shadwick — Joseph Stout — Warren Hawkins—Albert McGonigle 324
Wm. A. Delong—Emmet Goss—Orloff Norton...................... 325
Charles V. Hyde... 326
Rev. Richard Vernon... 327
John Miller—Elder Williams—G. L. Gove 328
James Nelson Smith.. 330
H. C. Covil... 332
Harvey G. Young—Daniel Handley—Nicholas Brown—George Grinold —McClure Martin—C. H. Budd................................ 333
Lou Selkin—Merrick D. Race 334
James Mayrers—Aaron Cook 335
David Fults 336
Major-General S. R. Curtis 339
Hon. James H. Lane 342
Brigadier-General John McNeil................................. 345
Battle of the Little Osage.................................... 348

ARMY OF THE BORDER.

CHAPTER I.

INTRODUCTORY.

WHILE east of the Mississippi River success crowned our arms during the entire current of the eventful year 1864, west thereof we were generally defeated: two splendidly equipped armies almost routed, each only saving themselves by great loss of material, as well as of men. At the same time, in a portion, at least, of the Trans-Mississippi region, over which our rule had most successfully re-established, by reverses to our arms the rebels succeeded, if not in reinstating themselves, at least in rendering our control precarious, and confining the Federal garrisons within the limits of their posts.

When 1864 opened upon the western scene of war, it looked on much of the States of Arkansas and Louisiana under control of our arms; on the rebel

Indians and their allies in the territory west of Arkansas, broken and discomfited; upon attempts to re-organize loyal state governments in the aforenamed states, and upon an apparently discouraged and defeated foe.

Major-General Banks commanded the Department of the Gulf, which included Louisiana and Texas. Major-General Fred'k Steele commanded the Department of Arkansas (which was included in the Division of the Mississippi, under General W. T. Sherman). Major-General Rosecrans that of Missouri; and Major-General S. R. Curtis that of Kansas. The latter comprised the State of Kansas, the Indian Territory and the Territories of Nebraska and Colorado. At this time General Banks was earnestly engaged in reconstructing the Louisiana State Government. In Arkansas the Union people were engaged in the same laudable task. Our armies in both States had been hitherto successful.

This was the position when, in March, the Red River expedition set forth under General Banks. In April following, a conjoint movement, or what was presumed to be such, was made by General Steele from Little Rock and Fort Smith, in the direction of Camden. The results of those ill-starred movements is now historic. It becames necessary to allude to to them, however, in order to make complete the position in which we stood at the time the rebel Lieut.-General Sterling Price made his last great raid—one which, in distance from base, extent of country traversed, and objects aimed at, was hardly less stupendous in character to those whose magnificent success have illumined with new lustre the name of General Sherman. The similitude ends, however, when success is named.

By the disastrous results of the spring campaigns under Banks and Steele, the rebel forces in their Trans-Mississippi Department, from the position of defense were enabled to assume the offensive. Our forces in the Department of the Gulf were at once concentrated by their new commander, General Canby, who was also intrusted with the direction of affairs in Arkansas and the Indian Territory, which latter region had been annexed to General Steele's department. The rebel forces numbered about 50,000 men. The Confederate General, Kirby Smith, in supreme command. Lieutenant-General Magruder commanded in Texas; General Dick Taylor in Louisiana; while General Sterling Price commanded what remained of the rebel Missouri army, consisting of Marmaduke's division of cavalry, Major-General Shelby's old brigade, the infantry under General Parsons, and the Arkansas rebel regiments under General Fagan. General Cooper had command of the rebel Indians, in the territory between the Red and Arkansas Rivers, assisted by a couple of Texas brigades, under Generals Gano and Maxy.

Price had about 10,000 veteran troops, well armed, equipped and clothed. Jackman, Dobbins, Brooks, and others were busily engaged bushwhacking and conscripting in all sections of Arkansas, except the immediate vicinity of the posts held by General Steele. During the summer he succeeded in conscripting about 8,000 men, a large number of whom were boys and old men, unfit for and incapable of withstanding the fatigues and hardships incidental to all military service; but especially so to that of the Trans-Mississippi Confederate armies with their ill-supplied quartermaster bureau. From the spoils of Red River and Camden, General Price received a good share of transportation, clothing, small arms, several Parrott guns; two captured at Pleasant Hill, La., and two from the 8th Indiana battery, Captain Rabb, captured at Poison Spring, near Camden, Ark.; four guns taken by Fagan at the Mark Mills, Ark., fight, and several howitzers, also taken in the same campaign.

During the summer, the utmost activity prevailed among the rebels in Western and Northern Arkansas. Our forces were stationed principally at Fort Smith and Little Rock. We had been compelled to withdraw the troops from all smaller stations. Nothing of importance, therefore, interfered with the perfecting, by General Price, of the army with which it was rumored he projected an invasion of and wintering in Missouri.

General Rosecrans found himself actively engaged in ferreting out and providing against the great rebel conspiracy which threatened, at one time during the summer of 1864, to plunge the States of Indiana, Illinois, as well as Missouri, into civil war. This treasonable organization, known as the "Order of American Knights," had received its impetus in Missouri; alike from Northern sympathizers and from the agents of General Price; as elsewhere in the Northwest, the impelling force was the Vallandigham Democrats. It is well established that the movements of Price were expected by those connected with the order. There is no doubt the great raider relied upon receiving aid from this source by movements not only in Missouri, but also in Illinois; and that through them he confidently hoped to revolutionize Missouri again and re-establish the Confederate State Government. What is known in the local military and political history of Missouri as the Paw-Paw rebellion, was, without doubt, originally intended to aid Price's movements. Its premature disclosure, however, prevented this, and caused its speedy suppression.

For months rumors were rife in sympathizing circles, and among the bushwhackers in Missouri that "Pap Price" (as the general is familiarly known by his admirers) would soon be in the state with a large army. It was generally credited by our troops stationed on the river and elsewhere in Arkansas, that the rebel general intended an advance northwards; yet this was hardly deemed possible by the distinguished soldier commanding at St. Louis. If General Steele knew or credited the rumor, it does not appear that he took action thereon. As for General Curtis, in command at Fort Leavenworth, fully occupied with the important duties entrusted to his inadequate forces, it is not surprising that he should have deemed it both monstrous and impossible that a rebel army could march unchecked in the slightest degree, for over two hundred miles beyond our advanced lines, into the very heart of our territory; not only without resistance, but almost unknown to the commanding officer of the department immediately concerned.

In Kansas, the military force looked miserably insufficient to successfully cope with the enemy, so soon to threaten the security of that state. The nomadic Indian tribes roaming near the important Santa Fe and California roads, had become suddenly and fiercely hostile, committing simultaneously savage atrocities and depredations upon life and property along, not only the overland routes, but the unprotected settlements in Kansas, Nebraska and Colorado.

To meet this emergency, as well as to guard the eastern and southern borders of Kansas, and protect the posts and depots of the army, General Curtis' force consisted of about 4,500 men. The vast territory and the long lines of inter-communication rendered the handling of this small force, for the objects to be accomplished, one of extreme difficulty.

The troops in the Department of Kansas consisted partly of the 1st and 3rd Colorado volunteer cavalry (the latter an hundred day regiment, since mustered out); a portion of the 1st Nebraska cavalry, Colonel Livingston; some three months Nebraska troops; a battalion of the 7th Iowa cavalry, and about 300 unassigned recruits of the 3rd Wisconsin cavalry. These troops were all employed upon the overland mail routes, and in protecting the Frontier and Colorado settlements, and were in themselves inadequate for that purpose. In Kansas itself were the 11th regiment Kansas Volunteer Cavalry, Colonel Thomas Moonlight; the 15th Kansas Volunteer Cavalry, Colonel Charles R. Jennison; a small battalion of the 3rd Wisconsin Cavalry, with a section of the 2nd Kansas Battery, at Fort Scott, which post was under command of Colonel Charles W. Blair, 14th Kansas Volunteer Cavalry; the 16th Kansas (at Fort Leavenworth and Northern Kansas;) a new cavalry organization just completed; and the 17th Regiment (a battalion of six companies, one hundred day men): these, with McLain's Independent Colorado Battery, and Captain Dodge's 9th Wisconsin Battery, constituted the entire volunteer force under command of General Curtis.

At the beginning of September and the date of Price's movement northward, Major-General Curtis was in the vicinity of Fort Kearney, with an hastily gathered force of volunteers and citizens, endeavoring to find the Indian enemy. Major-General Jas. G. Blunt, who had just assumed command of the District of Upper Arkansas (a command created from the region threatened by Indians in Western Kansas and Colorado, south of the Solomon River,) was at this time out beyond Fort Larned, in pursuit of a large force of warriors whom he met and defeated.

Major-General Sykes was in command of the District of Southern Kansas, with head quarters at Lawrence. This section was divided into three sub-districts under command of Colonels Jennison, Moonlight, and Blair. The supplies for Forts Gibson and Smith on the Arkansas, both for troops and Indian refugees, were mainly furnished from Fort Scott. The protection of route and trains engaged all the force stationed in South-Eastern Kansas. At this time great activity prevailed, owing to the constant alarm and danger to trains on our Southern border, created by the energy of the rebel General Gano, who was operating in the Cherokee nation, along the route to Fort Gibson. Such was the state of affairs in the Departments of Kansas, Missouri and Arkansas, at the time the rebel General commenced his northward march from South-Western Arkansas.

CHAPTER II.

GENERAL PRICE CROSSES THE ARKANSAS—ORGANIZATION OF THE REBEL ARMY.

LIEUTENANT-GENERAL STERLING PRICE, C. S. A., crossed the Arkansas River at Dardennelles, a village in Pope county, Arkansas, about equi-distant from Little Rock and Fort Smith, the two principal posts occupied by our troops. It is a position of military importance, and before the spring campaign of '64, was held by the 3d regiment Arkansas Volunteers.

The rebel army has been variously estimated at from 5,000 to 15,000 men. General Steele's first telegrams, announcing their advance, estimated them at 5,000, all mounted. He again reported it from 5,000 to 10,000, mostly infantry, and later, at 15,000 mounted men, with 20 guns.

Their operations showed the rebel army consisted, at the time of crossing, of about 18,000 armed men, nearly all of whom were mounted. Some three or four thousand recruits and conscripts were added in Northern Arkansas.

This force was organized into three divisions, under the command respectively of Brevet Major-Generals Fagan, Marmaduke and Joe Shelby.

Fagan's troops were in the main, veteran Arkansians. His brigades were commanded by Brigadier Generals Cabell, McRae, Slemmons, and Colonel Dobbins. Among the Colonels and Regimental Commanders, were Munroe, Hills, Gordon, Reeves, Baker, Crandall, Crawford, Witts, McGee and Anderson; Lieutenant-Colonels Reefe, Crabtree and Corcoran. The division had two Parrott guns, two rifled guns, made in Texas, six howitzers, and one inch-and-a-half rifled gun, used for picking off artilleryists, and said to be very effective; in all eleven.

The second division was commanded by Marmaduke, and consisted of the cavalry of the Missouri State Guard, an organization which, under Price, has from the beginning seen much service. Its brigade commanders were Brigadier Generals Clarke, Graham and Tyler. Its regimental commanders were Colonels Freeman, Lowe, Bristow, Green, Jeffries, Burbridge, Fauthers and Kitchen, with Majors Wood and Wolfe. It had four Parrott and James' rifled guns, captured on the Red River, and two or three light howitzers.

Shelby's division was composed mainly of the old bushwacking, raiding force of Southern Missouri, increased by a rigorous conscription in Northern Arkansas. The notorious partizan leader, Jeff. M. Thompson, commanded Shelby's old brigade, and the infamous guerilla, Colonel Jackman, commanded the other. Among the Colonels, were Smith, Hunter, Slayback, Coffey, Coleman and Schnable. Lieutenant-Colonels, Irwin and Elliott, with Major Shaw, and Captain Smith commanding the artillery, which consisted of six guns, two of them captured Parrotts. General Tyler was afterwards placed in command of a division, composed of the recruits and conscripts gathered in Missouri.

The route of this army in Northern Arkansas was through the counties of Pope, Van Buren, Searcy, Izard, Fulton and Lawrence. The rebel movements were unmolested and conducted in the most leisurely manner.

The contradictory intelligence which for two or three weeks reached St. Louis and Little Rock, served only to confuse Generals Rosecrans and Curtis. General Steele, who had been largely re-inforced by several thousand infantry, does not seem to have been very active. The rebels showed great activity in the neighborhood of our posts in Western Arkansas, and by demonstrations in the vicinity of Forts Smith, Gibson, at Cane Hill, Clarksville, Fayetteville, and along the supply route in the Indian Territory. General Gano moved along the latter line with two brigades of cavalry, one of Texans and the other of Indians, under Stand Waitie, the rebel Cherokee leader. The rebels, Colonel Brooks and Major Buck Brown, whose operations in Washington and Benton counties, Arkansas, had kept our troops at Fayetteville on the alert all summer, were reported at Clarksville, while other forces, marauding parties mainly, were reported at Cane Hill, Crawford county. By these means and this activity, our intelligence was confused, and the attention of our officers directed from the rebel line of march.

CHAPTER III.

INVASION OF MISSOURI—BATTLE OF PILOT KNOB.

General Curtis was encamped upon the Solomon River in Western Kansas, returning from an expedition against Indians, when Price crossed the Arkansas.

The despatch from Major-General Rosecrans suggested that their route northward was probably by way of Pilot Knob; whence they could overrun Southern Kansas, and join General Cooper in the Indian Territory.

The force under General Rosecrans was mainly new troops; most of the veteran regiments had been removed, a large portion to General Steele after the disasters of the previous spring. The commander in Missouri, warned, not of an expected rebel invasion, but by the Paw-Paw insurrection and the discovery of the Order of American Knights, had shortly before this period obtained authority to raise a number of provisional regiments for the period of twelve months. The organization of this force was under way, at the time Price's army entered the state at West Plains. These regiments and the state militia materially aided our subsequent success. At the same time the dispatch relative to the rebel advance was received, Colonel Blair at Fort Scott, Kansas, received dispatches from Colonel Wattles, 2nd Regiment Indian brigade, commanding at Fort Gibson, C. N., announcing that the rebels under Cooper, Gano and Maxy, were advancing through to the Choctaw Nation, with apparent intention of crossing the Arkansas. Colonel Wattles also reported Price's army at 15,000. General Curtis returned from the west on the 17th, and immediately commenced such preparations for defence as his very limited force would allow.

On the 19th of September a supply train for Forts Gibson and Smith, which left Fort Scott on the 12th, under Major Henry Hopkins, 2nd Kansas Cavalry, was attacked at Cabin Creek, Cherokee Nation, at midnight, by a rebel force under General Gano, numbering about 2,500, with several rifled guns. Our force consisted of one hundred and fifty cavalry, same of dismounted men (white), thirty mounted Cherokees and three hundred and thirty infantry (Indians); in all six hundred and ten. The enemy was held in check by four hundred of the escort from 1 P. M. to $7\frac{1}{2}$ A. M., when the rebel line advanced and ours was driven back, fleeing in disorder. They captured the train of three hundred wagons, about half belonging to Government, the balance, sutlers' and refugee supplies. The major portion of the train was burnt by the enemy. A number of our forces were killed, wounded and taken prisoners.

This event showed the perilous condition of the Southern border, with the small force at our disposal, and the activity of the enemy. It was a loss of great magnitude, depriving this supply route of its transportation, and put the garrisons on the Arkansas in danger of starvation. Reports were prevalent also, of Price's presence at Cane Hill, Arkansas.

On the 24th, Governor Carney was informed of the approaching danger, and requested to have the militia in readiness to co-operate for the defense of the State. Promises were made to the Governor, that, so far as possible, they should mainly be employed as garrisons, during the continuance of danger. On the night of the 24th, Gen. Rosecrans received information of the rebel advance into Missouri, by way of Poplar Bluffs and Bloomfield, through Butler and Stoddard counties.

Major General George Sykes, commanding the District of South Kansas, telegraphed on the 21st, a report of three thousand rebels marching on Fort Scott, and advised that Governor Carney call out the militia in the border counties. He also suggested the concentration of the 15th Regiment Kansas Volunteer Cavalry, at Fort Scott. Two companies of the 17th Regiment (100 days men,) Kansas Volunteers, were sent to Paola, under Lieutenant-Colonel Drake.

The Governor made a call upon the border militia as requested.

The telegraphic despatches came faster and still more contradictory from General Rosecrans at St. Louis, while nothing seemed definitely known of Price's movement, though his army at this time, was within a few miles of the south line of Missouri.

On the 24th, General Rosecrans telegraphed General Curtis, "that he does not credit" General Steele's dispatches that "Price with 5,000 to 10,000 mounted infantry, and seventeen pieces of artillery, was at Pocahontas on the 22d. On the 25th he found reason to believe "that Price is north of the Arkansas line in South Missouri." On the next day, that his "present" impression is, that Price will move toward Jefferson City, between Rolla and Lebanon, and pass out towards Kansas. He advised against any movement too far South, but urged waiting till Price's strength and intentions in Missouri were developed. On the 28th, he was again incredulous. Shelby had been reported at Pocahontas, and was known to be in the vicinity of Frederickstown, Mo. Under date of the 26th, Price and Shelby were seen together, between Pocahontas and Curent River. In Rosecrans' opinion, Shelby seemed to be operating to draw troops off to the south-east. Price had a train of from three to four hundred wagons, principally loaded with ammunition and ordnance stores. His army lived on the country and conscripted rigorously as they moved. It is evident that General Rosecrans believed the rebels only intended a great raid up to the central region, keeping his main force south of the Osage River, and then westward to Kansas, joining Cooper and Gano for a raid therein.

Brigadier General Sanborn, was in command of the District of South-west Missouri, with head-quarters at Springfield. The force in his district (cavalry), consisted of about 2,000 men, mainly Missouri State Militia; it also embraced the 2d Arkansas Volunteer Cavalry, under Col. Phelps, Jr.

The district of which Rolla is head-quarters, was under command of Brigadier General John McNeil, well known for his radical and active policy as a soldier, and his uncompromising loyalty as a citizen. Rolla is the terminus of the south-west branch of the Missouri Pacific Railroad, and one of the most important depots in that State. It has been the object of many efforts on the part of rebel raiding forces, and appeared to be again threatened by this movement. General McNeil prepared his small force for a vigorous defence. The post is well fortified.

Brigadier General Thomas Ewing, Jr., was in command of the District of South-east Missouri, head-quarters of which are at St. Louis, and in which is included the Iron Mountain Railroad, with the famous Arcadia Valley and the posts of Pilot Knob, St. Genevieve, Cape Giradeau, New Madrid, and others upon the Mississippi River. The rebels marched through this district, in the counties of

Butler, Stoddard, Wayne, Madison, and Iron, where was the terminus of the Iron Mountain Railroad, at Pilot Knob.

During the early preparations to meet Price, General Rosecrans had succeeded in temporarily detaining two brigades of the veteran 17th corps, under General A. J. Smith, then passing down the Mississippi River to Memphis. They were landed at Jefferson Barracks, below St. Louis. On the 24th, General Ewing was ordered to take the 2d Brigade, patrol and garrison the Iron Mountain Road

The enemy were reported at Fredericktown, Madison county. General Ewing proceeded to Pilot Knob, held by Major James Wilson, 3d M. S. M. All the troops stationed in the Third Sub-District had been withdrawn and concentrated here. Ewing's instructions from Gen. Rosecrans were to have Major Wilson hold the post against detachments, but evacuate if Price's army should appear. The entire force concentrated under General Ewing was 1,051 volunteers and one hundred and fifty citizens, enough to man the works, which were quite strong.

Pilot Knob is eighty-six miles south of St. Louis. It lies in a plain of three hundred acres, with Cedar and Rock mountains to the North, Pilot Knob to the East, and Shepherd mountain on the South and West. These are from five to six hundred feet high, rising abruptly from the valley and covered with rocks, gnarled oaks and undergrowth. The slopes of Shepherd mountain are accessible. A creek flows along its base, and through a gap between it and Pilot Knob, into a larger valley beyond, in which is the town of Ironton. Throug this gap runs the Fredericktown road, passing out of the larger valley by what is called "Shut-in-Gap." These valleys are known as Arcadia. The position is not considered defensible against a large force with serviceable artillery. Fort Davidson, defensive work lying on the plain south of the village, is about six hundred yards from the Knob, six hundred from Shepherd's mountain, and one thousand from the gap at Stout's creek. It mounted four thirty-two pound seige guns and three twenty-four pound howitzers. During the night preceding the attack, six pieces of field artillery were mounted—all *en barbette*.

General Ewing reached Pilot Knob at noon, September 26th. Strong reconnoitering parties being sent out, met Price's advance at "Shut-in-Gap." They were driven back to Ironton, where a stand was made till night. At midnight it was evident the enemy were in large numbers, their column having been all the night moving in strong force into the larger valley. Believing the advantage of delaying the enemy's northward march would be great, Ewing determined on a stubborn resistance. He forwarded by railroad all stores not needed; sent off the rolling stock and all empty Quarter-Master wagons. Telegraphic communication was kept open all night with General Smith at De Soto. The battle commenced at daylight on the 27th, and was obstinately fought all day, our well-served artillery, and the deadly fire of our small arms, driving the rebels back every time they ventured to attempt an assault. Two divisions, General Fagan's and Marmaduke's, were engaged. Both suffered terribly, as must needs be in an attempt to cross an open plain of three hundred acres, from the fire of eleven well-served guns, and the musketry fire of a thousand men. Marmaduke's Division made a charge from the south and west, but were broken and disordered, both by the inequalities and our heavy fire, before they reached the plain. Most of the assaulting force took cover in the creek bed, from which they kept up an incessant fire. Only about one hundred ventured on assault, but were driven back before reaching the ditch.

Simultaneously with Marmaduke's movements, General Fagan marched over Pilot Knob to the East. Stronger, and less disturbed by our fire, this Division swept back disordered, or cut off, the companies which had held the town and part of the mountain side. Their own lines became disordered by our fire, but hastily reformed, were led by General Cabell in person. We opened, as they came in sight, at four hundred yards, and with grape and canister from seven pieces. The rebels moved gallantly, but were confused, broken and swept down by our well-directed and destructive fire. The advance had reached the ditch, when the whole force fled, leaving a large number of killed and wounded. While the assault progressed, a large cavalry force was sent to occupy the Mineral Point Road, over which was the most available line of retreat for Ewing and his gallant troops. Prisoners stated that the enemy numbered 12,000 men with 10 guns, Shelby's Division having gone from Fredericktown to Farmington, Francois County, north-east of Pilot Knob. General Ewing, finding himself unable to hold the mountain sides, without which the works would be untenable, determined to evacuate. The Potosi (Washington Co.) Road was the only one now open. At midnight preparations began, and before daybreak the entire command was on its road North. The magazine was blown up about an hour before day, the enemy being then at Ironton, busily engaged in making fascines and scaling ladders for the assault, confident that General Ewing was hemmed in. In the meanwhile Shelby had moved over to Potosi the evening before. Price ordered Shelby down to join in the attack. Learning of this, General Ewing left the Potosi Road, and moved by that through Webster, towards Rolla, in a direction almost due West. A small squad struck Shelby's advance at Caledonia, killing several. This induced that commander to halt two miles north of the village to give us battle. Several hours were thus lost to them of which Ewing took advantage to press his retreat. Marmaduke left the Knob at 8 A. M., and joined Shelby in the pursuit. At sundown our forces reached Webster, having marched thirty-one miles, and rested till midnight. It was determined to march to Leesburg on the South branch of the Pacific Railroad, about thirty miles East of Rolla. The road to the latter place was open to cavalry movements, while by the Leesburg road General Ewing had the advantage (protecting his flanks) of a spur in the Ozark Hills, separating the Huzzah and Courteois rivers, and the gorge of the Huzzah, walled by precipitous cliffs. Besides, to Leesburg (Harrison) was but thirty-five miles; to Rolla, fifty-five. A detachment of ten men under Captain Dills, 10th Kansas, was sent forward to Franklin, to telegraph to General Rosecrans at St. Louis, and to General McNeil at Rolla, informing them of the situation.

Our little column, after marching through the night, were overtaken by the enemy at eight on the morning of the 29th. Major Williams, 16th Kansas, Acting A. D. C., was placed in command of the rear, and by occasional rounds of grape and canister kept the enemy in check, making good the retreat. The skirmishing was constant until within four miles of Harrison. We then entered a high sweep of gently rolling woodland, and had to fight doggedly thereafter for every step we gained.

Harrison was reached just after dark, the march of sixty-six miles being made in thirty-nine hours. The position was naturally strong, being on the crest of a ridge, with no timber for two hundred yards to obstruct the range. A railroad cut sheltered the horses. A large number of ties made into breastworks, and the adjacent houses, afforded a good means of defense. The wearied command had barely time to form, when an assault was made, which was gallantly repulsed. Just then the Eastern train arrived with cars enough to move the troops. They were placed on board, and were about to start for St. Louis, when the stations north and south of the position were seen in flames. The night was then spent in fortifying. On the 30th the enemy appeared in force, making demonstrations throughout the day as if to assault. The defence was maintained by musketry, less than thirty rounds to the gun remaining with the field pieces, which was reserved for the moment of assault, or the emergencies of a further retreat. The day passed in fighting and unremitting labor on the defense. At night another assault was made and repulsed. At midnight a messenger was sent to Rolla for help, and Lieutenant-Colonel Maupin, accompanied by Captain Schenck and Lieutenant Fletcher, sent to Franklin to advise General Rosecrans of our position, and endeavor to rally and bring back some mounted militia, our cavalry being completely exhausted. The messenger reached Rolla, but Colonel Maupin and companions failed, barely escaping capture.

The morning of October 1st opened anxiously. The skirmishing was renewed vigorously. The enemy thoroughly reconnoitered our position, and made every preparation to capture the heroic

3

command. General Shelby, who commanded the rebel force, evidently respected the pluck exhibited by General Ewing, and hesitated, letting—I would, wait upon I dare not. At two P. M. the enemy withdrew, and at four, Lieutenant Colwel Beveridge, 17th Illinois Cavalry, arrived from Rolla with five hundred men. Strong pickets were immediately posted on the roads occupied by the enemy, and towards midnight General Ewing withdrew in the direction of Rolla, leaving a hundred men to reinforce the pickets, and destroy the few stores left. The infantry were left at Rolla as garrison, and the cavalry turned over to General McNeil, who, on the 4th, marched to Jefferson City; General Ewing, with a small escort, passing around the rear of the enemy to St. Louis.

Thus ended the brief but brilliant services of General Ewing in the campaign against General Price. The defence of Pilot Knob, retreat to and defence of Harrison, are in themselves events which deserve great credit. The result was also good. It delayed the rebel march, and enabled all concerned in defeating them, to gather more force and better arrange their plans. The gallant action of General Ewing in all probability saved St. Louis. The delay caused in the rebel march enabled our forces to effect a junction there and prevent its capture. Our loss was about one hundred and fifty killed and wounded, and fifty captured and paroled. The rebel loss is estimated at 1,500. This appears from the evidence of Surgeon T. W. Johnston, left in charge of our wounded. At Ironton, there afterwards fell into our hands, Colonel Thomas, General Fagan's Chief of Staff, three Majors, seven Captains, twelve Lieutenants, and two hundred and four enlisted men, representing seventeen regiments and batteries. The balance of the wounded were sent South under escort of Colonel Rain's Regiment. Those in the hospital were all dangerously, many of them mortally, wounded.

In the meanwhile, General Curtis was straining every nerve. Upon the 2d of October, General Sykes was directed to concentrate troops at Olathe, gathering such of the militia as he could in that vicinity. The 2d Colorado Volunteer Cavalry were at Independence, making preparations to march to the Department of Kansas. Colonel Ford was directed to move to a point near Paola, Colonel Blair at Fort Scott, Colonel Jennison at Mound City, and Colonel Moonlight, were directed to concentrate all their forces. Bushwhackers were bolder in North Missouri and the section contiguous to Kansas.

CHAPTER IV.

MOVEMENTS IN THE DEPARTMENT OF KANSAS—PROCLAMATION OF MARTIAL LAW.

On the 2d of October, General Rosecrans reported to General Curtis, that the rebel army was moving west, and had intersected the railroads south-west and west of St. Louis, the south-west branch at Franklin, and the Pacific Road at Washington. Both points are in the county of Franklin, the one next west of St. Louis, and each seventy miles from that city.

Shelby, after withdrawal from Ewing's front, had proceeded north-east along the line of the road, destroying bridges and other property, until reaching Franklin, where he united with the other divisions, which meanwhile, had marched northward along the line of the Iron Mountain Road, destroying everything valuable, consuming all supplies, and conscripting all the semi-secessionists, and as many Union men as they could lay their hands on. By the time Price reached Missouri River, at Washington, there can be no doubt the rebel force had increased about four thousand. Thus, from the time they left the Arkansas River, of the eighteen thousand men who crossed at Dardennelles, the statements of rebel prisoners, as well as of Union spies, scouts and prisoners, unite in saying that only 15,000 were armed, and that arms of different kinds and character were obtained by the time they reached Washington, to indifferently equip five or six thousand more. The arms used by their veteran troops were of the best character, mainly Enfield rifles, obtained through Mexico from England.

By the movement along the lines of railroad, Price was enabled to throw all the force concentrated at St. Louis, several days march to his rear. This included the two brigades (veterans) which General A. J. Smith had landed in obedience to orders, as also other troops, that, under General Mower, had been sent to the assistance of Rosecrans, The latter believed that St. Louis was the prize sought by the daring raider.

Jefferson City, the State capital, was in the greatest danger. Brigadier-General Clinton B. Fisk, commanding the District of North Missouri, headquarters at St. Joseph, rapidly concentrated what force he had and could spare from posts necessary to be protected, and threw himself into Jefferson City. Brigadier-General Brown, commanding the Central District, head-quarters at Warrensburg, Johnson County, had previously assumed command there with all his available force, consisting of less than 2,000 enrolled militia. General Fisk took command, and General Curtis immediately opened communication with him, the telegraph to St. Louis having been destroyed by the rebels. General McNeil also united his forces (cavalry), after relieving General Ewing from his perilous position at Leesburg. This was on the 5th of October. General Sanborn reached the same point next day from Springfield. The force at Jefferson City then numbered 6,000. Four thousand were cavalry, and with eight guns and with the addition of Winslow's Brigade of the 17th Army Corps, formed the Provisional Cavalry Division commanded by Major-General Alfred Pleasanton, in the subsequent pursuit of Price, and the battles of the border.

In the meanwhile the rebels were steadily advancing westward, destroying, foraging and conscripting as they marched; General Rosecrans was making cautious movements out of St. Louis. The forces gathered at Jefferson City were resisting strenuously the movements of Price, while General Curtis, in Kansas, was actively employed in working, preparing and counselling. October 4th, an order was issued forbidding the transit of boats below Kansas City. Colonel Ford, at Independence, was untiring and energetic, keeping stations at Hickman's Mills and Pleasant Hill, while scouting thoroughly to the east.

Colonel Thomas Moonlight, commanding the

Northern Sub-District of the District of South Kansas, made a call on Brigadier-General Fishback, K. S. M., for two regiments of State Militia to assemble at Olathe without delay.

The notorious guerilla, Bill Anderson, who had operated along the line of the North Missouri Road, kept North Missouri in a continual ferment. During the first week in October, he attacked several trains on the Hannibal & St. Joseph Railroad, robbing the passengers, and committing other depredations.

On the 3d the rebels held Hermann, an important German settlement on the river, where they captured a train and three locomotives. Colonel Chester Harding, Jr., 43d Missouri Infantry Volunteers, with four hundred men, left St. Joseph on the 4th, on the steamer West Wind, with the intention of proceeding to Jefferson

The Governor of Kansas, in response to a request for the calling out of State Militia, asked that a written demand should be made upon him. This request was promptly complied with on the 4th inst., when it was known that Jefferson City was in peril. On the 6th, General Rosecrans was urged to push his force in rear of the enemy, as delays were disastrous.

Colonel Ford then held the advanced posts of the Department of Kansas, and the ones from which information, it was certain, would first come. General Curtis hoped the rebels might still be checked at the Gasconade and Osage Rivers, and to this end counselled General Brown, at the capital of Missouri, to burn the bridges on those streams. Eight companies of the 2d Colorado were at Pleasant Hill, under the Colonel, two at Independence, under Captain Moses, and two at Kansas City, under Major Pritchard.

General Fisk telegraphed on the 6th, that he held the enemy at the Moreen, upon the road to Castle Rock, and that no force was pressing their rear. Our troops from St. Louis marched in a leisurely manner considering the imminent peril ahead, and the obvious advantage to be gained by attacking the rebels at or near the Osage River, where the force in Jefferson City could co-operate. General Curtis deemed this the proper action to be taken. Governor Carney was kept constantly advised as intelligence was received, and was urged to hasten the call for the militia. Naturally disliking to take the citizens of a whole State from their peaceful avocations, this was not promulgated until longer delay would have been fatal.

The 7th and 8th of October passed. Sharp fighting was reported by General Fisk in front of Jefferson City; our forces withdrawing to the trenches. The telegraph lines between Sedalia and Lexington were cut on the evening of the 8th, the guerilla Anderson having been reported the previous day at Lexington, with five hundred men. The same day all the wires were cut east of Pleasant Hill, indicating the westward advance of the rebels.

On the 7th of October, Major Samuel S. Curtis, 2d Colorado Cavalry, A. D. C. to General Curtis, took possession of the steamer Benton for Government purposes. Three Companies of the 43d Infantry Missouri Volunteers, under Major Davis, were on board. Three more companies were on the steamer West Wind, Colonel Chester Harding being in command. Major Curtis was directed to proceed with them to Jefferson City.

On the 8th, the following despatch was received:

FORT SCOTT, Oct. 10.
To MAJOR-GENERAL CURTIS:
Lamar was burned last night entire—not a house left. Supposed to be done by a large force of bushwhackers. Lamar is forty six miles south-east of here.
(Signed) C. W. BLAIR, Col.

The peril being imminent, an urgent letter was sent by General Curtis to the Governor, which was responded to by that functionary in the following proclamation:

No. 53.
STATE OF KANSAS, EXECUTIVE DEPARTMENT, }
TOPEKA, Oct. 8, 1864. }

The State is in peril! Price and his rebel hosts threaten it with invasion. Kansas must be ready to hurl them back at any cost.

The necessity is urgent. The extent of that necessity the subjoined communications from Major General CURTIS to me will establish.

HEADQUARTERS, DEPARTMENT OF KANSAS, }
FORT LEAVENWORTH, Oct. 5, 1864. }
His Excellency, Governor Thomas Carney:
The rebel forces under Gen. Price have made a further advance westward, crossing the Gasconade, and are now at

the railroad bridge on the Osage, about fifteen miles below Jefferson City. Large Federal forces about St. Louis and below tend to drive him towards Kansas. Other motives also will induce his fiendish followers to seek spoils and vengeance in this State. To prevent this, and join in efforts to expel these invaders from the country, I desire that you will call out the entire militia force, with their best arms and ammunition, for a period of thirty days. Each man should be provided with two blankets or a buffalo robe for comfort, and a haversack for carrying provisions. No change of clothing is necessary. I want this force assembled on the border, mainly at Olathe, as soon as possible. For that purpose let farmers' teams, with provisions and forage, be employed to hurry them forward. I will do all in my power to provide provisions and public transportation, but hope every man will be as self-sustaining as possible, and ready to join me in privations, hardships and dangers to aid our comrades in Missouri in destroying these rebel forces before they again desolate the fair fields of Kansas. It is necessary to suspend business and labor until we are assured our property and earnings are not within the grasp of unscrupulous marauders and murderers.

Confidently believing, Governor, that your Excellency and all loyal citizens will concert with me in the propriety of this very important demand, and give me your hearty co-operation and assistance. I have the honor to be, your very obedient servant,

R. S. CURTIS,
Maj. Gen. Com'dg Department.

UNITED STATES MILITARY TELEGRAPH,
FORT LEAVENWORTH, Oct. 8, 1864.

To GOVERNOR CARNEY:

The line is now cut this side Sedalia. This indicates a rebel move by some body west or south. Hurry the militia. R. S. CURTIS, Maj. Gen.

UNITED STATES MILITARY TELEGRAPH,
FORT LEAVENWORTH, Oct. 8, 1864.

To GOVERNOR CARNEY:

I request that you issue the call. Let the Militia turn out. If not needed, they will of course be discharged. Their call and collection would enable us, at least, to give an impetus to Price's departure. In your prompt responses to my requests heretofore, I am sure we have saved the State from desolation. Let us do it now. The enemy is now near Sedalia, and a fight is expected there to-night. They have burned Syracuse, Lamine and Otterville depots to-day. You see, they seem moving steadily westward. Delay is ruinous. R. S. CURTIS, Maj.-Gen.

Kansas, rally! You will do so as you have always promptly done, when your soil has been invaded. The call this time will come to you louder and stronger, because you know the foe will seek to glut his vengeance upon you.

Meet him, then, at the threshold and strike boldly; strike as one man against him.

Let all business be suspended. The work to be done now is to protect the State against marauder and murderer. Until that is accomplished we must lead a soldier's life, and do a soldier's duty.

Men of Kansas, rally! One blow, one earnest, united blow, will foil the invader and save you. Who will falter? Who is not ready to meet the peril? Who will not defend his home and the State?

To arms, then! To arms and the tented field, until the rebel foe shall be baffled and beaten back.

THOMAS CARNEY, Governor.

N. B.—Major-General Deitzler will lead the brave men of Kansas and issue the necessary orders. Commanding officers of brigades and battalions will see that their respective commands are in readiness for immediate service.

THOMAS CARNEY, Governor.

This was followed by an order from the General in command of the State militia, arranging the places of rendezvous, etc.

In pursuance of this call of the Governor, the militia of Kansas will turn out and rendezvous immediately, as follows:

HEAD-QUARTERS, DEPT. KANSAS STATE MILITIA, }
TOPEKA, KANSAS, Oct. 9, 1864. }

General Order, No. 54.

In pursuance of the order of the Commander-in-Chief, of the 8th inst., the militia of Kansas will turn out and *rendezvous, immediately*, at the points indicated below:

Doniphan, Brown, Nemaha and Marshall counties, at Atchison, under Brigadier General Byron Sherry.

Atchison, Leavenworth, Jefferson, Jackson, Pattawatomie, Riley, Davis, Waubaunsee, Shawnee, Douglas and Johnson counties, at Olathe, under Brigadier-General M. S. Grant.

Wyandotte, at Wyandotte, under Major E. S. Hubbard.

Miami, Franklin, Osage, Morris and Lyon counties, at Paola, under Brigadier-General S. N. Wood.

Bourbon, Allen and Woodson counties, at Fort Scott.

Commanders of brigades and regiments will promptly prepare their respective commands for active service for thirty days, unless sooner discharged, and see that each man is supplied with two blankets, a tin cup, knife and fork, and a haversack; and, also, a coffee pot and frying pan for every five men.

Let each regiment or detachment bring its own transportation and all the rations possible, *but there must be no delay on any account.* The General Government will undoubtedly pay all proper charges for such transportation and supplies, and will furnish rations and forage as far and as soon as possible, at the points indicated in this order.

Let each man come with such arms as are at hand and a full supply of ammunition. As this campaign will be a short one, no change of clothing will be necessary.

Until further orders, the head-quarters of the militia will be at Olathe, to which point all returns and communications will be sent. By order of

GEO. W. DEITZLER,
Maj. Gen., K. S. M.

JOHN T. MORTON, A. A. G.

Both orders were embraced in one from Department head-quarters, under date of the 9th, and which concluded as follows:

General Orders, No. 53.

All Federal Officers in this Department, will aid in giving circulation and success to this effort to concentrate troops for immediate service.

Quarter-masters and Commissaries, will aid to the utmost of their abilities, to have requisite provisions accumulated as fast as possible.

An earnest and united movement should animate officers and men, volunteers and militia.

Let business and personal strife be suspended; partisan discussions and political animosities be avoided; and instead of impatience, fault-finding and detraction, too common among raw recruits, let every man display the fortitude, patience and endurance which distinguish the patriotic soldier engaged in the defence of his home and his country.

The sooner this call is met, the more certain will be its success; and the General earnestly appeals to soldiers and citizens, to unite all their moral and physical energies in this effort to stifle the fiendish hordes that again threaten the people of Kansas and the peace of our country.

By command of Major-General Curtis,
C. S. CHARLOT,
Assistant Adjutant-General.

The annexed dispatch was sent to General Sykes, and all commanding officers in the State:

"The Governor has called out the entire militia of the State. I want this given the widest circulation and the most prompt action.
"S. R. CURTIS, Maj. Gen."

The same day reports were received of the taking of Lexington, and that Independence was threatened. This was by conscripting parties from Shelby's Division. Major-General Blunt, returned from his Indian expedition, reported to head-quarters, and was ordered to Olathe for orders, reporting his arrival by telegraph. Major-General Sykes' health was such that he could not stand the fatigue of the impending campaign, and even General Curtis' rendering it probable that he too might break down, the necessity of a younger and more active man was apparent.

General Sykes not liking the ordering of General Blunt to Olathe for the the purpose of field operations, asked to be relieved, which was done, and General Blunt was placed in charge of that district. He assumed command by telegraph upon the 11th inst.

Captain Moses, 2d Colorada, reported a small force threatening Independence. Quite an excitement was created at Lawrence on the 9th, which was caused by the accidental discharge of firearms. On the 10th, the work of fortifying Leavenworth was commenced. It was determined by General Curtis, in order to secure unity of operation and harmony in management of the forces called out, to to proclaim martial law throughout the State, and at the same time call into active service those not reached by the Governor's call:

   Head-Quarters, Department of Kansas,
  Fort Leavenworth, Kansas, Oct. 10, 1864.
    General Orders, No. 54.

The better to carry out the object of the Governor's Proclamation, issued this morning, and to secure prompt and united military organization and action, martial law is proclaimed to extend throughout the State of Kansas, and the country occupied by the troops moving therefrom, and all men, white or black, between the ages of eighteen (18) and sixty (60), will arm and attach themselves to some of the organizations of troops, for temporary military service.

In all the principal cities and towns, business houses will close as directed by the Governor's Proclamation, except where General Officers may give leave to such houses and special establishments as may be considered necessary for the public subsistence and health.

As this order is only designed to continue while danger of invasion is apprehended, the proper functions of civil officers will not be disturbed, and especially Courts of Justice and their processes will not be interrupted by the military authorities.

All troops, volunteers and militia, are clothed with the powers, and are subject to the duties and penalties prescribed in the Articles of War, and soldiers and citizens must expect very summary punishment of crime, and burning, robbing and stealing in the field will be severely and promptly punished. Private property and peaceable citizens must be protected. Our object is Price and his followers. His forces are now reported as retreating from Jefferson City in this direction. My advance to meet him is already moving. Let troops of every organization press forward to join in his repulse and pursuit.

By command of Major General Curtis.

C. S. CHARLOT,
Assistant Adjutant-General.

[OFFICIAL.]

The same day the latest received from General Rosecrans was as follows:

HEAD-QUARTERS, ST. LOUIS,
Oct. 10.

Price's movements are not known, but he has avowed his intention to go to Leavenworth. If he will try this, it will enable our columns under Mower and Smith and our cavalry to get between them and the Osage, and they will suffer. They spread and stretch out for subsistence; therefore your cavalry can forcibly strike the heads of their columns and hurt and retard their march. The telegraph lines are so interrupted it will be difficult to communicate with you.

(Signed)   W. S. ROSECRANS,
Major-General.

Hon. Jas. H. Lane, United States Senator, who had for some days been in consultation with General Curtis, having, with his usual sagacity, perceived the great peril of the State, now tendered his services, which were accepted in the following order, assigning various duties to officers who had reported for duty:

HEADQUARTERS, DEPARTMENT OF KANSAS,
FORT LEAVENWORTH, KANSAS, Oct. 10, 1864.

General Orders, No. 55.

The following temporary assignments to duty are published to the command. They will be obeyed and respected accordingly.

I. Major F. E. Hunt, Chief Paymaster, is also appointed Acting Aid-de-Camp, and will take charge and command of all artillery in and near the county of Leavenworth, consistent with the general arrangements of District Commanders, Generals Blunt and Davies.

II. Major Henry Almstedt, in addition to his duties as Additional Paymaster, will report to Major F. E. Hunt for artillery duty.

III. Hon. Jas. H. Lane, having tendered his services to the Major-General Commanding, they are accepted, and he is assigned to duty as Volunteer Aid-de-Camp.

IV. Captain James L. Rafferty, 2nd Kansas Colored, having reported for duty, will take charge of the general organization and command of persons of African descent; all of proper age and ability are included in the proclamation, and will be organized as other troops for immediate service.

V. Captain J. M. Mentzer, 2nd Kansas Volunteers, cavalry, reports being here *en route* and unable to reach his command. He will report for temporary duty to Brigadier-General T. A. Davies, commanding District North Kansas.

VI. Rev. J. B. McAfee, Chaplain 2nd Kansas Colored, having reported for duty, will have charge of Contrabands in the field, and will also report to Captain Rafferty as Acting Adjutant in the organization of troops of African descent. By command of Major-General Curtis.

C. S. CHARLOT,
Assistant Adjutant-General.

CHAPTER V.

GRAND UPRISING OF THE PEOPLE OF KANSAS.

Never was there heartier response to a demand of such a character, than that of the citizens of Kansas to the call of the Federal and State authorities. In the history of the present war no similar instance occurs. Rebel armies have invaded other loyal States. Twice have the veterans of Lee entered the State of Pennsylvania. The daring partisan, John Morgan, galloped through one half of Ohio and Indiana. Kentucky has been debatable ground over and over again. Maryland, like Missouri, has been fought for, and over, by contending armies.

For four years the people of Kansas had stood, a wall of fire, round about their border. Not only sending more troops in proportion to population than other States, but compelled also, from her exposed position, to do duty at home; a large body of her citizens have constantly been under arms for the protection of the eastern and southern borders. The calls have been frequent—the danger often imminent. Peril waited by every man's door, and invasion was the skeleton at many a farmer's fireside. Every border cabin has its tale of suffering and sacrifice, while the waste places in Lawrence yet bring brooding memories unto all. Nor was it alone on the East and South that the dark days of warfare rested like a thunder cloud. Along the long line of sparse settlements upon the western frontier dwelt the haunting terror of hostile Indians. For months the horrors of savage warfare had been added to the desolation of civil strife, with its worst concomitants of guerilla and partisan atrocities. As along the eastern border the militia stood sentinel to watch the murderous bushwhacker, so upon the western frontier, the settler—half farmer and half hunter—did a ranger's duty in guarding the scattered cabins which were slowly feeling their way out over the plains and along the valleys, until they could clasp hands with the mountain settlements.

Thus exposed, and thus wearied, though still prepared, the settlers sprang to arms with a wonderful unanimity, which set the nerves tingling and made the blood run like flame. The order flew from one end of the State to the other. Each man vied in rapidly communicating the imperious demand. Flaming, like the Highlanders' ancient symbol—the cross of fire—the cry, "To Arms," pealed over the prairies, along the streams, in every workshop, and met reply in every town and hamlet. The roads were lined by men, who, leaving the plow and plane, axe and flail, reaper and thresher, from every quarter were pouring to the rendezvous appointed for the different regiments.

From the State Adjutant-General, Colonel C. K. Holliday's report is given the following extracts, to show officially that in thus writing no overdrawn picture is presented.

"Never was appeal for help answered so promptly.
"In most instances on the next day, or the second,
"after the receipt of the proclamation at regimental
"head-quarters, the regiment itself, in full force,
"was on the march for the rendezvous designated
"by the commanding general. and it was only in
"exceptional cases—where the regimental district
"embraces several counties in extent—that the third
"or fourth day was required before the command
"could take up its line of march.

"But promptness alone was not the only com-
"mendable feature in the movement. Its univer-
"sality was equally marked. * * * Nor
"was this earnest enthusiasm confined to those
"within military ages; but very many outside of
"those ages—under 21 and over 45—voluntarily
"stepped into the ranks, and hastened "to the
"front" with their commands. All this occurred
"before there was the remotest intimation that the
"services of those outside the military ages would
"be required."

Colonel Holliday proceeds, after referring to the call under the proclamation of martial law:

"No where, at no time, and under no circumstances, has such an uprising been witnessed. It was widespread and complete. It was as thorough as there was material out of which it could be composed: as extensive as the limits of the population among whom it took place." * *

The following tables show the number of regiments reporting for active service; their commanding officers; the counties to which they belonged; the number of effective men in each; the places of general rendezvous, and the general officers under whose direction they were:

COMMAND OF BRIGADIER-GEN. M. S. GRANT.

NO. OF REG'T.	COMMANDING OFFICER.	COUNTY.	NO. OF MEN.	RENDEZVOUS.
1st,	Col. C. H. Robinson,	Leavenworth,	503	Olathe.
2nd,	" G. W. Veale,	Shawnee,	561	"
3d,	" Chas. Willemson,	Douglas.	643	"
4th,	" W. D. McCain,	Jefferson,	777	"
7th,	" Peter McFarland.	Leavenworth,	705	"
12th,	" L. S. Treat,	Atchison,	460	"
13th,	" J. A. Keeler,	Johnson,	400	"
14th,	" J. M. Harvey,	Riley, Waub'sa, &c.	560	"
15th,*	" J. T. Price,	Davis, Dickinson, Salina, &c.	400	"
18th,	" Matthew Quigg,	Atchison,	400	"
19th,	" A. C. Hogan,	Leavenworth,	548	"
20th,	" J. B. Hubbell,	Jackson,	340	"
21st,	" Sandy Lowe,	Douglas,	519	"
			6816	

* Of this force the 15th Regiment was, by order of Colonel Holliday, retained at Fort Riley; the 7th was stationed at Leavenworth City and Fort, until the 22d, when they were sent to the front. Other small detachments were detained at Lawrence and Topeka. The duty of garrisoning, in the main devolved upon those called out by the order of the Department Commander. At Leavenworth City some fifteen hundred were thus organized. Four full companies of able bodied negroes were organized there, and stationed at the Fort until the 21st, when they also moved to the front. One company was retained, composed of exempts. They were under command of their own officers.

The following force assembled at Atchison, under BRIGADIER GENERAL SHERRY:

NO. OF REG'T.	COMMANDING OFFICER.	COUNTY.	NO. OF MEN.	RENDEZVOUS
9th,	Col. Frank M. Tracy,	Doniphan,	554	Atchison,
17th,*	" E. C. Manning,	Marshall, Washington, Republic, Clay.	—	"
22d,	" Jas. P. Taylor,	Nemaha,	400	"
Ind'pt Bat'n.	" J. A. Pope,	Brown,	200	"
			1154	

The Border counties were ordered to assemble at Paola, under BRIGADIER GENERAL FISHBACK.

NO. OF REG'T.	COMMANDING OFFICER.	COUNTY.	NO. OF MEN.	RENDEZVOUS
5th,	Col. G. A. Colton,	Miami,	471	Paola,
10th,	" Wm. Pennock,	Franklin and Anderson,	751	Paola and Mound City.
11th	" A. J. Mitchell,	Lyon,	300	Paola,
Ind'pt Bat'n.	Lt. Col. M. M. Murdoch,	Osage,	250	"
			1772	

The Anderson County Battalion of this regiment, assembled at Mound City, as being more convenient than Paola, but soon after joined the regiment, and with it moved into Missouri.

At Mound City assembled the following regiments, who were ordered to report to Brigadier General S. N. Wood. General Wood, however, failed to report for duty.

* The 17th Regiment, Colonel Manning, was the only organization which did not respond to the calls. They presented a reasonable excuse in the fact of the exposure of their section to Indian attacks. The rule which governed the State Adjutant General, in directing the 15th Regiment (Colonel Price), to remain at Fort Riley, would have applied to the 17th.

NO. OF REG'T.	COMMANDING OFFICER.	COUNTY.	NO. OF MEN.	RENDEZVOUS
6th,	Lt.-Col. J. L. Snoddy,	Linn,	530	Mound City.
16th,	Col. F. W. Potter,	Coffery, Woodson.	560	"
			1090	

At Fort Scott, the militia were under BRIGADIER GENERAL J. B. SCOTT.

NO. OF REG'T.	COMMANDING OFFICER.	COUNTY.	NO. OF MEN.	RENDEZVOUS.
24th,	Col. J. Stadden,	Bourbon,	500	Fort Scott.
Bat'n,	Lt.-Col. Eves,	"	350	"
"	Col. C. P. Twiss,	Allen,	200	"
			1050	

The 22d Regiment (Wyandotte county) rendezvoused at Wyandotte City, five hundred and fifty strong. It reported to Major E. S. Hubbard. Wm. Weer, late Colonel of the 10th Kansas Volunteers, was elected Colonel and commissioned by the Governor.

To recapitulate: the force assembled at Olathe was, - - - - - - - - 6,816
That at Atchison, - - - - - 1,154
" Paola, - - - - - - 1,872
" Mound City, - - - - - 1,180
" Fort Scott, - - - - - 1,050
" Wyandotte, - - - - - 550

Total, - - - - 12,622

These are the figures of the Adjutant-General's report. Out of the Olathe force must be deducted from those actually at the front, the 7th and 15th

Regiments, (the former being on important service at Leavenworth, and reaching Westport on the evening after the battle that saved Kansas was over; and the latter being on duty at Fort Riley,) a force of 1,105; thus leaving a force under Grant of 5,715, of whom 4,500 crossed the Missouri line, and the others were garrisoning posts in the State.

At Paola, the 11th and 16th Regiments were retained. Both took active part in the flanking movement of the 2nd Brigade. At Fort Scott, Colonel Stadden with the 24th Regiment, exempts and negroes, did garrison duty. Of the 12,622 of the enrolled militia, at least 10,000 were concentrated south of the Kansas River, in the section threatened by the invading army, along the line of its march in the battles against and in pursuit of its retreating columns. Yet the force in the field under the calls of the Federal and State authorities was actually larger than these figures show. Some further extracts from Colonel Holliday's report will show this, and the reasons therefor:

"Portions of some of the foregoing regiments
"were detailed for special duty at several points in
"the State; such as Leavenworth, Lawrence, Topeka,
"&c., which number thus detailed, together with the
"old and young men, and the colored troops organ-
"ized under the martial law proclamation, are not
"included in the above exhibit, and would probably
"swell the count by several thousands. These latter
"troops were generally organized at their local ren

"dezvous, and were held in readiness to march to "any point that emergencies might require. The "whole number who thus responded for active "service exceeded 16,000, or a larger number than "appears upon the returns of the enrolled military "forwarded to this office."   *   *   *   *

The general disposition of the militia, so far as the points of rendezvous were concerned, was wisely arranged. Modifications had afterwards to be made. These will be given in the course of the narrative.

CHAPTER VI.

AFFAIRS IN THE CITY AND AT FORT LEAVENWORTH.

The excitement in Leavenworth was naturally greater than elsewhere in the State. That city had larger interests at stake; while the proximity of the Fort, with its immense stores of all kinds, rendered it certain that its possession was Price's main aim. The total cessation of business, the departure to the scene of action of so many of its citizens, the rigidity of martial law, and the manner of its enforcement, rendered the period during which the city was threatened one of the most intense interest.

The 1st Regiment, Kansas State Militia, Colonel Charles Robinson commanding, was among the first to respond to the Governor's call, and was, on the second day thereafter, marched to Olathe, the place of general rendezvous. With it went the Leavenworth Battery, manned by a company of the most respected German citizens. Another regiment, the 19th Cavalry, commanded by Colonel Hogan, followed, leaving on the 11th, and reaching Olathe

the same evening. It was soon afterwards ordered to the front, and until after the battle of Westport, when it returned home, was among the most efficient.

A battery was organized, with guns from the United States Arsenal, which was manned by a company commanded by Captain Zesch, a German merchant of the city, who had seen service. After doing duty in the protection of the city, the battery was ordered to the front, and participated in the movements upon the Big Blue, and in the severe battle of the 23rd near Westport.

The 7th Regiment, Kansas State Infantry, Colonel Peter McFarland, was left as garrison, in conjunction with several companies of exempts and a battalion of colored men.

The 7th did their whole duty. Lieutenant-Colonel Hershfield thereof, was, by order of General Davies, placed in command of the post of Leavenworth. The city had been declared such by orders from District head-quarters. This gentleman, one of the most popular and active business men of the city, threw himself into the work of appreciating the crisis. He showed a rare aptitude and energy, and was a most efficient co-worker with the regular military authorities. The position of Post-Commander was no enviable one, nor was it rendered more inviting by the annoyance produced through efforts to evade the military duties imposed upon all alike. Colonel Hershfield's tact, as well as firmness, tided him over these difficulties, and he won general esteem by his course. A long line of rifle-pits and earthworks on the south and east sides of the city were rapidly completed. All were alike compelled to take their share in the common labor. Much amusement was created by the organization of the "Sneak Company," under Captain Pendry, a well-known lawyer. The negroes who were not already on duty in Camp Sully, at the Fort, were organized as "The Iron-Clads," under Captain Harvey Edgerton. A strict system of Pickets, Provost Guards and Patrols was arranged and maintained with the utmost diligence. Fears were entertained of an attempt to cross the river by the rebel brigade under General Clarke, known to have crossed into North Missouri. The "Veteran Scouts," a company of discharged soldiers, were charged with the duty of patroling the river banks. Upon the bluffs, south of the city, were planted some heavy siege guns, sixty-pounders, brought from the Fort for that purpose.

The wild excitement, produced by the wilder reports and rumors constantly in circulation, kept the public pulse to fever heat. Every man who returned from the front brought fuel for this restless flame. The intense political excitement, which this necessity found in the State, added much to the difficulties of the occasion. Partizan prejudices strengthened the natural dislike of business men to service such as they were now compelled to perform. One of the city papers added to this feeling, by making it appear that there was no necessity for martial law; that Price was moving to the southwest; and that it was only sought to use the people for political purposes. These things caused dissatisfaction, both in the city and among its militia then upon the border.

Up to the 20th of October, nothing definite had been known of the enemy's whereabouts. At that date dispatches were received announcing the fight of General Blunt, at Lexington, with the entire rebel army. It thus became apparent that Price was advancing westward, and the wise forecast of General Curtis, in organizing the militia, was made evident. Before this, owing to the political excitement, a great diversity existed as to the necessities of the case, and many were induced to denounce the Department Commander and his co-adjutors. The effect of General Deitzler's dispatch was immediate. The sense of danger was realized, and all went to work with a will. Troops were immediately relieved from duty in the city and defences, and ordered to report daily at their different head-quarters, ready for an immediate movement.

On the succeeding day (Friday 21st), dispatches were received from Generals Curtis and Deitzler, announcing the battle of Little Blue, and the falling back of the troops to the line of Big Blue, six miles east of Kansas City. These filled all with dread. Words fail in painting the gloomy uncertainty. Over the thousands of homes, from each of which some loved one had gone forth at the call of duty, hung sadness and fearful anxiety. But, impressed by the urgency, one common purpose now animated old and young.

The Governor telegraphed the following order:

IN THE FIELD, BIG BLUE,
October 21, 1864.

To COLONEL R. N. HERSHFIELD, *Commanding Post:*

Send all deserters back to their commands at once. All that have left without leave must return. Now is the time for every Kansan to do his duty. Let no man hesitate. Price is upon us. Now is the time to save our homes and assist our comrades.

THOMAS CARNEY,
Governor and Commander-in-Chief.

An order was issued and rigorously enforced, directing the impressment of all males, between fifteen and sixty, who were not already in service. Other measures were taken, adapted to the emergency. The 7th Regiment, the Veteran Scouts, and Captain Zesch's Battery left for Kansas City. The Steamers Benton and Tom Morgan were used as transports. The Morgan was used to patrol the river. Officers had arrived from General Curtis' Head-Quarters, to aid in the rapid forwarding of troops. At the Fort, the utmost activity was displayed. At District Head-Quarters, General Davies, and his efficient Adjutant, worked energetically. Lieutenant Colonel Stark, A. A. A. G., Captain John Willans, A. A. G., were in charge of Department Head-Quarters, and worked night and day to meet the emergency. While their associates were at the front, in the position most dear to the soldier, these officers and others, were filling no less important and laborious positions at home. Captain Hodges, Depot Quarter-Master, was untiring; the veteran Paymaster, Major Hunt, Captain McNutt, Ordnance Officer, in charge of the Arsenal, Colonel Werter R. Davis, Post-Commandant, all did their whole duty. Large amounts of ordnance stores were forwarded; transportation promptly supplied; militia were armed. The "Iron Clad Battalion" had already left under Captain Rafferty. A detachment of Light Artillery (colored), just recruited, had been sent with two guns, Parrots, under command of Second Lieutenant P. H. Minor, (colored).

In the city, an impromptu gathering was held for counsel. Major Heath, Provost Marshal General of the Department, who had just returned from St. Louis, urged the calling of the citizens together for the better placing of the emergency before them. This was immediately done. The bells were rung, the cannon fired, and soon they rallied in front of the Market House. The meeting was addressed in stirring appeals by Judge Sears, Dr. King, Major H. H. Heath, and other gentlemen. At the first sound of the bells and cannon, wild anxiety was aroused in the city. Few were acquainted with the object, and reports of a rebel force threatening to cross the river, or advancing from the South, spread like wildfire. The real purpose of the alarm, however, was soon known.

Two days passed, and the sound of battle at Big

Blue and Westport, could be distinctly heard. The wires were in constant use, and the most exciting reports reached the city. It was known on Saturday night that our lines had been forced, and that the right and centre were falling back. Sunday morning came, and with it the certainty of a decisive engagement. The hours seemed ages. From Kansas City were sent constant bulletins, and the varying fortunes of that morning met as varying emotions in the streets of Leavenworth. At last, as the afternoon waned, came news of victory, and later, the certainty thereof, in the order abolishing martial law north of the Kansas River.

Thus ended the excitement and anxiety consequent upon the imminent danger in which Leavenworth had been placed. When all did so well, it would be invidious to distinguish individuals; but too much praise cannot be accorded to the ladies of the city, who organized relief and aid societies, worked unremittingly to relieve the distress among the poorer classes, occasioned by the stoppage of work and the absence of the men in the field, and by the preparation of supplies for the sick and wounded.

Thus has it ever been. The annals of war are gilded by the devotion of the women of the land, who, shut out from sterner duties, have filled their lives with sacrifice, and gone out, blessing and cheering, making beautiful its dreary ways with the light of charity, and the glory of inspiring devotion.

CHAPTER VII.

GENERALS CURTIS AND BLUNT TAKE THE FIELD—ORGANIZATION OF TROOPS.

Major-General Blunt assumed command on the 10th inst., and telegraphed to head-quarters suggesting the concentration of all available force at Olathe and Paola. Not believing that Price would attempt to cross the Kansas River, he deemed it more likely that he would strike as far up on the south side as possible. A concentration would meet this, while a forward movement into Missouri would enable us to strike his right flank, and if he turned southward, join the pursuit. These views were also those of General Curtis. Orders had been received from General Halleck directing the concentration of troops in the vicinity of Fort Scott, under the supposition that Price would be turned south before reaching Lexington.

General Curtis made every preparation, previous to taking the field in person. Such reports and dispatches from General Rosecrans, Colonel Ford, etc., as would, without injury to the service, arouse the people to a sense of their danger, were published by his orders. The movements of the 2d Colorado Cavalry were then of the utmost importance. The following dispatches show its position:

HEAD-QUARTERS, 2ND COLORADO CAVALRY,
HICKMAN'S MILLS, Oct. 12, 1864.

Major-General S. R. Curtis, Commanding Department of Kansas, Olathe, Kansas:

I have the honor to inform you that at ten o'clock P. M., yesterday, I left Pleasant Hill for this place, reaching here just before daylight. My reasons for this move were, that from all I could learn of Price's movements, he evidently means to strike north of Pleasant Hill, probably between there and Independence, leaving me in danger of being cut off from your main command. * * * I was over thirty miles from your main army, and part of the country between dangerous for small parties to travel through. At this place I am only six miles from Oxford, on the Kansas line, sixteen from Pleasant Hill, fourteen from Independence, and thirteen from Kansas City; and moreover on the route Price must come on account of water and forage, which in this vicinity are plenty. Another reason for thinking that Price will come this way is that guerillas have told some of their friends that they have positive orders from Price not to destroy any forage in this neighborhood. * * * When I left Pleasant Hill, I sent Captain Green, with one hundred men, north and north-east, to scout well Cedar Creek and the Little Blue, reaching this place by way of Raytown. He arrived about noon to-day. He had seen no fresh signs of any large body of guerillas, though he could hear of occasional small bodies of five or six in a gang. He ascertained that it was their intention to capture this place from the citizen militia to-night, taking their arms from them, but not destroying any forage. I have sent Captain Elmore and fifty men towards Pleasant Hill to-day, Lieutenant Keith, with fifty men east and north-east, and Company "D." (forty men) to Independence, all to return to-night. I propose to keep Captain Moses and his two companies at

Independence for the time being, as an extreme outpost, to be ready to move in a minute, and, as I am now in his rear, to fall back and reinforce me if necessary. Hoping that my actions meet the approbation of the Major-General-Commanding, I am, General, very respectfully, your obedient servant,

(Signed) JAS. H. FORD,
Colonel 2nd Colorado Cavalry, Commanding.

Colonel Thomas Moonlight was directed to place himself in communication with Colonel Ford.

On the 11th, General Curtis proceeded to Olathe, accompanied by the following members of his staff: Major C. S. Charlot, A. A. G.; Major T. J. McKenny, Additional A. D. C.; and Major R. H. Hunt, 15th Kansas, Chief of Artillery. Captain Meeker, Lieutenant Fitch, U. S. Signal Corps, and Lieutenant Hubbard, A. S. O., were also in attendance with their command. Honorable James H. Lane, Volunteer Aide-de-Camp, accompanied the General. Honorable S. C. Pomeroy and Colonel W. H. Roberts, Volunteer Aides, reported on the 15th.

For the purpose of obtaining wood and water, the rendezvous was changed to Shawnee Town, still nearer the State line. General Blunt was ordered to Hickman's Mills, Missouri. General George W. Deitzler, commanding the State militia, reported at Olathe that evening, and regiments from Leavenworth, Lawrence and contiguous districts, arrived. Every disposition was made for the prompt organization and equipment of these forces. The 1st, 2nd, 3rd, 4th, 13th, 14th, 19th, 20th, 21st and 22nd Regiments, Kansas State Militia, arrived during the three next days. General Grant was very active in discharge of his duties. A depot for ordnance, subsistence and quartermaster stores was established at Wyandotte. The 23rd Regiment, Colonel William Weer, was stationed there; Major Hubbard being in command of the post. The cavalry portions of the 2nd and 3rd Regiments were consolidated into one command, under Colonel George W. Veale, 2nd Regiment. The infantry were placed under Colonel Williamson, of the 3rd. A portion of the Topeka Battery, under Captain Handley, with a twenty-four pound howitzer, was also attached to Colonel Veale's command, whose experience as Major of the 6th Kansas Cavalry was deemed of value. Lieutenant-Colonel Abernathy, formerly of the 8th Kansas, acted as Chief-of-Staff to General Grant. General Deitzler's Staff was announced: Chief, Lieutenant-Colonel O. E. Leonard; Cavalry, Lieut.-Col. A .W. Spicer, (both, formerly of the 1st Kansas); Adjutant, Major John T. Morton; Quartermaster, Lieutenant-Colonel William Rosenthall; Engineer, Major L. E. Wilmarth; Judge Advocate, Major John J. Ingalls; Paymaster, Major Charles Chadwick; and as Aides, Lieutenant-Colonel William Crawford, Majors E. G. Moore, A. R. Banks, and A. S. Hughes.

General Grant's command was moved forward to Turkey Creek, beyond Shawnee. A dispatch was received on the 13th, announcing General Rosecrans as having taken the field. Shelby was reported in Howard and Randolph Counties, with four thousand men. Springfield not disturbed. Pleasanton at Jefferson City. Rebels reported moving on the North Missouri Road; also Standwaite, near Humboldt, Kansas. Price was moving on the Georgetown and Booneville Road; Sanborn six miles from the latter point, which Shelby occupied. The statements in relation to North Missouri and Standwaite, were deemed and proved untrue. General Curtis directed that the militia (being without uniform) should wear as a distinctive badge, a piece of red material of some kind. Most of the men found badges in the scarlet leaves of the Sumach, which at this season flamed along the creeks and on the prairie's edge. Nicknames are always plenty wherever men assemble. They learned to good humoredly designate themselves as "Kansas Tads," or "The Sumach Millish." The staff officers were employed on the work of Inspection. General Lane, Senator Pomeroy, Col. Roberts, of the Volunteer Staff, with Major McKenny, attended to this duty, visiting Wyandotte, Shawneetown, Hickman's Mills, Kansas City and Independence. Major Hunt hurried forward the ordnance stores and amunition with great activity. Lieutenant Fitch, of the Signal Corps, was detailed as Quarter-Master.

At daylight of the 14th, Major General Blunt moved from Paola towards Hickman's Mills, Mo. He took with him the 11th Kansas Cavalry, Colonel Thomas Moonlight, Commanding; Company "L," 5th Kansas Cavalry, Captain Young; Company

"A," Captain Ames, 16th Kansas; the Independent Battery, Colorado Volunteers, Captain George McLain; and a portion of the 5th (Colonel G. A. Colton), and 10th Regiments (Colonel Wm. Pennick), K. S. M. These troops were all mounted.

On the 15th, Colonel Jennison arrived from Mound City, with the 15th Kansas Cavalry; Colonel C. W. Blair, 14th Kansas, from Fort Scott, with a battalion of the 3rd Wisconsin Cavalry—portions of Companies "A," "C," "D," "F" and "M,"—under Captain Carpenter, Company "A:" also Companies "D," "E" and "L," 14th Kansas Cavalry; Company "D," Captain Kendall, 16th Kansas, and the right section of the 2d Battery, Kansas Volunteers, Lieutenant Knowles. Captain Geo. J. Clark, Ordnance Officer, accompanied Colonel Blair, with ammunition train, and four mountain-howitzers—twelve-pounders—in charge of Lieutenant William B. Clark, Company "E," 14th Kansas Cavalry, with sixty men of his company. These troops had been directed to join, by forced marches. With Colonel Blair, were a battalion of militia (mounted) from Bourbon County, under Lieutenant Colonel, G. P. Eves, and a Company of Scouts, under Captain John Wilson. The 6th Regiment K. S. M., Lieutenant Colonel Snoddy, also reported. The entire force numbered about forty-two hundred men, with eight Parrot guns, and nine mountain-howitzers, the latter attached to the Cavalry.

Major Smith, 2d Colorado Cavalry, who had been

sent by Colonel Ford to Independence, returned, reporting a force under Colonel Page, 1,200 strong, within a short distance of that place. He was again sent out after dark, with two hundred men, to reconnoitre. No other information was received. Active scouting was maintained to the East and South-East, but no evidence of rebel advance in force visible. In Henry County stragglers were seen, supposed to be men on furlough, visiting their homes. Advices from St. Louis, located Price's columns at or near Booneville, during this period of suspense. The cavalry belonging to the Districts of Generals McNeil, Sanborn, Brown and Fisk, were hanging on his rear under General Pleasanton. Colonel Winslow's Brigade of the 17th Army Corps, General A. J. Smith, joined the pursuit.

General Curtis having determined on a forward movement into Missouri, arranged his forces in two divisions; the main body of the militia, under Major-General Deitzler, constituting the left wing, to move from Shawneetown towards Lexington, by way of Independence. The right wing, under Major-General Blunt, consisting of the Volunteer Cavalry and the Southern Border Militia, to move by way of Warrensburg.

The successful execution of this plan was frustrated by the opposition manifested by the militia to crossing the State line. A portion of the Cavalry Brigade organized by General Grant, consisting of the 19th and 4th, were directed to report to Colonel

Ford at Independence. On reaching the State line at Oxford, a part of the 19th refused to cross, declaring that there was no power to compel them. They were appealed to by Generals Deitzler and Grant. The 4th Regiment, Colonel McCain, crossed without hesitation, and at last the balance took its line of march to Independence.

Colonel Ford, with ten companies of the 2d Colorado, had already preceded them, in obedience to orders from General Blunt. Major Pritchard, of the same regiment, was in command of the post at Kansas City.

At Hickman's Mills, similar difficulties occurred with the border militia. On the 15th, General Blunt issued an order brigading his force as follows:

1st BRIGADE, Colonel C. R. JENNISON, 15th Kansas Volunteer Cavalry, Commanding.
15th Regiment Kansas Volunteer Cavalry, Lieutenant-Colonel George H. Hoyt commanding.
3rd Regiment Wisconsin Volunteer Cavalry Battalion, of five companies, Captain Carpenter commanding.
Four twelve-pound mountain-howitzers.
2D BRIGADE, Colonel THOMAS MOONLIGHT, 11th Kansas Volunteer Cavalry, Commanding.
11th Regiment Volunteer Cavalry, Lieutenant-Colonel Plumb.
Company L, 5th Kansas Cavalry, Captain Young.
Company D, 16th Kansas Cavalry, Captain Kendall.
Four twelve-pound mountain-howitzers.
3RD BRIGADE, Colonel C. W. BLAIR, 14th Regiment Kansas Volunteer Cavalry, Commanding.
5th Regiment Kansas State Militia, Colonel G. A. Colton (Miami County).
6th Regiment Kansas State Militia, Lieutenant Colonel J. D. Snoddy (Linn County).
10th Regiment Kansas State Militia, Colonel Wm. Pennock (Franklin County).

Detachment of Company E, 14th Kansas Cavalry, Lieutenant Wm. B. Clark.

Battalion Bourbon County Militia (four companies), Lieutenant-Colonel Eves.

Independent Battery, Colorado Volunteers, Captain McLain, six guns; and right section of 2d Kansas Battery, Lieutenant Knowles.

Brigadier-General Fishback, Kansas State Militia, to have immediate command, reporting to Colonel Blair.

This last order was issued on a supposed agreement of General Fishback to waive the question of rank. Dissatisfaction, however, was soon manifested by that officer and Colonel Snoddy. General Fishback issued the following order:

> HEAD-QUARTERS 5TH BRIGADE, K. S. M., }
> HICKMAN'S MILLS, OCT. 15, 1864. }

Colonel Colton, of the 5th Regiment K. S. M., Colonel J. D. Snoddy, 6th Regiment K. S. M., and Colonel Pennock, of the 10th Regiment K. S. M., are hereby ordered to march their regiments to Rockville, via Aubury, with the discretion to march from Aubury too, if in their judgment the enemy are likely to attack Paola.

By order of Brigadier-General Fishback:

H. McBRIDE, A. A. G.

Lieutenant-Colonel Snoddy, in common with others, had been directed to report to division head-quarters the number of men, arms, amount of ammunition, etc., in his command. He did so, and also forwarded the following request:

> HEAD-QUARTERS 6TH REGIMENT, K. S. M., }
> HICKMAN'S MILLS, MO., OCT. 15, 1864. }

CAPTAIN GEO. S. HAMPTON, A. A. G.:

In view of the fact that all the effective men of Linn County, Kansas, are now here in my command, and that in consequence that county is now left entirely without protection, and that the men of my command are poorly prepared to endure a campaign, from the want of camp equipage, I most respectfully ask that I be ordered with my regiment to the border of Linn County.

Very respectfully, your obedient serv't,

JAS. D. SNODDY,
Lieutenant-Colonel commanding 6th Regt. K. S. M.

An endorsement was returned, as follows:

HEAD-QUARTERS 1ST DIVISION, ARMY OF THE BORDER, IN THE FIELD,
HICKMAN'S MILLS, Oct. 15, 1864.

Respectfully returned—application refused. The General commanding will make such disposition of the troops under his command as in his judgment he thinks best. Everything will be done that is possible to supply the militia of your command with whatever is required for their comfort, when application is made through the proper channels.

By command of Major-General Blunt:

GEO. S. HAMPTON, A. A. G.

Early on the 16th, the dissatisfaction culminated in an attempt to march the 6th Regiment to Kansas. The regiment was already on its way ere General Blunt was informed. Prompt measures were taken. The 15th Kansas was ordered out. General Blunt, in person, stopped the regiment, and placed General Fishback and Colonel Snoddy in arrest, ordering them to Paola, and marched the militia back to camp. They returned most willingly, greeting the General's action with cheers, and displaying an enthusiastic desire to meet the enemy. Colonel James Montgomery, formerly of the 3d Kansas Volunteers, and latterly of the 2d South Carolina Volunteers (colored), who had distinguished himself greatly in South Carolina and Florida, having arrived at head-quarters to tender his services, was by the 6th Regiment unanimously elected Colonel. No further conflict of authority occurred. General Fishback was released from arrest by order of General Curtis, on the ground of a misunderstanding between him and General Blunt. He afterwards served gallantly with his brigade at the Big Blue, Westport, rendering efficient service prior thereto in forwarding troops. Colonel Snoddy was retained a prisoner at Paola, till after the army of the border moved south in pursuit of Price.

At four P. M. of the 16th, General Blunt received orders to move with all his mounted force towards Pleasant Hill. At seven the same evening, the 1st and 2d Brigades, 2,000 men, with eight howitzers, took up the line of march. Before marching, the Division Staff was announced: Captain G. S. Hampton, A. A. G.; Captain B. F. Simpson, 15th Kansas, Acting Quartermaster; Captain Geo. J. Clark, Ordnance Officer (he remained with Colonel Blair); Captain A. J. Shannon, Division Provost Marshal; Volunteer Aide-de-Camps, Lieutenant-Colonel J. T. Burris, late of the 10th Kansas, Major R. G. Ward, 1st Kansas Colored Volunteers, Captain Milhoan, late of the 10th Kansas. Captain R. J. Hinton, 2d Kansas Colored Volunteers, A. D. C. on the regular staff, reported for duty to General Curtis, being unable to reach division head-quarters till after the engagement at Lexington. Major Penny, late of 31st Missouri Volunteers, Volunteer

A. D. C., was assigned to duty after that battle. General Lane remained on duty with General Blunt, by direction of General Curtis. Colonel Blair, with the 3d Brigade, moved to the west side of the Big Blue, where he encamped. Colonel Ford, with the 2d Colorado, held Independence, six miles further east. He had with him there his own regiment, under Major J. Nelson Smith, and several companies of the 16th Kansas Cavalry (Colonel Werter R. Davis, Commanding Post at Fort Leavenworth), under Lieutenant-Colonel Sam. Walker, one of the best officers and most gallant soldiers in the service. The 4th and 19th Regiments Kansas State Militia (cavalry), commanded by Colonels Hogan and McCain. Colonel Hogan commanded the brigade.

Orders were issued directing militia then concentrating at Paola, Mound City and Fort Scott, in view of the probability of Price's moving south from the vicinity of Lexington, to remain there, holding themselves in readiness to march at any moment. Lieutenant-Colonel Drake, 17th Kansas, with two companies, garrisoned Paola. He was shortly after joined by the 12th Regiment Kansas State Militia (Lyon County), Colonel Mitchell, the 16th (Coffey County), Colonel Potter, and a mounted battalion from Osage County, under Lieutenant-Colonel M. M. Murdoch. This latter, in obedience to orders, moved up the line in the direction of Westport, and opportunely arrived in time to participate in the engagement of the 22d.

At Mound City, Captain Greer, 15th Kansas, was in command. He had as garrison sixty men, convalescents, 15th Kansas, and five companies of the Linn County Militia, two mounted. At Fort Scott, Captain Vittum, 3rd Wisconsin Cavalry, was in command. He had with him about two hundred volunteers, mostly 2d Kansas Cavalry. Two regiments of militia under Brigadier-General J. B. Scott were also assembled there. About three hundred colored men, called out under the proclamation of martial law, were placed under command of Lieutenant Wm. D. Matthews (colored), Light Artillery, United States Colored Troops, who, with his command, were put in charge of a portion of the defences.

At various other points in the State, militia were assembled. Those regiments rendezvousing at Atchison were ordered to the front, but owing to a misunderstanding and conflict of authority, they did not move till after the battle of Little Blue, aroused all to a realizing sense of the danger in which the State was placed. The 15th Regiment was retained at Fort Riley. The 14th, under Colonel Harvey, formerly of the 10th Kansas Volunteers, exhibited great alacrity in concentrating and marching, having over one hundred miles to travel. They reached the State line on the afternoon of the 22nd, while an engagement was in progress. Thence they marched to Westport and Kansas City. They made this march in six days. The 18th Regiment, infantry,

Colonel Matthew Quigg, formerly of the 10th Kansas Volunteers, left Atchison and marched to Wyandotte, where they remained in camp till the 22nd, when they moved to Big Blue. The 12th Regiment, cavalry, Colonel L. S. Treat, was among the foremost in usefulness. Two days after receipt of orders, Colonel Treat, with four hundred men, was in the saddle. On the 16th he reported at Wyandotte to General Curtis, and thence to Colonel Ford, at Independence.

While troops were thus concentrating, and the 1st Division was marching towards Lexington, the commanding General was moving to the different rendezvous, reconnoitering the country, and making other dispositions to meet the enemy. It having been found almost impossible to move the State troops as a unit upon the Lexington road, it was wisely determined to turn all efforts to holding them together at the next most available line of defence. General Curtis confidently hoped the troops under Rosecrans would overtake the rebel army at or near Lexington, turn them on a retreat, and thus enable him, with the irregular forces at his disposal, to attack their flank, disorder and pursue their retreating columns. The main difficulty was in obtaining accurate intelligence. Head-quarters were successively made at Wyandotte, Kansas City and Independence.

At Kansas City, Lieutenant-Colonel Wheeler, 13th Kansas, and Captain Hinton, of General Blunt's staff, reported for duty. Lieutenant-Colonel Sears, 18th U. S. C. T., at home on furlough, also reported. He was announced as Provost Marshal. Captain Edgar Seelye, A. Q. M., stationed at Kansas City, was announced as Acting Chief Quartermaster. From Fort Smith, Arkansas, arrived Colonel Wm. F. Cloud, 2nd Kansas Volunteer Cavalry, Colonel S. J. Crawford, 2d Kansas Colored Volunteers (now Governor of Kansas), and Colonel John Ritchie, 1st Regiment, Indian Brigade, who with Lieutenant S. S. Prouty, Regimental Quarter-Master 3rd Regiment, Indian Brigade, reported to General Curtis for duty, and were assigned; the Colonel as Volunteer Aid-de-Camp, and Lieutenant Prouty to the Quarter-Master's Department.

Other members of the department staff arrived. Lieutenant G. T. Robinson, Chief Engineer, was placed in charge of the preparation of defences upon the lines chosen by General Curtis. Major S. S. Curtis, 2d Colorado, A. D. C., reported on the 18th at Kansas City, with the Steamer "Benton," on board which, he had run the blockade of the Missouri River, established by the rebels at Lexington and elsewhere. The whole trip was of so daring a character as to be worthy of mention.

Major Curtis, in obedience to orders, took possession and charge of the Benton, on the 7th of October. Had on board three companies of the 43rd M. S. M., under command of Major Davis. Three companies of same Regiment were on the West Wind; all under command of Col. Chester Harding. Started immediately for Jefferson City; were much delayed by low water and hard winds, and only reached Brunswick at 10 A. M., of the 11th inst. Found the town occupied by Captain Kennedy, of Price's Army, with eighty men, mostly raised in the place. A guerilla, named Ryder, with one hundred men, had left the preceding evening. We landed, driving the enemy from the town at the first fire. Colonel Harding seized all the serviceable horses, mounted and sent in pursuit eighty men, who returned during the night, reporting having come up with the enemy, who again fled without fight. Lieut. Brunswick next day saw a few of the enemy at Cambridge. Arrived at Glasgow on the 13th; found Captain Mayer, of 9th M. S. M., with about three hundred cavalry, and as many more armed citizens, throwing up intrenchments, intending to hold the place as long as possible. Learned that Price was at Booneville, conscripting every man fit for duty, and had possession of the steam ferry boat. Colonel Harding decided to remain at Glasgow. Believing the boat would be wanted at Leavenworth, Major Curtis concluded to return, and in view of the weakness of the garrison, without a guard, feeling confident the boat could not be taken with small arms. He left Glasgow on the 14th; was fired into that evening at Miami City, and at Plains City, and again the next morning, when the mate of the boat was slightly wounded. Fired into near Waverly, by about fifty rebels, and also at Lexington. Here the boat was under a heavy fire from two hundred bushwhackers; the shot fell thick and fast, without however, doing material damage. Besides the above, was fired into repeatedly by small parties. The boat was struck by over six hundred shots; probably three or four thousand more were fired at her, before arriving at Kansas City. Though bringing up the boat was considered hazardous, the capture of Glasgow the next day by Price, proves it better than to have remained there.

The following order was issued, owing to the reported connivance with rebels, of the commanders of certain captured boats:

HEAD-QUARTERS, DEPARTMENT OF KANSAS,
Fort Leavenworth, October 15, 1864.

GENERAL ORDERS,
No. 56.

Commanders and owners of Steam-boats and Ferry-boats on the Missouri River, in this command, will see that their boats do not fall into rebel hands in a condition for rebel service, under the sure and swift penalty of the loss of boat, and the forfeit of the life of the commander and pilot.

By COMMAND OF MAJOR-GENERAL CURTIS:

W. H. STARK,
Acting Assistant Adjutant-General.

CHAPTER VIII.

MARCH TO LEXINGTON—PREPARATIONS AT THE BIG BLUE—MOVEMENTS OF MILITIA.

On the 18th, General Curtis' Head-Quarters were at Camp Charlot, Kansas City. Information was constantly received of the movements of General Blunt, who, with the volunteer cavalry of his Division, was moving by the Warrensburg Road towards Lexington. On leaving Hickman's Mills, Major Anderson had been sent towards Warrensburg, with instructions to move east until he obtained reliable information. Bushwhackers were reported in the vicinity of Pleasant Hill. Captain Allen, of the 7th E. M. M., with one hundred and fifty men, held that point. At Warensburg, all the militia had been removed to Jefferson City by General Brown. Major Emory S. Foster assumed command, taking active measures to defend the place. He succeeded in arming about one hundred and twenty men in all, and obtained 5,000 cartridges. The Court House was occupied as quarters, and defences made around it of wagons and cord wood belonging to the quartermaster's department. Major Anderson reached the town on the 16th inst., and returned to Pleasant Hill on the 17th. Captain Palmer, 11th Kansas, with twenty men, was sent on a scout to Knob Noster, ten miles east of Warrensburg, but till after the 17th, was not heard from. One of our spies, who had been within Price's camp, reported him as having a force of over 20,000, daily augmented by conscripts and recruits. Camp rumors stated Price's intention to move on Kansas City by way of Lexington, following the river, and thence through Kansas and the Indian Territory to the Arkansas. General Blunt believed this would be their route; all information obtained, confirmed it. Hopes were entertained of communicating with Sanborn, who, on the 14th, was at Georgetown. On the 17th, Blunt moved to Holden; the same night twenty miles towards Lexington; on the afternoon of the 18th, reached that city.

In the meanwhile, Major J. Nelson Smith, 2d Colorado Volunteer Cavalry, had been ordered on a scout towards Lexington, the results of which are thus reported by him:

INDEPENDENCE, Mo., Oct. 18, 1864.

Robert L. Roe, A. A. A. General, 1st Brigade, 2nd Division, Army of the Border:

SIR:—For the information of the Colonel commanding, I have the honor to report that in pursuance to instructions received from him I left this place on the afternoon of

Sunday, the 16th instant, at eight o'clock, with a detachment of the 16th Kansas Cavalry and 2nd Colorado Cavalry, viz.: Companies H, K and L, 16th Kansas, commanded by Major Ketner, and Companies C, E, G, K and L, 2nd Colorado, numbering in all about three hundred men. I proceeded east on the Lexington Telegraph Road, and when out nine or ten miles from this place found the telegraph line down and cut, which continued for every two or three miles until I reached Lexington. * * *

When within ten miles of Lexington, I commenced making inquiries in regard to the force, and kind, at that place, and the invariable report was from five hundred to seven hundred men, about half Confederate troops and the rest bushwhackers; and not till I got within a mile and a half or two miles could I learn anything to the contrary, when I learned that it was reported that the enemy's force had left late the night before. I dashed with my command into the town on the morning of the 17th, a little after sunrise, but found the town evacuated. I was informed by the citizens that a strong picket of the enemy had been posted in the town during the night previous, and had left at daylight. Also, that a small picket force had left the town as I occupied it. I found but very few citizens in the streets, and they all women and children; but as soon as they learned that "Feds." occupied the town, what few male citizens there were left commenced crawling out of their holes, and the citizens generally commenced crowding around us—some in tears, some in smiles, and some in rags. They generally appeared much rejoiced at our arrival, and offered us the hospitalities of the town, inviting us to their homes, and acting as if they could not do too much for us. I immediately posted a strong picket about the town and sent out scouts in different directions, as I had learned that a force, from five hundred to seven hundred, of Confederates had been in camp only six miles from town at daylight, intending, if such a force was there, if not too strongly posted, to make them show their hands or else throw up ours. My scouts proceeded in a south and south-easterly direction a distance of nine miles, and found no force except a picket of the enemy six miles from town, which the scouts fired upon, killing one and wounding two. I learned that quite a large force of the enemy had been at Dover, a distance of eight miles, but that the pickets had been driven in from Lexington by the Federal troops, and reported them in large force there and more coming, and that the Confederates had got up and "skedaddled."

I also learned in Lexington, from what I consider pretty reliable authority, that a force from 2,000 to 3,000 strong (said to be Shelby's force, and commanded by General Fagan, C. S. A.) was down the river at Waverly. The citizens of Lexington have had a reign of terror, both loyal people, McClellan people, and rebels. The enemy have plundered and robbed indiscriminately, taking everything of value they could carry away, and have left many poor families very destitute. I captured thirty (30) double-barreled shot guns, brought by the enemy to Lexington, to arm their conscripts with; also, one thousand rounds of ammunition, all of which I destroyed, as I had no transportation to carry them away. I sent a dispatch to Captain Eads, 1st M. S. M., who I learned was at Richmond, across the river, and who was in command at Lexington, with his company, and two full companies of citizen guards, at the time that it was evacuated, advising him to return, which he did just as my rear guard was leaving town. Being well satisfied that he could hold the place, if he chose to, I left the place with my command at about four o'clock, being out of rations, the citizens pleading with me to stay, and telling me that they would feed my whole command so long as I chose to, or could stay there. I returned eighteen miles by the same route on which I came in, and went into camp, it being now dark. Just before going into camp, my advance ran into six mounted men, which I supposed to be the enemy's bushwhacker pickets, and who after getting into the brush some distance, discharged two shots, probably signals for the force to which they belonged. It being quite dark, my command and their horses being tired and worn out, I did not think it advisable to pursue them. I here had my telegraph operator "tap" the wire, so that I might communicate with you, but he reported that he could get no circuit, and I had to abandon it.

Hearing that a force of from seventy-five to one hundred bushwhackers had passed south of us just before we went into camp, I sent Captain Greene with his company (E), and companies G and L, 2nd Colorado Cavalry, this morning just before daylight, to see if he could find their whereabouts, and if so to give them a turn. His (Captain Green's) report accompanies this, and is marked "C," also notice marked "A," published by Captain Bedinger, C. S. A., at Lexington, October 14th, 1864, and orders marked "B," by Captain George S. Rathburn, same date and army. Most of the recruits enlisted by Captains Rathburn and Bedinger, as well as most of their conscripts, deserted and returned to their homes.

In conclusion, I would remark that too much credit cannot be given to the officers and men under my command for their good behavior and prompt obedience of orders. No complaints whatever came to me of the misconduct of any man of my command. I broke camp at daylight this morning, and arrived here at twelve o'clock M.

(Signed) J. NELSON SMITH,
Major 2d Colorado Cavalry, Commanding.

NOTICE.

HEAD-QUARTERS, LEXINGTON, Mo., Oct. 14th.

I hereby notify the citizens of the city of Lexington and vicinity, that I am here now for the purpose of enlisting all those who are subject to military duty, and organizing them into companies, battalions, &c., with authority from Major General Price. All those subject to duty will report to me at the Court House, immediately.

L. L. BEDINGER,
Captain and Recruiting Officer.

GENERAL ORDER.

HEAD QUARTERS DETACHMENT SHELBY'S BRIGADE, }
LEXINGTON, Mo., Oct. 14th.   }

The city of Lexington having this day surrendered to me by the Mayor thereof, in the name of the Confederate Government, I have the honor to issue the following General Order:

I. The rights of non-combatants and private property must be respected and preserved.

II. All male white citizens between the ages of seventeen and fifty are ordered to report to head quarters at the

Court House, within twenty-four hours after issuing this order.

III. All public property belonging to the Federal Government in this city is taken possession of, in the name of the Confederacy, and the citizens are required to report the same to head-quarters at the Court House, immediately.

IV. If any shots are fired from houses in the city upon Confederate troops, or any force under my command, such houses are ordered to be burned to the ground.

V. Proper vouchers to be issued for all property taken for the public use in the Quartermaster's Department.

This order to be rigidly enforced.

GEO. S. RATHBURN,
Capt. Com'd'g Detachment Shelby's Brigade, Recruiting Service.

INDEPENDENCE, Mo., Oct. 7, 1864.

SIR:—I have the honor herewith to report for the information of the Major-Commanding, that I scouted in a southeast direction through Texas Prairie, and found a large trail going east, supposed to be Todd's command. Said trail was in the vicinity of Judge Gray's. We then struck for Fire Prairie, by the way of Robinson's; thence west, crossing the Blue at Franklin's. From there we struck the Lexington and Independence road, four miles from this place. After leaving the large trail, we heard of two parties, one of six and one of three, traveling in all thirty miles from the time of leaving your command on same date.

Respectfully, your obedient servant,
(Signed) W. H. GREEN,
Captain Company E, 2nd Colorado Cavalry.
To Lieutenant J. W. Stanton, Bat.

While these movements were progressing, the difficulty of advancing the militia to the points most essential for practical resistance to Price, daily became greater. The aim now was to concentrate force enough at some particular point sufficiently strong to effectually hold the rebel army in check until General Pleasanton could co-operate. To this end Colonel Blair was stationed at the Big Blue, and with the engineers, actively engaged in fortifying that line, by means of formidable abattis and breast works at salient points, rifle pits to cover the line of advance, and such other means as would materially strengthen the natural advantages of the west bank of the stream. At Kansas City martial law was rigidly enforced, and all available force set to work constructing a long line of intrenchments on the east and south, thus creating a formidable obstacle to the rebel army. Officers were sent to hurry all troops to the front. Among these, Captain R. J. Hinton received orders to take general charge of the movements and organization of the colored men. The Leavenworth Battalion, under Captain Rafferty, accompanied by a section of Parrott guns, with thirty men, under Lieutenant P. H. Minor (colored), two companies from Wyandotte, and three from Shawneetown, were sent to the front under the general direction of Captain Hinton, with the assistance of Lieutenant-Colonel O. E. Learnerd and Captain Simpson, Kansas State Militia. These troops, with companies attached to other regiments, were organized as a brigade, and placed under command of Captain Rafferty, 83d United States Colored Troops. It numbered over one thousand men, who deserve, with their officers, great credit for uniform zeal and gallantry. Meanwhile the handling of the militia became more difficult. Since Price moved from Jefferson on the 9th, no positive information had been received of his whereabouts. This tended to increase the difficulties. They are strikingly illustrative of the obstacles caused, even in a loyal community, by the mischievous theory of State sovereignty, and show the necessity of remodeling our militia system, and adapting it somewhat to the wants of a nation, instead of being now fit only for the loose ties of a confederation.

A dispatch from General Deitzler to General Curtis, illustrates forcibly the great trouble in the way of effective organization:

> INDEPENDENCE, Mo., Oct. 17, 5 P. M., 1864.
>
> GENERAL:—I have the honor to inform you that the militia regiments ordered to repair to this post from Shawneetown yesterday, refused to cross the State line this morning until after I made them a speech explaining the object of the movement, and promised to accompany them, and see that they are "not ordered too far in this State." They are arriving here as I write, and seem to be in good spirits. I apprehend considerable difficulty in inducing them to march further into Missouri, and I shall regret if the necessity arises to make the effort. They know their rights under the militia laws of our State, and will not tamely submit to an effort to move them far from their homes, unless the necessity is great and apparent. General Blunt passed through Pleasant Hill to-day, moving towards Warrensburg. Major Smith has not yet returned, but is expected in during the night. He will doubtless bring some reliable information respecting the strength and whereabouts of Price's army. I cannot persuade myself to believe his army is moving in this direction in considerable force. A few days will certainly determine this perplexing business."

The 1st Regiment Kansas State Militia refused to cross the line. The Leavenworth Mercantile Battery deserted, taking their guns. On the 19th, over one-half the 1st Regiment returned to Leavenworth. The others moved to Wyandotte. Afterwards, a small number crossed the river, and participated in the battle of Westport. They were induced to this by the action of Lieutenant-Colonel McCarthy and Adjutant Frank S. Drake. A small number afterwards moved over with Colonel Robinson, who also removed his shoulder-straps and took a musket.

To return. The force at Independence has already been given. General Deitzler, at Shawneetown, was reinforced by the 9th Battery Wisconsin Volunteers, under Captain J. W. Dodge and Lieutenant Hicks, who had left Fort Riley on the 14th, making a forced march of one hundred and forty miles, and reporting on the 18th. He was afterwards attached to Colonel Blair's Brigade.

At the Big Blue, every preparation was being made. At Kansas City, Colonel Coats commanded the Missouri Militia. Colonel Van Horn, M. C. elect, was of great service in rallying and organizing the loyal people. At Wyandotte, a large militia force was assembled. Major Hubbard, Commanding the post, was untiring in the discharge of his duties. The 18th Regiment, Colonel Quigg, was in camp, as also the 23rd. At Shawnee, was General Deitzler's Head-Quarters. A large force was assembled there.

On the night of the 18th, General Curtis received dispatches from Blunt, announcing his arrival at Lexington. Near that place, Colonel Moonlight's advance (the 11th) run on a small guerilla force, drove them through the town, killing and capturing three. Shelby was known to be at Waverly on the 17th. Price was at Marshall, Saline County, and moving up the river. His head-quarters, reported at the Kizer farm, thirty-two miles east of Lexington. Conscripting was going on briskly. Blunt urged the sending of troops, and the repair of telegraph from Independence. Captain Geo. West, with thirty-six men of Company "F," was sent with dispatches. At 11 A. M., of the 19th, a party was sent to repair the telegraph.

At 4 A. M., of the 20th, a dispatch was received by General Curtis, announcing an engagement at Lexington that afternoon, with General Price, and the falling back of Blunt towards Independence.

This intelligence was immediately communicated to Fort Leavenworth, to all posts and the forces at the Big Blue, Shawnee, Wyandotte and Kansas City. It was now evident that Price's entire army was moving westward, aiming directly at Kansas. Lieutenant Smith, Company M., 3rd Kansas State Militia, was ordered to scout thoroughly towards Blunt's advance on the Lexington Road. Captain Hinton was sent forward with dispatches to General Blunt, whom he reached about sunrise. Major McKenny was dispatched to Colonel Ford, with orders for him to keep open the road to Kansas City. Captain Hyde, 16th Kansas Volunteer Cavalry, was directed to take the Steamer Tom Morgan, and with a guard of twenty men proceed down the river as far as Lexington. If fired upon by artillery, to turn back and report at Kansas City.

CHAPTER IX.

BATTLE OF LEXINGTON.

GENERAL BLUNT, with two Brigades of Cavalry, moved from Hickman's Mills on the 16th, by way of Pleasant Hill and Holden, to Lexington. At Holden a party of citizens and militia from Warrensburg, were met, under command of Major Foster. They were sent back to Warrensburg; Major Foster reaching that place first, and telegraphing that no rebel force had been there. Nothing of special importance occurred on the march. Company "B," Captain Green, 11th Kansas, held the advance, when our troops entered the city. At Lexington, the General learnt the rebel's whereabouts. Price was near Waverly, twenty-two miles east, busily engaged in concentrating his army for the purpose of resisting Rosecrans' advance. General Curtis was immediately informed of the position, and requested to send the 2d Colorado and 16th Kansas Cavalry. Owing to the militia difficulties, the General was unable to send forward the desired reinforcements. This

ADVANCE OF THE ENEMY. 85

information was received at 11 A. M. of the 19th. Messengers were sent to General Sanborn, but failed to reach him.

The two brigades were disposed to meet the rebel advance. The 1st Brigade was encamped on the Fair Ground, south of town, and the 2d Brigade near the College Buildings, famous for their bloody defence by Mulligan in 1861. Companies "A" and "F" of the 11th Kansas, under Captain Palmer, were stationed on the Dover road, and Company "B," Captain Green, was stationed on the Warrensburg road.

Early in the morning General Blunt, assisted by Hon. Jas. H. Lane and Lieutenant-Colonel Burris, acting as Aides, made a thorough inspection of the ground, and approaches to the city. They had but just returned to head-quarters when information was received that our pickets had been driven in. The enemy were reported advancing in three columns by the Dover, Camden and Warrensburg road. All was put in readiness for resistance. The pickets fell back, stubbornly contesting every foot of ground. The 1st Brigade immediately formed to the south of the Fair Ground, along a road running through the camp. The 2d Brigade took position in line with them. General Blunt, with the officers of his staff, was everywhere present. Strong parties were sent forward to make a thorough reconnoissance of the ground at our front. Our line of battle was formed to the south-east of the city, with open and undulating country in our front and open fields extending for two or three miles; the Independence road being in our rear. It thus offered a good opportunity for active skirmishing, and enabled us to keep open a line of retreat, all flanking movements being visible. The direct attack was made by the Camden road. A portion of the 15th Kansas, under Lieutenant-Colonel Hoyt, had been sent forward. The balance of the brigade, with howitzers, was posted on the southern edge of the city, but were soon after ordered back to the Fair Ground. Companies "E" and "F," under Capt. J. A. Curtis and 1st Lieutenant J. T. Smith, were moved to the right of the line upon the Sedalia road, with one howitzer, under Lieutenant J. Murphy, Company "B," 15th Regiment. Capt. Curtis moved forward rapidly, and soon became actively engaged with the rebel advance, four hundred strong, whom he drove back to the columns. The skirmishing was sharp and severe, firing with small arms being continuous, while the howitzer was used with considerable effect. The enemy was several times repulsed, not only here, but on our left, where the 2d Brigade was actively engaged. While thus engaged, General Blunt, with his staff, was forming a second line of battle, and withdrawing the troops to take this position. The 2d Brigade was thus withdrawn. Captain Curtis, outflanked, had been cut off. He did not rejoin the main column until after dark, having gallantly cut his way through, meeting on his retreat a detachment under

Captain West, 2d Colorado, who was bearing dispatches to General Blunt. But for this opportune rencounter, Captain West with his thirty men would have entered Lexington, then occupied by the rebels.

By the time we were actively engaged, it became evident from the steady movements as they massed themselves in our front, that their whole force was present. At the same time they brought forward a battery, and soon convinced us of their possession of Parrott guns. Their artillery did not do us much damage, while our howitzers, well and rapidly served, were kept well in front, and loaded at short range with canister, did considerable execution, as was evident from the caution with which they advanced, in spite of their overwhelming numbers and the disparity of our force, the small strength of which was plainly visible.

General Blunt's object was, by persistent resistance, at the same time falling back, to delay the enemy and ascertain their strength. An irregular firing, with occasional artillery practice, was kept up for about two hours. Their rifled guns being brought into play, it became necessary for us to move off, which was done with the utmost coolness. General Blunt, General Lane, Captain Simpson and Colonel Burris had been throughout this engagement on the skirmish line, directing and participating in the fight. General Lane dismounted, and with a Sharp's carbine took his place in the ranks of the skirmishers, in front of the 2d Brigade.

The command was directed to withdraw on the Independence road. This was done in excellent order, though the enemy pressed forward rapidly to prevent its success. The movement was covered by the 11th Kansas Cavalry, Colonel Moonlight, with about five hundred men and four howitzers, checked the pressing columns. General Blunt and Colonel Moonlight personally directed the use and firing of the howitzers. The conduct of this force was beyond all praise. They fought and fell back, forming four different lines of battle, retiring only to the main column, when almost enveloped by the enemy. A retreating fight was maintained for over six miles, until the head of our column reached the forks of the roads to Independence and Wellington. Our loss was inconsiderable—about forty killed, wounded and missing. Many cases of individual bravery made the engagement brilliant. The action of Captain Jack Curtis, in cutting his way out of the rebel lines, and rejoining the division was worthy of all praise. A small body of Kansas State Militia, and Captain Grover's Company Enrolled Missouri Militia, from Warrensburg, did excellent service. The troops engaged were, the 11th and 15th Kansas, the 3rd Wisconsin Cavalry Battalion, under Captain Carpenter, which occupied the left of the 1st Brigade, and Companies "A" and "D," of the 16th, under Captains Ames and Kendall, who behaved like veterans. The entire objects sought in this movement to Lexington, had been successfully accomplished. The enemy's force had been developed; his position, strength and location ascertained, for the first time since Price had left Pilot Knob. Our loss was small. An army of 28,000 had been in check for at least twenty-four hours, by a cavalry column of 2,000. Through this stubborn resistance, an important gain in time was made. General Curtis was enabled to disseminate reliable information to his militia, thus re-uniting them, and producing harmony of spirit and action. At the same time, it enabled him to bring forward a considerable body of troops, who had been held back, and also to fully arrange and prepare his chosen lines. The check was the most serious, when the advantage to be taken by General Rosecrans' troops, but thirty miles east of Price, was to be considered.

The Division engaged by General Blunt was that of Joe Shelby. A characteristic story was afterwards told by a deserter to this effect, that considerable disputing occurred among the rebel officers while in Lexington, as to who commanded our troops in this engagement. Some declared that it could not be General Blunt, as he held no command. During the discussion Shelby is reported as saying: "Well, gentlemen, I've only one thing to say: it was either Blunt or the devil."

Among the acts of coolness, is one given by Colonel Jennison in his published report:

"The retrograde movement was conducted with "the utmost good order, notwithstanding the difficul-

"ties of the road and the darkness of the night,
"during which nothing of consequence was aban-
"doned, and officers and men discharged their duties
"with as much equanimity as though there was not
"an army of 30,000 pressing closely upon their rear.
"An incident to the credit of Lieutenant Murphy,
"15th Kansas V. C., and Sergeant Patterson, 14th
"Kansas V. C., attached to the battery, may be men-
"tioned here: Owing to the darkness of the night
"and the inequalities of the road, an accident occurred
"by which the limber of one of the howitzers was
"broken, and before it could be repaired the entire
"column had passed. Lieutenant Murphy and Ser-
"geant Patterson remained with the piece, and
"succeeded in bringing it away in the very fire of the
"enemy's pressing columns."

Colonel Moonlight records also the breaking of the tongue of a howitzer while covering the withdrawal, and the lashing of the same to another piece under a heavy fire of the enemy.

After dark the command was marched leisurely towards Independence, bivouacking a few miles from the Little Blue, at 2 A. M.

Dispatches were received at sunrise, directing the division to move to Independence, leaving a battalion to hold the bridge at Little Blue till the enemy appeared, and then burn it. General Blunt urged that the Little Blue be held as our next line of battle, confidently announcing our ability to hold the same. There is little doubt that if our militia force had been easily handled and willing to move forward, that this plan would have been advantageous, as in that way Pleasanton's cavalry would have closed up sooner on the rebel rear, and the fighting necessary on his part to regain Independence and cross the Big Blue have been avoided.

As, however, the militia could not be moved forward, it was necessary that our lines on the Big Blue should be regarded as the main one. Another objection to the Little Blue was the character of that stream, which, being easily fordable, was considered not of sufficient extent to warrant prominent movements. Colonel Moonlight, with the 11th Kansas, was left at the crossing of the Little Blue, and the 1st Brigade, with the balance of the 2d, moved into Independence. The bridge commanded the main road to Lexington.

Had it been possible to have, at this time, extended our right by way of Lone Jack, and thus united with Rosecrans' left, throwing the main portion of the Army of the Border, with that of Missouri, on the east and south of Price, leaving sufficient to the west to check him temporarily, it is certain that we should have succeeded in bagging the prey, and bringing him to grief. The character of the main portion of our force precluded this.

CHAPTER X.

BATTLE OF THE LITTLE BLUE.

As before stated, General Blunt moved to Independence on the 20th, leaving Colonel Thos. Moonlight with ten companies of the 11th Kansas Cavalry to resist the approach of the enemy as long as possible. Two companies of the 5th Kansas Cavalry, under Captain Young, had been left on the State line to watch the guerillas, and Companies "A" and "D," of the 16th, which had been with the 2d Brigade at Lexington, were, on arrival at the Blue, ordered to report to Lieutenant-Colonel Samuel Walker, commanding their regiment. This left Colonel Moonlight with about six hundred men, and the four twelve-pound mountain howitzers, attached to the 11th Kansas.

As the stream was fordable at almost every point, it was no easy matter to hold the west bank. Major Martin Anderson, with two companies was stationed

ADVANCE OF THE ENEMY. 93

at the bridge, with directions to hold the same as long as possible, and burn it before retreating. Captain Green, with Company "I," was stationed at a ford two miles south of the bridge, with instructions to hold the same. Captain Huntoon, with Company "H," was stationed at a ford four miles distant. Colonel Moonlight's Head-Quarters were in the vicinity of the bridge. Heavy pickets were thrown out on the Lexington Road, and every preparation made that the necessities demanded. Though the stream was shallow and easily forded, the heavy timber and broken ground, extending west for two miles, with advantages afforded by the fences, walls, &c., rendered it peculiarly adapted to resisting an advance. A low range of hills run back from the stream, and, for the possession of these, Colonel Moonlight contested stubbornly every foot of ground.

About 7 A. M., the enemy's advance was fairly developed, and a brisk firing opened. Information was immediately dispatched to head-quarters at Independence. It found the Generals actively engaged in preparing to move out the 1st Division (General Blunt's), to which a Fourth Brigade, under Colonel James H. Ford, consisting of the 2d Regiment Colorado Volunteer Cavalry, Major J. Nelson Smith; the 16th Regiment Kansas Cavalry Volunteers, Lieutenant-Colonel Sam Walker, and the Colorado Battery, Captain McLain, in all about nine hundred men, with six guns—had been added.

Other preparations had been made—both to

resist the rebel advance, and to evacuate Independence—a perfectly untenable position, easily flanked were the Little Blue once carried in force. General Deitzler, Kansas State Militia, who commanded the 2d Division, was ordered to the Big Blue, and took general direction of the defensive preparations. The 4th, 12th and 19th Regiments, Kansas State Militia, Colonels McCain, Treat and Hogan, were relieved from duty under Ford, and sent to the same point. Captain McDowell (then Mayor of Leavenworth) 19th Regiment, was, with his company, detailed as escort to the ammunition train, and did good service, supplying the troops engaged.

At 10 A. M. (Colonel Moonlight having been for some time actively engaged) the 1st and 4th Brigades left Independence, and proceeded at a gallop to the scene of conflict. They reached it within the hour, a distance of eight miles.

Here they found Colonel Moonlight had fallen back, fighting stubbornly for over two miles. When the engagement opened, the rebel advance Division, under General Shelby, moved on the main road. Major Anderson set fire to the bridge, and held it until fairly burning. He then fell back to the hills, where the balance of the regiment was already in position. Captain Green also returned to the main command. The rebels had deployed to the left of the road, and were fairly swarming across the stream, compelling the abandonment of Green's position, without possibility of resistance on his part.

Colonel Moonlight immediately opened on the enemy with his howitzers. The west bank of the stream was fairly in their hands, they having succeeded in putting out the fire at the bridge, so as to cross it with their artillery. Without hesitation, and with no other thought than to contest every foot, the gallant 11th, with enthusiastic shouts, swung earnestly to their work.

The rapid deployment and overwhelming strength of the enemy, who moreover were all mounted, soon placed our small force in danger of being flanked and surrounded. Colonel Moonlight's instructions had been fully obeyed, and the objects for which he had been left being accomplished, he commenced a slow retrograde movement, taking advantage of every fence and wall to check the rebel onset by deadly volleys of small arms and rapid canister firing. Every man dismounted, and horses were led to the rear. From some of the walls and fences in our front, behind which the enemy had ensconced themselves and were sending a destructive fire into our thin ranks, they were, by a daring movement, dislodged and driven back in confusion.

At this time General Blunt arrived on the field, and assumed command. A new line of battle was formed. The 11th took the left; the 16th Kansas on its right; McLain's Battery, the centre; the 2nd Colorado on the right of it; with the 1st Brigade in line on the extreme right; the 3rd Wisconsin, under Lieutenant J. B. Pond, and the 15th Kansas, under

Lieutenant-Colonel Hoyt, in order, each to the right of the other.

Dismounting, we advanced immediately into the timber, becoming actively engaged with the rebel army. Our whole line of battle thus formed did not exceed 2,500. General Curtis, accompanied by Major Charlot, his Adjutant; Captain Meeker, Lieutenants Hubbard and Quimby, of the Signal Corps; General J. H. Lane, and Colonels Crawford and Ritchie, arrived upon the ground. Major R. H. Hunt, 15th Cavalry, Chief of Artillery, had preceded them, in charge of Company "G," 11th Kansas, Captain Gove (Escort to General Curtis), and four howitzers, and immediately went to the front and centre, placing McLain's battery in position to check the rebel advance across a deep ravine, seven hundred yards to our front. The place thus designated was in immediate range of a four-gun battery. The Colorado boys unlimbered with great rapidity, and getting in battery, commenced showing the quality of their metal. Their firing was quick and accurate, and in a very few minutes, "Johnny Rebs" were glad to get out of that; three guns being withdrawn and one abandoned, though afterwards recovered by the enemy. Prisoners declared that the fire of our guns was so destructive as to wound nearly every horse, and compel the men to run the guns off by hand, with a considerable loss in killed and wounded. The firing against the rebel guns was directed by 1st Lieutenant G. S. Eayre, commanding right section. The left and centre were directed against a heavy dismounted force, which was advancing upon our left. After ten minutes rapid firing, by direction of General Curtis, the battery fell back, their position being too exposed. One man was wounded and one horse killed. In the meantime Major Hunt had gallantly taken position in an open field, four hundred yards in advance, with the Body Guard and four howitzers, under Captain Johnson, 11th Kansas, and Lieutenant Gill, 15th Kansas. Finding this position much exposed to sharpshooters, he moved, supported on the right by the 2d Colorado, under Major Smith, to the shelter of some farm buildings, and opened with canister and spherical case, with damage to the enemy. The timber was filled with sharpshooters. It is reported by prisoners, that these were generally bushwhackers, who had reported to Price at Lexington. They knew every foot of ground over which we were fighting, and were all excellent marksmen.

Among those who fell at this point of the contest, was the gallant Major J. Nelson Smith, 2nd Colorado, who, while encouraging his men, under a heavy fire and against these great odds, was shot through the heart. His body was brought from the field by the men, though most of our dead and wounded had to be left to rebel care.

On our left, Colonel Moonlight, hardly pressed, and with failing ammunition, had held his own most stubbornly, as did Colonel Jennison, on our right, though at last the 1st Brigade was pressed back by overwhelming numbers. For some time then, the 11th, being out of ammunition, was held in line, the men cheering lustily, and occasionally breaking into the stirring refrain of

"Rally round the flag, boys."

As Colonel Moonlight fell back, he was requested by Major Hunt to support his howitzers. This was promptly acceded to, though the command depended only upon their revolvers and sabres. The enemy, as then deployed, outnumbered our force ten to one. Captain Huntoon, with Company "H," of the 10th, had just joined his command. This gallant officer held his position at the ford, where he was first stationed, against a large force, though the volleying musketry, retreating sound of the howitzers, and advancing and increasing shrill scream and report of rifled ordnance told him that we were falling back, and the enemy advancing on his left.

The 1st Brigade, Colonel Jennison, had been actively engaged. The men were dismounted. Here the firing was rapid and spirited during the whole engagement. The battle raged along the right with the same varying success which attended the day elsewhere. Before this overwhelming force, our small command could do no more than slowly fall back. The enemy brought up a number of rifled guns, and the firing was heavy, though mainly ill-directed, doing damage to detachments at our rear.

FAILURE OF AMMUNITION.

Lieutenant-Colonel Hoyt distinguished himself greatly at several periods of the battle, leading his men, when opportunities occurred, to dislodge or punish the foe. The small battalion of Wisconsin Volunteers won warm encomiums. Lieut. Dixon, Company "M," fell severely wounded, at the head of his command. Lieutenant W. H. Bisbee, Company "E," Acting Regimental Adjutant, 15th Kansas, was wounded in the left shoulder, but remained on the field throughout the engagement, though several times urged to retire.

Our entire line had now fallen back to a position about a half mile west of the one where McLain opened. Here his battery was again placed in position to the left of the road, and directed to shell the woods at the front and right, through which the rebels were then advancing. Our fire had a good effect, as it checked this movement for the time being. Again the battery fell back, going into position under the direction of General Curtis, at several points where the angles of the road afforded openings for checking the rebels' forward movement.

Orders had been given to withdraw and mount. Colonel Moonlight's command, being out of ammunition, accomplished this with great difficulty, having to do so in face of the enemy, giving up to them a long line of stone wall, of which cover they availed themselves to open a galling fire. Colonel Walker, with the 16th, covered their withdrawal with a brisk flank fire, under direction of Colonel Moonlight.

This looked like the turning point for our left. Exhausted and worn out, without ammunition, it seemed at one time hardly possible to prevent the withdrawal from becoming fatal. Yet it was done. The ammunition train, by some error, had been ordered towards Independence, near which Colonel Moonlight afterwards found it and replenished his cartridge boxes. General Blunt, with the members of his staff, was every where at the front, encouraging and directing the movements. Cheering the men with the tenacity so characteristic of this officer, and with usual seemingly reckless, but cool audacity, exposing himself to the storm of bullets, he was the animating spirit of the battle. His presence was inspiring, and as the men regarded him, they ceased to heed the whistling shot and screaming shell, which fell and exploded all about them.

Colonel T. J. Burris, Volunteer Aid-de-Camp, with Major Penny, were most conspicuously useful. The Colonel, an old and tried soldier, seemed ubiquitous, and was to be found every where, with cool and calculating manner, noting every thing that occurred, and directing the operations under the General's orders. He was sent to find and halt the ammunition train, which he did a short distance to the east of Independence. All the staff officers were active in the deployment of troops and the conveyance of orders. Not one failed to display the spirit befitting the occasion. Time was what we were fighting for, and gallantly was that object won.

Another position was taken about two miles from Independence; McLain going into battery to the right of the road. The ground was open to the front and right of our guns, while to the left, was a heavy body of timber. Through this, our troops were falling back. The enemy developed heavy lines at this point. The volleying musketry was almost incessant. General Blunt superintended the placing of the guns, and as soon as our troops had fallen back sufficiently, directed them to open on the timber. This was done with telling effect, with canister and case shot. The howitzers well advanced, were also brought into play; in a few minutes the rebel musketry fire slackened, and then ceased. A charge was ordered and gallantly executed, the rebels being driven back from our left and front; the timber was cleared, and the battery, with the 11th Kansas, enabled to pass to the rear successfully.

The 4th Brigade received orders to cover the retreat towards Independence. This was done by forming one half our line across the road, resisting until too hardly pressed, when this advance was withdrawn to the rear of a second line, which had in the meanwhile been formed in rear of the first. In this way the enemy's advance was hotly contested up to the very outskirts of the town. Throughout the whole engagement, Major Hunt, with his howitzers, was at the extreme front of our lines. Lieutenant Gill, under his direction, did great execution.

Here a last line of battle had been formed, the guns placed in position, and the division deployed. nearly all of our militia force, supplies, etc., had been removed to the Big Blue. General Curtis had been actively engaged in directing the evacuation. General Lane and Colonel Crawford of the Volunteer staff, remained on the field, having reported to General Blunt.

The last line of battle being thus formed on the outskirts of the town, the formidable advantages accruing to us from the possession of the walls, fences, houses, etc., as well as from the bloody punishment already given them, made the enemy temporarily stay their movement. Advantage was immediately taken to withdraw all but the 16th Kansas, through the town, towards the Big Blue. The 11th Kansas was to relieve the 16th, so soon as supplied with cartridges. The conduct of the 16th, with its gallant commanders, Colonel Walker and Major Ketner, was such under this fiery ordeal as to win the highest praise. Being heavily pressed, it fell back to the 2d Colorado, by which it was supported. Its ammunition became exhausted, yet it received the rebel fire without flinching, falling slowly back, as if on battalion drill, until in the town, when it was relieved by the 11th, who covered the retreat through the streets unto the railroad bridge on the east, when, it being then quite dark, the enemy ceased pursuit.

The battle had lasted for eight hours. For the first three the enemy were held at bay by less than six hundred men. For the remaining five, 3,000 men fought over six miles of ground, against an enemy increasing in numbers, until the three divisions of Price's army were developed, thus outnumbering us ten to one. The great advantage gained to our arms, and one which materially insured our subsequent victories, was the delay thus made. The cavalry of General Pleasanton was thus brought within striking distance. Besides, the punishment given the rebels in some sort compensated our loss. Prisoners taken afterwards reported the rebel loss, killed and wounded, at not less than five hundred.

General Blunt estimated our loss in killed, wounded and missing, as about two hundred. Of this the 2d Brigade lost one half. The Fourth also suffered heavily; Colonel Ford estimating his loss at sixty. The 1st Brigade suffered the least. Lieutenant Gill, of the howitzer battery, had fifteen horses killed; he fired the last shots on the retreat.

Quite a number of officers were wounded. Captain N. I. Gregg, Company "M," received a severe gun-shot wound in the right arm, which resulted in a permanent disability. Francis J. Gould, Esq., acting as Volunteer Aid to Colonel Ford, was mortally wounded. Lieutenant Spencer, 2d Colorado, was severely wounded in the foot. Other officers were injured.

Many noteworthy and striking incidents occurred during the day. Towards the close of the fighting, General Curtis received a telegram from the War Department, announcing Sheridan's splendid victory at Fisher's Hill, Va., with the capture of forty guns, and a large number of prisoners. This was read by the General to the volunteers and militia, at Independence, by whom it was welcomed with enthusiastic cheers for the Nation, and as an augury of the success ultimately to crown the campaign on the Union's right flank, in which they were now engaged.

An incident occurred which showed the malevolent and treacherous character of that smouldering rebel sentiment, that in Missouri festered beneath a sullen submission. The 2d Colorado had for many months been stationed at Independence. Its officers were humane men, mainly conservative in their tendencies. They had, however, severely punished the bushwhackers and their harborers. While the regiment was passing through the town, some cowardly hand, and that a woman's, fired from a window, wounding a Lieutenant. The family residing in that house had long enjoyed the protection of the regiment. The dastardly act was suffered to go unpunished, the exigency rendering a halt impossible. Others of the citizens appeared on the streets to scoff at our retiring troops, and welcome their congenial traitors.

George Todd, a notorious guerrilla of Jackson county, was shot in this battle—it is believed by Lieutenant-Colonel Hoyt, of the 15th Kansas. He was the leader of the "Sam Gaty" Massacre, in 1863, when a number of contrabands were taken and murdered in cold blood. He was also Quantrille's second in command, at the terrible butcheries of Lawrence and Baxter Springs, in August and October of the same year.

It was long after dark when our exhausted troops reached the Big Blue. Many of the troops were without subsistence for several days, owing to the trains being sent to Kansas City.

CHAPTER XI.

MARCH OF ROSECRANS' CAVALRY FROM JEFFERSON CITY TO INDEPENDENCE.

Leaving the Kansas Volunteers and Militia encamped upon the west bank of the Big Blue, anxiously awaiting the dawn of the 22d, we turn towards the forces of General Rosecrans, and mark their progress in the rear of the Rebel army.

After that army was withdrawn from Jefferson City, October 8th, Brigadier-General John B. Sanborn was ordered by Major-General Alfred Pleasanton, who had arrived and assumed command on the 6th, to take command of the cavalry there concentrated as a corps of observation, and follow the enemy.

This force consisted of regiments and detachments as follows: First, 3rd, 4th, 5th, 6th, 7th, 8th and 9th Regiments Missouri State Militia; 6th and 7th Provisional Enrolled Militia Regiments; 2d Arkansas Cavalry; 1st Iowa (Veteran) Cavalry, and 17th Illinois Cavalry; Battery "H," 2d Missouri Light

Artillery, and one section of "L" Battery, same regiments; the guns under Captain Thurber. The force numbered four thousand one hundred effective men, with eight guns, and was at once organized into the following brigades:

First Brigade, consisting of the 1st, 4th and 7th M. S. M. Cavalry, and the 1st Iowa Cavalry, under command of Colonel John T. Phillips of the 7th M. S. M.

Second Brigade, consisting of the 3rd, 5th and 9th M. S. M. Cavalry, and the 17th Illinois, with a battery of mountain howitzers, under command of Colonel Beveridge, of the 17th Illinois Cavalry.

Third Brigade, consisting of detachments of the 6th and 8th M. S. M. Cavalry, 6th and 7th Provisional E. M. M. and the 2d Arkansas Cavalry, under command of Colonel J. J. Gravelly, of the 8th M. S. M. Cavalry.

In addition to this force, General Rosecrans was concentrating a force under Major-General A. J. Smith, consisting of 4,500 veteran infantry, belonging to the 17th Army Corps; the 136th, 134th, 135th, 136th, 139th, 140th and 142d Illinois Volununteers (100 days' regiments); the 14th Iowa; the 47th Missouri Infantry (Colonel Fletcher's); and the 1st, 2d, 3rd, 4th 10th, 11th, 13th, 80th and 85th Regiments Enrolled Missouri Militia, and the National Guard of St. Louis. The latter were not taken to the field. This division numbered nearly

10,000 effective men. It was moved to Jefferson City, and immediately thereon marched westward.

General Sanborn moved on the 8th. Colonel Phillips marched towards Versailles and Warsaw, upon the Springfield road. The brigades of Colonel Beveridge and Colonel Gravelly, moved along the line of railroad towards California and Tipton. Phillips reported the enemy in a strong position at the crossing of the Moreau. Colonel Gravelly, with one section, was ordered from the California road, to reinforce Phillips. The enemy, in the meanwhile, evacuated their position, with some loss in killed and wounded, and seventy horses.

Colonels Phillips and Gravelly bivouacked near the Moreau that night; the 2d Brigade, Lieutenant-Colonel Beveridge, on Gray's Creek, ten miles west of Jefferson.

On the 9th, the division moved towards Versailles on the Springfield road. The 3rd Brigade, which had moved in direct pursuit, soon became engaged. The 2d advanced to its support. The armies were then passing through heavily timbered country east of Russellville. The 3rd Brigade was dismounted to act as skirmishers of the division. The nature of the ground admitted of sharp resistance. A charge was made through the rebel skirmish line, and their rear guard reserve attacked by Lieutenant R. B. Riggs, Company "K," 6th M. S. M., who fell in its execution. The enemy moved rapidly through Russellville, leaving their dead and wounded in our hands.

ENGAGEMENT AT CALIFORNIA.

The road was clear to the open prairie, where the rebel column and train could be seen. Being within range, our guns opened on them. They continued to move forward to Versailles, passing all roads turning towards the right to California, except that of High Point.

Believing the enemy would move by this to Booneville, General Sanborn determined to take the shortest route to California, hoping to strike their right, and also by a night march to move past their flank, and reach Warsaw before the enemy.

At 5 P. M., the column reached California, but found a large rebel force already there; a portion busy in tearing up the railroad, and the remainder in line of battle, awaiting our approach. Colonel Phillips' Brigade formed in close column of squadrons, in rear of crest-ridge running east and west. It dismounted, the right extending to the road in which our troops were marching, and the left south-westerly to the High Point Road. Our artillery opened immediately. Three squadrons of the 1st Iowa Cavalry were sent to the left to watch that flank. The other brigades, excepting two regiments, were held in reserve. Our lines then advanced rapidly, and a brief, but vigorous engagement ensued. As the left entered the town, the enemy retired, leaving five dead in our hands. Our loss was one wounded. We bivouacked for the night, it being quite dark when the firing ceased.

The main rebel force camped on the Monteau, and at daylight moved out on the Booneville road. Shelby's Division occupied Booneville that night. This body of troops constituted the advance of Price's army during its westward march. The larger number were originally from the counties through which he passed.

On the 10th General Sanborn started at daylight, marched all day, bivouacking at night nine miles from Booneville. General Fagan was reported moving that afternoon into the town.

Early on the 11th we demonstrated on the various roads leading to Booneville. The 6th Provisional Regiment, E. M. M., Lieutenant-Colonel McMahon, was ordered to take the Pisgah and California road. Colonel Gravelley moved on the Tipton Road. Colonel Eppstien with the 5th M. S. M. was sent west to the Georgetown Road, advancing till he reached the enemy's pickets, and found whether they had moved west.

The 2d Arkansas encountered the rebel pickets on the Tipton road, three miles from town. They were driven in a spirited manner. The rebel skirmish line extended for two miles. The 6th Regiment E. M. M. joined the 2d Arkansas. Lieutenant Gideon, Company "H" of this regiment, advanced into the outskirts of the town, driving the enemy. Artillery was opened by the rebels. Our line withdrew a short distance, and again advanced. A dispatch from Colonel Eppstein announced that the enemy had not moved west. Our forces then retired to the south side of the Petit Saline. Our loss was three killed and twelve wounded. The enemy's is known to have keen fifteen killed and twenty-eight severely wounded, besides others who could be moved.

On the 12th the division was moved back to California, where four days rations having been obtained, it again moved on the 13th. Here it was reinforced by a brigade of veteran cavalry, under Colonel Catherwood, 13th Missouri. It numbered 1,500 effective men, and consisted of the 13th Missouri, the 7th Kansas Cavalry, under Major Malone, and a detachment of the 2d Missouri Cavalry, under Captain Huston. At 10 A.M. the division resumed its position in front of Booneville. A reconnoissance by Captain Turley, 7th Kansas, shewed the enemy moving west, crossing the Lamine river at Dug and Scott fords.

From General Sanborn's published report to General Pleasanton, the following is given, which tersely and clearly states the position of the forces under his command, immediately anterior to General Blunt's engagement at Lexington. General Sanborn says:

"My apprehension was that the enemy would move by rapid marches to Lexington and into Kansas, and thereby prevent the organization and concentration of the troops of that Department on the border against him, and at the same time place so great a distance between his army and the infantry and cavalry of this Department, then moving to the front in support of my command, that it would be impossible for them to join me if I should follow him, and thereby avoid a battle with the large number of troops then being marshalled for that purpose, or with any command larger than my own.

"Hence, all my movements, after the enemy left Booneville, were made with the view of holding the enemy in or near Saline county, until the Kansas troops were organized and on the border, and Winslow's Brigade of Cavalry and General A. J. Smith's command of infantry and artillery should be within striking distance. I therefore moved my command, with the exception of a small force under Captain Turley, which was ordered to follow the enemy's trail, by Neb's Church, through Georgetown, up the Georgetown and Lexington Road to Cook's store, arriving at this point at three P.M. on the 15th day of October, with the view of resisting the advance of the enemy and attacking his flanks if he should advance immediately. After the first day's march from Booneville, the enemy moved slowly, portions of his command halting a short time near Marshall, Arrow Rock and Waverly. Detachments from my command reconnoitered the position and movements of the enemy daily. On the 17th day of October some movements were reported that indicated a design on the part of the enemy to move south-east through Marshall, and his advance not having appeared at Dover, I moved south to the Black Water, to be in a better position to strike the enemy if he should move in that direction. Subsistence supplies had also been exhausted for two days, and it was absolutely necessary to get a train from Sedalia.

"Immediately upon my command moving south to the Black Water, the enemy commenced moving west rapidly.

"Subsistence was obtained and issued on the 19th day of October, and on this day I received the first dispatch from General Blunt, giving the force and position of the troops from Kansas, and indicating a state of readiness on the part of General Curtis and himself. On the same day I received information from your head-quarters of the arrival of Winslow's Brigade of Cavalry and General Smith's Corps at Sedalia, and your order re-organizing the cavalry and taking immediate command.

"I sent a dispatch to Major General Blunt immediately upon receiving his dispatch, informing him of the position of the enemy, and of all our forces and intended movements, and having on this day, by order of the General commanding, moved the 1st Brigade to Booneville and the 2d Brigade to Kirkpatrick's Mills, I moved with the third Brigade to Cook's Store and halted.

"At 3 P.M. I received a dispatch from Major-General Blunt, then in Lexington, and sent one immediately in return.

"I ordered Colonel John E. Phelps, 2d Arkansas Cavalry to move forward on the Dover road at midnight, till he should strike the main body of the enemy or reach the Missouri river.

"At 3 A.M. a dispatch from him announced that the rebel army had been moving through Dover West during the afternoon and evening of the 19th, and that cannonading was heard late in the evening in the direction of Lexington — adding that he would move forward and attack the force remaining at Dover.

"This information was immediately communicated to the General commanding, and the entire force at once commenced advancing.

"I sent dispatches to General Blunt on the evening of the 19th, and again on the morning of the 20th. None of these dispatches reached him, and I consider it the most unfortunate thing of the campaign that he did not know our position and plan at this time."

An obvious criticism on General Sanborn's movements, is, that he was compelled to lose valuable time in obtaining supplies; an accident which, the country east of his march being in our hands, should not have been allowed. It would appear also, that from five to six thousand well appointed cavalry should have more successfully impeded the enemy's movements. General Blunt, at Lexington, with two thousand men, fought the rebel advance for six, and hindred their movements for twenty-four hours. Again at the Little Blue, with three thousand, Generals Curtis and Blunt, obstinately resisted them one day, and by this means enabled Pleasanton to attack them at Independence.

On the 19th, General Pleasanton arrived at Dunksburg, and assumed command. It was re-organized into four brigades; the 1st, under Brigadier-General Sanborn; the 2d, under Brigadier General Brown, and the 3rd, under Brigadier General John McNeil; the 4th, Col. Winslow, consisting of veteran cavalry, belonging to the 17th Army Corps. At this time, Gen. Rosecrans was at Sedalia. General Smith, with the Infantry, moved on the 19th towards Lexington.

At 2 P. M. of the 19th, our troops moved in the same direction. General McNeil being in advance, camped that night ten miles from that place. Being ordered to occupy the town, General McNeil moved, and at midnight entered Lexington. Lieutenant-Colonel Eppstein, with the 5th M. S. M., being in advance, were fired upon by two separate parties in the suburbs of the town. Seven were captured. The city was evacuated by the rebels, and the brigade bivouacked in the streets. The command had marched twenty-four hours without forage— none was found in the place—and at day-break McNeil moved *via* Waverly to Fire Prairie, where he again bivouacked without forage or food.

On the 22d, at 5 A. M., the division moved to the crossing of the Little Blue. The bridge was found destroyed, and the ford impracticable for artillery. General McNeil still led the column. A temporary bridge was hastily constructed under the direction of General Pleasanton, and the artillery and train passed. General McNeil, with a part of his brigade, moved rapidly forward, attacking the rebel rear guard, consisting of two brigades of Arkansians, Major-General Fagan's Division, which held the eastern approaches to Independence. McNeil deployed and steadily pressed forward, driving Fagan from each position for several miles, though the enemy were supported by a well-directed fire from Parrott guns. General Sanborn was sent to McNeil's support. The skirmishing was severe. A charge being ordered, General McNeil mounted his regiments as they came up, ordering Colonel Catherwood, with the 13th Missouri, to fall upon the rebel rear with the sabre. The order was brilliantly executed. Forming in close column of companies, Catherwood, supported by the Veteran 7th Kansas, Major Malone, and the 17th Illinois, Lieutenant-Colonel Beveridge, charged through the streets, capturing a number of prisoners, killing and wounding many, and taking two Parrott guns, formerly belonging to the 2d Regiment Missouri Light Artillery, which were captured at Pleasant Hill, La., by General Dick Taylor. About forty of the Kansas wounded, left on the field the day before were found in Hospital. Colonel Phelps, of the 2d Arkansas, participated in this charge, leading his regiment on our right and to the left of the enemy's position. He captured a staff officer of General Cabell, with that officer's sword. It is reported that one time General

Marmaduke himself, was within our advanced lines, but escaped. The rebel line gave way, falling back to Sponge creek, where they re-formed on the western bank. General Sanborn immediately moved by a circuitous route for the purpose of turning their position, but Colonel Winslow's Brigade had already driven them back, and continued fighting them towards the Big Blue, though it was then dark.

General McNeil moved out at midnight, under orders to march to the junction of the Independence and Hickman's Mills, on Santa Fe road. The 3rd M. S. M., Lieutenant-Colonel Mathews, being left at Independence, as Provost Guard.

The following rebel officers, were captured in this gallant action of General McNeil. Several were taken near Lexington:

Colonel W. D. Baber, 45th Arkansas; Lieutenant F. Curtis, of M. Jeff. Thompson's Staff; Major H. Carrolton, Inspector General Slemmon's Brigade; Captain F. Davidson, 10th Mo. S. G.; Lieutenant A. W. Smith, Coffey's Regiment; Lieutenant-Colonel Young (since dead), and Lieutenant J. Kinder, Lowther's; Captain H. W. Lenmox and Lieutenant S. B. Hickough, Crabtree's; Major William Cook, Freeman's Brigade Staff; Captain Wm. M. Morrison and Lieutenant P. M. Little, Gordon's; Lieutenant T. H. Morwin and Lieutenant M. C. Thornburn, 1st Arkansas; Captain J. B. Moore, Slayback's. Lieutenant W. B. Walker, Elliott's; Adjutant Wm. A. Redd and Lieutenant J. S. Plattenberg, Goodwin's. Colonel Young was a former resident of Jackson County, Missouri, and an active bushwhacker in '61-62.

The treatment of our wounded left at Lexington and Independence, by the rebels, was not such as to materially improve the reputation for chivalry of which they boast so hugely. An instance of this was seen in the case of James Thomas, Company "C," 11th Kansas Cavalry, left severely wounded in the outskirts of Lexington. He was unable to move, and after being stripped naked, was ridden over several times by the rebels, and otherwise injured, while not one offered to aid him. He remained thus exposed, until found by General A. J. Smith, on occupying the town, who had him carefully attended.

At night, on the 22d, General McNeil occupied a position upon the road from Independence, leading south-west. Colonel Winslow was in advance, west on the road to Byrom's Ford. The balance of the command of General Pleasanton in the rear, ready to move at peep of day. General Rosecrans was at Lexington, with General Smith. General Curtis had fallen back to Westport and Kansas City. The main rebel army was concentrated on the Blue, west and south of Westport.

No communication had yet been had with General Pleasanton, since the failure of Sanborn's messengers to reach Blunt before the battle of Lexington. The first intelligence was received at sundown by a volunteer scout, Daniel W. Boutwell, 2d Regiment K.

S. M., who on the night of the 21st, started to obtain information. Boutwell was formerly a member of the 6th Kansas Cavalry, but had been discharged. We give the story as told by himself:

"He received his instructions from General Deitzler, and without papers or arms, dressed in the army uniform, left the General's Head-quarters on the Blue, about 7 o'clock at night and rode to Kansas city. Leaving his horse there he took a skiff and started down the river, but had not proceeded but a few miles, when his boat stuck on a bar and he was compelled to abandon it. He made his way to the shore the best way he could, and now found that he had reached the rebel lines and was fired upon by the pickets, the ball passing but a few inches from him. Carefully concealing himself in the brush, he moved stealthily along and passed the pickets. From this point, he went above the lower ford of the Big Blue, which was held by the rebels, and finding the mud very deep, threw in rails and lying down attempted the passage. About half way over he slipped off the rails and was immersed in mud, thin and slimy, three or four feet deep. By dint of hard work and perseverance, he succeeded in reaching the other side, and passed on by Independence, carefully avoiding roads, pickets and guards. About daylight, for miles below Independence, he came within sight of the rear of Price's army, five thousand strong, left to oppose Pleasanton.

Passing to the left of this, he had proceeded but a few miles through the timber, when he was ordered to halt, and turning, saw three men with guns drawn on him. They beckoned for him to come up, and asked who he was. He replied, that he supposed he was their prisoner. They examined his uniform and wished to know if he was a federal soldier. He replied, that he was, and much to his surprise was told he was "all right then."

These three men proved to be George Smiley, and two other members of the Rush Bottom Company of Missouri State Militia, who had been cut off from their command the day before, in the fight with Blunt at the Little Blue, and had not been able to get out of the rebel lines. One of these guided our hero on through the country four or five miles and took him to a house, where he was furnished breakfast. A short time after he left this man, he came within sight of the rebel pickets, and evading them passed to one side, one of the rebel pickets coming within twenty yards of him. When nearly opposite them, Pleasanton's pickets commenced firing upon the rebels. After the firing had ceased, Boutwell went up to the road, but seeing no one, and the tracks showing the federals had advanced, he proceeded towards the main army. He had travelled about a mile, when he met a soldier who conducted him to the General's Head-quarters, at the ford of the Little Blue. The army was moving slowly along, intending to camp soon for the day. Boutwell was introduced to the presence of Generals Pleasanton, McNeil and Sanborn.

"Boutwell asked the Generals if they 'would receive a verbal message from a muddy man.' Pleasanton replied that he would, and he proceeded to deliver his message. The General examined, re-examined and cross-examined his informant, until fully satisfied of the correctness of his statements, and said that he had been ready to attack for several days, and not having heard any thing from above, and realizing that it was slow business to organize militia, feared that they were not ready for him to move."

Upon the information brought by Boutwell, General Pleasanton determined to press forward energetically. The engagement at Independence followed. Messengers were sent to General Curtis, who reached him at sundown.

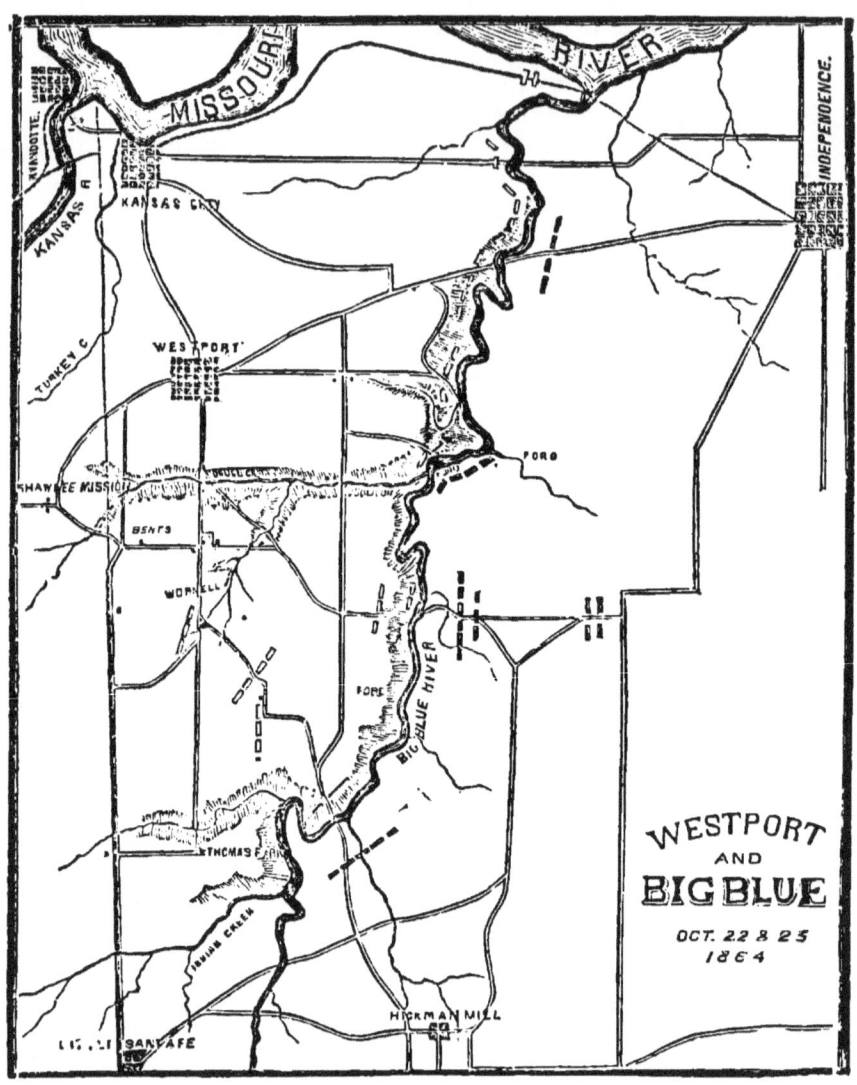

CHAPTER XII.

BATTLES ON THE BIG BLUE AND STATE LINE.

The entire force under General Curtis rested on the night of the 21st, upon the west bank of the Big Blue, the main body at and adjacent to the road leading from Independence and Kansas City. Pursuant to order, General Deitzler retired to this point during the forenoon of the 21st, from Independence. He found Colonel Blair, with a considerable force of militia, two sections of the 9th Battery Wisconsin Volunteers, under Captain Dodge and Lieutenant Hicks, and a section of the 2d Kansas Battery. A great deal of work had been done to render this very strong position more defensible. The east bank was open country to the front and right, while the west bank rose abruptly as precipitous bluffs, well covered with timber and brush, quite difficult of access, and makes a defile for the road to pass through. South of the road the timber was dense—ground broken. North of the road, were open fields sloping moderately to within twelve or fifteen feet of the stream. The roads from fords crossing the Blue, all converged to Westport and Kansas City. North of the main ford, was one other at the mouth, three miles above. Here a small steamboat was stationed, as also a battalion of the 19th Kansas State Militia, Col. Hogan, two hundred and fifty strong. The 4th and 19th had reported to Colonel Blair, Commanding 3rd Brigade, 1st Division, by order of General Deitzler.

Every thing being in readiness for the expected emergency, transportation was all sent back to Kansas City. At that point and Wyandotte, by direction of Colonel Weir, 23rd Regiment K. S. M., alarm guns were fired at midnight, and the militia aroused. A considerable body of colored troops moved during the night, as did the 10th and 23rd Regiments, also militia and volunteers from Kansas City.

The main line, our left and centre, extended for six miles. The 19th Regiment held the extreme left, when, on the morning of the 22d, the troops waited the rebel approach. North of the road was formed the 6th Regiment K. S. M., Colonel James Montgomery; then the colored volunteers, about six hundred strong (the mounted companies being retained with their local militia regiments). Immediately to their rear, in the open ground, was stationed the 9th Wisconsin Battery, and to the right, under direction of Captain Dodge, the two Parrotts of Lieutenant Minor. The guns were supported by the 5th Regiment K. S. M., Colonel Colton, and Lieutenant-Colonel Eves' Battalion from Bourbon county.

Above the main crossing, McLain's Colorado Battery held a commanding position. The 4th Brigade was formed to support it, with the 12th Regiment K. S. M., Colonel Treat. The second Colorado supplied the pickets to the east. One was advanced to Rock Ford, four miles from Independence. Six companies, under Captain Green, were thrown across as skirmishers, and remained until the left and centre retired to Kansas City.

At Simmons' Ford, two miles south, the 10th Regiment K. S. M., Colonel Wm. Pennock, was stationed, supporting a section of the 2d Kansas Battery. Early on the morning of the 22d, Colonel Moonlight moved to this point with the 11th Kansas and assumed command. Above this a cattle ford—known as Hinkle's—was left comparatively unguarded. Three miles from Simmons' Ford is Byrom's. This proved to be the main point of attack. Roads to Independence and Raytown cross here, and to the west run roads which diverge to Kansas City or Westport, striking between both, or moving out towards the State line.

Colonel Blair had, the evening previous, directed Colonel McCain, with mounted battalion of the 4th K. S. M., to proceed to this ford, hold the same, and scout thoroughly the eastern bank and roads; also to open communication with the force at Russell's

COLONEL McCAIN'S MOVEMENTS.

Ford on the Hickman's Mills road, some miles to the south. It was late at night when the 4th Regiment proceeded to its destination. Compelled to cross the Blue, it moved almost in the face of the enemy, over a rough country, and by blind and broken roads. At 1 P. M., Colonel McCain halted his command in the bottom near Byrom's Ford, to await daylight, and thus enable him to ascertain his whereabouts.

In the morning at break of day, he occupied his assigned position. Dispatches were sent to Hickman's with an escort of twenty-one men. This party was attacked soon after daylight, two miles from the Ford, and all but one taken prisoners. He escaped by the fleetness of his horse. Aaron Cook, one of the prisoners, was murdered in cold blood.

Major Hazen was sent with a detachment to hold another ford, long disused, some distance above. He came across a rebel straggler, played "secesh" on him, obtaining much valuable information, and then brought him into camp. At nine A. M., Colonel Jennison, with the 1st Brigade, took position at Byrom's Ford.

Still further above was the ford known as Russell's, or Hickman's Mills Crossing. This was of considerable importance. General M. S. Grant, through General Deitzler, had been directed to hold this position with militia; two regiments of cavalry and one gun being detailed for that purpose under the following order:

HEAD-QUARTERS KANSAS STATE MILITIA,
CAMP AT SHAWNEE, KANSAS,
Oct. 20th, 1864.

SPECIAL ORDER,
No. 15.

I. The commanding officer, 1st Brigade, will, on receipt of this order, move the 2d K. S. M., Colonel Veale commanding, and the 21st K. S. M., Colonel Lowe commanding, to the crossing of the Big Blue, near Hickman's Mills, Missouri.

II. The officers commanding this force, on arriving at the point designated, will proceed at once to fortify that crossing for defensive purposes, and picket thoroughly the country on the opposite side.

* * * * * * *

By order of Major-General Deitzler, K. S. M.

JOHN T. MORTON, A. A. G.

The Leavenworth Battery was designated as part of this force, but as elsewhere stated, it abandoned the field and returned home. Colonel Veale's immediate command consisted of the cavalry of the 2d and 3rd Regiments, numbering about seven hundred men. The 21st, Colonel Lowe, numbered about five hundred. A brass twenty-four pound howitzer, belonging to Company "A," 2d Regiment, under Captain Ross Burnes, was attached. Colonel Veale moved on the morning of the 21st, crossed the State line, marched through Westport and to the ford near Hickman's Mills, where he encamped. Here the guns at the Little Blue were plainly heard, and the militia fully realized that they were in face of an enemy, and about to fight for their homes. The same night a bushwhacking force, under Lieutenant Mears, said to be four hundred strong, surprised a company of Missouri Militia, under Captain Tate, at Hickman's Mills, and passed within range of our pickets.

At sunrise, Colonel Veale receiving a dispatch from General Grant, stating his inability to join at an early hour with balance of brigade, fell back, according to direction, to the Moccabee Farm (a well known Union man's), one and a half miles in the direction of Westport. This would give him an opportunity of supporting the force at Byrom's Ford.

Such was the position of our forces along the line of the Big Blue, before the enemy attacked our right. It extended for nearly fifteen miles, and could not be otherwise than weak at isolated points. The main body of the State Militia (infantry) were at Kansas City, or concentrating there from Shawnee Town and Leavenworth. A battalion from Osage County encamped the night of the 21st at Little Santa Fe, and moved up the line in time to participate in the engagements. A battalion of the 13th Regiment, and also one of the 23rd, under Lieutenant-Colonels Johnson and Guildford, participated in the movements on our extreme right.

About 9 o'clock A. M., a small body of cavalry demonstrated on the main road, east of the centre. It was a feint to cover movements to the south-west. Captain Green drove back this force. A small scouting party also appeared at the cavalry ford on our extreme left, but retired before the militia.

General Deitzler had command of the left, General Blunt the right and centre. General Curtis' Head-Quarters were about a mile from the ford, and afterwards further west, at the forks of roads to Kansas City and Westport. Early in the forenoon, becoming convinced that the rebels were moving up the stream, orders were sent through Major McKenny to General Deitzler, to reinforce Colonel Jennison. The 16th Kansas, Lieutenant-Colonel Walker, which had reported to General Deitzler, was ordered to Byrom's Ford, as was also Colonel Moonlight, with the 2d Brigade.

At Byrom's Ford, Colonel Jennison had timber felled to obstruct the crossing. The position was a strong one, and the ford was rendered almost impregnable. Two companies, 15th Kansas, under Captains Swain and Smith, were sent across the stream to scout. Afterwards, a battalion, under Major Laing, were sent up stream towards Hickman's Mills, and did not rejoin the brigade until after Price retreated south. Captain Smith returned to the main ford in safety, though narrowly escaping capture. Captain Swain retained his post at the forks of the Raytown and Independence roads, until the enemy had passed between him and the ford, as well as to the south, moving towards Hickman's Mills. He found himself in a perilous position, and almost surrounded. Swain determined to make an attempt to escape, hoping to pass between the moving columns as a part of the rebel force. This design was materially assisted by the fact, that many of the confederates wore blue overcoats, captured from our men. Addressing his men, he told them if they would obey orders and hold together, he could take them through. Moving to the west, skirting the timber, he passed a short distance without attracting attention, though the sound of artillery and other movements, showed that our position had been attacked. On the east and south, heavy columns could be seen moving and closing to his front, while the timber seemed to swarm with rebel scouts. The squadron was seen, pursued; the race became exciting and desperate, and our men, though holding well together, were almost headed off. They went by the head of the rebel column with a dash, sabre and revolver in hand, reins in teeth, passed the flankers, and succeeded in escaping without loss. The squadron moved rapidly beyond the enemy, reached and passed round Hickman's Mills, crossing the line into Kansas, rejoining their regiment at or near Little Santa Fe.

To return to Byrom's Ford, where Shelby's advance was attempting to cross, Colonel Jennison placed the howitzers in the road commanding the east bank, and deployed a strong skirmish line. For hours the rebels made but little progress, having commenced the attack at 11, and not forcing a passage till 3 P. M. It is certain that a portion of the attacking force crossed at cattle fords, both above and below Colonel Jennison's position. On finding itself flanked, the 1st Brigade fell back towards Westport, fighting at every available point. Dispatches were sent to Generals Curtis and Blunt. The latter, hearing the guns, had previously ordered Colonel Moonlight, and the 16th Kansas, to support the 1st Brigade. McLain's Battery was also withdrawn from its position and ordered towards Westport. It was found impossible to reach the Byrom's Ford road with artillery by any shorter route than this. Thus our lines were driven back, and the rebels crossed the stream in force, moving a heavy column, under General Shelby himself, towards the State line, passing round by roads south-east of Westport. Another body of rebels moved directly to that place, passing to the left of Colonel Jennison, by whom they were supposed to be Kansas Militia. Lieutenant-Colonel Sam Walker, moving with the 16th Cavalry, to the support of Jennison, discovered them and halted his command, sending back skirmishers under Captain Wright. He held them handsomely in check. They commenced to flank us on the left. Again the 16th fell slowly back to the outskirts of Westport, and with the assistance of a battalion of militia cavalry, under Lieutenant-Colonel M. Murdock, kept the enemy out until the arrival of Colonel Ford compelled them to retreat to the Blue. Major McKenny rallied the militia and placed them in a position to do good service.

The 1st Brigade moved steadily to the open prairie, four miles below Westport, near the State line. Upon reaching the line road, Colonel Moonlight, with the 11th Kansas Volunteer Cavalry, the 12th Regiment Kansas State Militia, two Parrott guns and four howitzers, joined the command. The head of Shelby's Division was then near the line, and almost into Kansas. Both brigades formed in line, and the action commenced fiercely. A body of militia (battalion of the 13th, under Lieutenant-Colonel Johnson), were formed in line of battle to the rear of the 1st Brigade. The engagement became sharp and general.

Our forces had been strengthened by the body guard of General Curtis, who, at Westport, had directed Major Hunt to reinforce Colonel Jennison. The Colonel directed him, as they met on the Byrom's Ford road, to fall back towards Westport and assist in holding that place against the rebel flanking column. Here Colonel Moonlight was joined by Major Hunt, and all passed out to the south. Two rifled guns had been brought up by Shelby, and the field was hotly contested; but we continued to drive them steadily for nearly four miles and until dark, back to the Big Blue. The 14th Regiment, Kansas State Militia, Colonel Harvey, on its march to Kansas City, arrived in sight of the enemy, and were deployed on the high prairie in support of our troops. Among the most efficient volunteers on this occasion, was an Aide of General Grant, Kansas State Militia, Dr. Dubois, of Leavenworth, who rendered Colonel Jennison great assistance in conveying orders, riding to the most exposed portion of our lines. The fighting was principally done by our skirmishers, eight companies being deployed for that purpose. Four or five companies of the 11th and the remainder of the 15th—the former under Lieutenant-Colonel Plumb, and the latter under Captains Wanless and Johnson and Major Hunt, who assumed command of our skirmish line after the engagement opened—composed our advance. The work was most gallantly executed. As the 1st and 2d Brigades came up at different parts of the engagement, no general direction was taken by either commander; Colonel Jennison being the senior officer, however, Colonel Moonlight formed on his left. Major Hunt took command of the skirmish line. Under his direction, the formation was completed, a steady forward movement made, and success insured. When the rebels withdrew, the Major was loudly cheered by the men, who realized that this result was largely due to his efforts.

When the sun went down, Shelby's Division had melted from the field. They had fallen back to the Big Blue, where a long line of fires and heavy columns of smoke told of the presence of a large army. Our troops retired to Westport, which was already occupied by the 16th Kansas; Colonel Ford with the 2d Colorado Cavalry, and McLain's Battery covering the roads to Kansas City.

Colonel Ford with a portion of his regiment and the 12th K. S. M. had been ordered from the centre to reinforce Jennison about 3 P.M.

REBEL DEFEAT AT SUNDOWN. 133

In this engagement our loss was inconsiderable, while the results were most conspicuous. Gallantry was never more heartily displayed. Each man felt he was defending his own fire-side. The consciousness of the devastation to which Kansas would be doomed in the event of a rebel invasion—the memory of Lawrence and other raids—nerved every arm, and filled the heart of our soldiers with fierce resolve not to be defeated, however great were the odds. The loss on the part of the enemy was reported at over one hundred. We captured one hundred and fifty stand of small arms from dead and wounded left on the field. Among the prisoners was a Lieutenant of Jackman's Regiment, who reported the entire rebel army on the Blue as numbering 30,000, and intending to fight in the morning for the possession of Kansas City.

To return to the force at the Hickman's Mills crossing—our extreme right—and the events which transpired there.

Colonel Veale having moved back to the Mocabee farm, formed his command in line of battle, covering the road to Byrom's Ford. Then, with his Adjutant, Lieutenant E. P. Kellum, and an escort of twelve men, he moved down the road to communicate with Colonel Jennison; Lieutenant-Colonel Greene being left in command of the Brigade.

General M. S. Grant, accompanied by the 21st K. S. M., soon after arrived on the ground. On the return of Colonel Veale, who reported all right at the ford, it was determined to move forward and occupy the position originally assigned them. Col. Veale, with six companies moved to the east side of the Blue, reconnoitering towards Independence; Captain Hindman, with the Douglas County Battalion, being left in charge of the train and ford.

A messenger had previously reached Grant, with the following dispatch from General Curtis:

> HEAD-QUARTERS, FORKS OF THE ROAD,
> 9 A. M., Oct. 22d, 1864.
>
> GENERAL GRANT:—Price is making very feeble demonstrations in front. Look out for your position. Send scouts on road to Pleasant Hill, and also towards Independence, to see if Price is moving towards my flank. Send me reports every thirty minutes.
>
> S. R. CURTIS, Major-General.

Lieutenant-Colonel Guildford with battalion of the 23rd Regiment Kansas State Militia, reached Westport about 10 A. M., and was ordered to report to Colonel Veale. Lieutenant-Colonel Johnson also reported with battalion of the 13th. Lieutenant-Colonel Abernathy was sent with a party to communicate with Colonel Jennison. On his return, Colonel Lowe was sent to the Rock Ford on the Little Blue, upon the Pleasant Hill road. At the crossing were retained, under command of Lieutenant-Colonel Guildford, his own battalion; that of the 13th, Lieutenant-Colonel Johnson; Captain Hindman's, 3rd Regiment, and the twenty-four-pound howitzer. Colonel Veale moved, as ordered, on the Hickman's Mills road, without finding the enemy. On his return he halted to feed, and was met by General Grant, who had also crossed the stream to examine the country. Returning with Colonel Veale, they were met at the crossing by dispatches directing Grant to reinforce Jennison, who had been driven from Byrom's Ford. Arriving at the west side, it was found that Colonel Guildford had moved without orders in the direction of Westport. The difficulty in the management of affairs here, seems to have been that General Grant scattered too much, sending out too heavy reconnoitering parties, and not keeping the troops well in hand. The gun had also moved back, and as was soon seen, was left with only the detachment belonging thereto, to protect and defend it. A dispatch was sent to Colonel Lowe, directing his speedy return. This reached him at Hickman's Mills. Major Laing, with four companies of the 15th Kansas Cavalry, was also with him. An Aide of General Curtis, Lieutenant Cyrus M. Roberts, found this force and returned to the Blue with it. Laing was charged with want of alacrity in moving as directed.

In the meantime it was found that our troops were engaged near the Mocabee farm, and General Grant, believing that Colonel Lowe would soon be up, determined, contrary to the recommendations of Colonel Veale, to push forward to the prairie on the Westport Road. The rebels, who had crossed between Byrom's and Russell Fords, attacked Cols.

Guildford and Johnson in the lane. Captain Hindman's battalion had fled, leaving the train. The others had been driven from the field in the direction of Westport. Lieutenant-Colonel Johnson afterwards moved out to the support of Colonel Jennison at the State line fight.

Captain Burnes, marching in rear of Guildford, was challenged in the lane by a rebel officer. A heavy line was deployed, and the rebels opened fire upon the little handful of twenty-one men who were with the gun. Private Race and the Captain returned to the gun, which, in spite of the odds, returned the rebel fire with a shell. At this time Colonel Veale, with a battalion, numbering in all not over two hundred and fifty men, formed to support the gun. The rebel force in our front was under Jackman, and in spite of the disparity of numbers, their advance was for some time checked. A rebel officer rode up to Colonel Veale, and, mistaking him for one of their own officers, was captured. It proved to be a nephew of General Shelby. The gallant militia formed under a galling fire, and maintained the unequal conflict for about forty minutes. Expecting the arrival of Colonel Lowe, General Grant hesitated to withdraw, though urged to do so by Colonel Veale. Our first line of battle was broken in some confusion, but speedily re-formed, and the men continued the conflict with the coolness of veterans, exhibiting none of the characteristics of raw militia. It was the very apotheosis of valor, and well deserves a place among the heroic actions of this war.

The continued resistance, so deadly and effective, of this puny handful, exasperated the rebels to madness, and finally their whole line, which had been strengthened until it numbered 3,000 men, charged with a yell, almost overwhelming the little band. This onslaught drove our force parallel to the lane. The rebels dismounted and occupied a locust grove on our right, pouring therefrom a deadly fire. Company "B," 2d Regiment, cleared the grove, and repelled a flank movement. Still Colonel Lowe did not arrive, and it became evident that an attempt at escape must be immediately made. The battery boys stood at their guns, each vying with the other, until all were shot down; all dead or wounded, or taken prisoners. Not a member of the detachment escaped. A flanking column had in the meanwhile passed around the Locust Grove, and extending almost to the Blue, poured in a most deadly fire, and the weak and wavering line fled towards the timber. Colonel Veale, Lieutenant-Colonel Greene, Captain Huntoon, and other gallant officers, remained almost to the last man. They had nobly striven against odds outnumbering them at least ten to one. The rebels charged with their wild and peculiar yell. Maddened by the gallant resistance they met, our men were shot down as they surrendered, or murdered as they lay wounded on the ground. True courage seems not to excite admiration, but rather to arouse their passions to madness.

Another line of battle was formed in the timber of the Big Blue, and Colonel Lowe arriving on the double quick, dismounted his men, sent the horses to the rear, and moved in good order to check the enemy's advance. They came on yelling, evidently intending to take in the entire force of "Tads." Major Laing, with battalion of the 15th Kansas, is reported as not acting with proper courage, and finally as moving off the field without in any way aiding the militia. He was arrested by order of General Curtis for this, and was afterwards tried, the court exonerating him, though dismissing him from the service on other disgraceful charges. The 21st was formed along the brow of the rise; the enemy were coming in hot haste through a narrow defile at the foot. Those of the 21st who could see the enemy commenced firing; the rebel advance fell back out of sight. Presently they moved forward again, when a heavy volley from our entire line drove them once more. At this time, some of the militia, seeing Major Laing leaving, also started to the rear; but Colonel Lowe, Lieutenant-Colonel Robinson, Major Still, and Lieutenant Roberts, A. D. C., weapons in hand, checked and turned them to the front. A brisk fire was maintained for half an hour, but the rebels gladly availed themselves of all possible shelter. Finding our position could not be forced, they returned, leaving our exhausted citizens to withdraw unmolested from their isolated and perilous position. The 21st lost three men—two killed.

To narrate the conspicuous acts of personal daring, at the Mocabee Farm fight, would be impossible. Where all done so well, it would seem invidious. Dan Handly, of the battery, fell at his gun, fighting even after being wounded and on the ground. Many, as before stated, were shot after surrender. It is probable, that but for the personal interference of General Joe Shelby, all would have been butchered by Jackman's bushwhackers. Lieutenant Wm. De Long was shot after capture, and died at Kansas City. Race of Company "A," was also shot, and died on the following Tuesday. Lieutenant-Colonel Greene, while with Captain Huntoon, endeavoring to form a line on the west bank of the stream, was taken prisoner. He was divested of nearly all his clothing and shot at three times, one ball taking effect in his hip, one glancing along the back of his head, and the other missing. The ruffian who fired, exclaimed as he did so—"There, d—n you, die!" Colonel Greene shortly after dark succeeded in dragging himself to a ravine on the left of the road, and lay there that night and following day. He heard the noise of the engagement at the State line, and distant thunders of the guns at Westport next morning. About 11 A. M., the forces of Marmaduke commenced moving by the adjacent road to the South. Colonel Greene, being discovered, was at first supposed to belong to their own command. A surgeon gave him some whiskey and water. Later in the day, when in response to close questioning, Colonel Greene assured a party he was a Federal officer from Kansas. Although displeasure was manifested, no threats were made or violence exhibited. Before night the rebels had passed. Our troops moved upon a road further to the west. Colonel Greene did not obtain assistance till Tuesday, when he reached a house, was fed and taken to Westport. Captain Huntoon was taken prisoner, as were many others. Two men of the 23rd were killed after surrender; three taken prisoners, who subsequently escaped. A portion of its train, nine wagons and eighteen horses, were captured; as also a portion of the train of the 19th, with the Brigade Quarter-Master, Lieutenant Marsh, of Leavenworth.

The simple, but vivid words of Colonel Veale's report, form a fitting close to this narrative:

"It is not for me to say upon whom rests the "responsibility of scattering our forces in such a "manner as to preclude the possibility of concert, or "unity of action. I can only say, I acted under "orders, and by so doing lost twenty-four brave "Kansans killed, about that number wounded, and "eighty-eight taken prisoners, among them four "officers; also one twenty-four pound brass howitzer, "and one hundred horses.

"The enemy's loss in killed and wounded in this "engagement was very heavy, as our prisoners "passing over a portion of the field a few moments "after the battle counted forty-three dead rebels.

"While our loss is very severe, I have to thank "God that the bold stand taken by my brave men "gave the enemy an afternoon job, which detained "them from marching into Kansas; and the next "morning they were confronted by an army that "neither yielded them ground nor spared their "ammunition, but put them on a hasty retreat "southward, and thus Kansas was saved.

"On the morning of the 24th, we gathered "together our dead (our wounded having been "already cared for), and took them to Kansas City, "where we obtained coffins for them, and on the "morning of the 25th we buried them at Wyandotte, "on Kansas soil. From there we marched home to "meet our mourning friends, and tell the story of "the fallen."

And there was mourning in many households. The brave had fallen. Their homes were bereaved. Widows and orphans were made desolate. Let any one think what a calamity the sudden death of two score of active citizens would be in any small community. Yet it was not this alone which affected Shawnee county. Three score and over were prisoners in the hands of the Philistines. Their fate was more pitiful; as, even if not murdered, there was the horror of lingering starvation, and all the foul and loathsome fear of the rebel prison pens, to haunt with dread the loving memories at home.

Soon afterwards the dead were gathered up and returned to Topeka, where they were re-buried with public honors. A monument is to be erected over their grave.

The number of prisoners captured by the rebels was one hundred and two. The number of killed was thirty, ten of whom were killed after surrender; one being shot for a bushwhacker by our own troops, through a sad error. The wounded in all would not number more than fifty. The following are the names of the wounded of the 2d Regiment: Lieutenant-Colonel H. M. Greene, Captain S. B. Miles, Captain H. E. Bush, Captain Ross Burnes, Lieutenant Wm. De Long (since died), Privates John P. Green, John A. Ward, Brook Crawford, John Keiser, Isaac Rickel, John Prater, Peter Fleck, Allen Blandon, John Thompson, H. M. Howard, Martin Dreck, James Norris, Wm. T. Thompson, John Branner, John Ward.

The prisoners were: Captain Huntoon, Lieutenants Hiram Ward, P. H. Gilland and John W. Brown, (Lieutenant Ward died after his release, from the sufferings endured while a prisoner;) Sergeant Geo. Duncan, Corporal J. H. Glenn, Privates G. H. Wood, F. Dawson, C. G. Howard, W. Flanders, A. McConnel, F. M. Fletcher, Nelson Young, S. Shaefer, J. S. Stansfield, E. B. Williams, Levi Williams, J. Warren, J. Reed, O. Nuylor, J. T. Gage, A. Quiet, J. Keiser, R. B. Hoeback, Wm. Marx, J. B. Taylor, A. G. Taylor, G. B. McKee, John Kempt, S. J.

Reader, J. W. Clark, Eph. Johnson, J. P. Majors, J. Bickel, D. Vaughn, J. Hudgins, T. Fleshman, Geo. Fix, H. Fix, W. True, H. Cunningham, L. T. Cook, S. Blandon, G. Wood, D. Stevens, Jerome Stahl, Eli Snyder, J. Russell, B. Ingrund, W. S. Hibbard, H. M. Denning, John Robinson, J. S. Markham, S. Kosier, H. Linn, E. Williams, G. G. Sage, C. G. Follansbee, John Link, R. Fitzgerald, Fred Mackey, J. Anderson, A. H. Holman, E. Pape and Jacob Klein.

Lieutenant Marsh, Brigade Quartermaster, was also captured, as were twenty men of the 4th Regiment, and others belonging to the 19th and 23rd Regiments.

After witnessing the withdrawal of the rebels from their front, the militia retired to Kansas, (whither they had been preceded by Major Laing,) following the timber of the Blue to Little Santa Fe. The 2d Regiment moved to Wyandotte and Kansas City next day. The 21st, with others, were stationed at the Fords on the Kansas River, under directions of General Curtis, through Senator Pomeroy.

While these events were transpiring, the left and centre of the army had fallen back to Kansas City by order of General Blunt. This movement was commenced about four P. M. General Blunt and staff moved towards Westport in advance. Directing his staff and Colonel Blair to station the troops as they arrived in the entrenchments at Kansas City,

General Blunt himself rode to Westport, where he found the other brigades of his command; the 1st and 2d with the 4th and 10th Kansas State Militia at the south side of the town; the 2d Colorado, 12th Kansas State Militia, and McLain's Battery, on the hill upon the Kansas City road, in line of battle. The militia were ordered to Kansas City and placed in the entrenchments till daybreak. The battery was also ordered back. The cavalry remained at Westport, the 16th Kansas holding the picket lines. The rebel camp extended for miles, far to the right and left of our bivouack fires. A night of anxiety and doubt, but not dread, was passed.

As our troops were falling back, a messenger arrived from General Pleasanton, at Independence, announcing the victory there, and his presence in our neighborhood.

The intelligence was greeted with wild cheers, as staff officers rode along the line communicating the welcome news.

As the rear guard left the crossing of the Blue, a party of rebels, about five hundred strong, who had lain concealed in the brush on the east bank, made a rush upon the rear, consisting of the 19th Regiment Kansas State Militia, under Colonel Hogan. The rebel dash was gallantly made, and as gallantly defeated. Wading the creek, they pushed through and over the abattis, logs, etc., up to Hogan's line. Our gallant militia turned promptly. A sharp but short skirmish ensued—partly in the bed of the river. The rebels fled, leaving twelve dead and ten prisoners in our hands, among whom was a Captain Von Valkenberg, brother to a member of Congress from New York. On being taken before General Curtis, he stated that it was Price's intention to occupy Kansas City; of his ability to do which the Captain seemed not to doubt.

The labor of placing the militia was of an onerous character. Not appreciating the importance of position, a large number of the companies sought to pass into town and obtain food. The scene grew animated. Staff officers galloped here and there, shouting hoarsely; portions of the militia obstinately insisting upon their right to do as they pleased; amusing colloquies and expostulations occurred, but at last the long line of works was occupied, and affairs began to assume a business shape. The guns were placed in commanding positions; the 2d Kansas Battery covering the main road to Independence; Dodge's (9th Wisconsin) Battery and the section under Lieutenant Minor occupying elevated ground, covering roads to the north and west; McLain being placed to cover the approach from Westport. By some mistake, the ordnance train and horses of the militia were removed towards the Kansas River, near the Wyandotte bridge, and were not found until nearly daybreak.

Head-quarters were established at the Gillis House. Very few obtained food, while many of the officers worked hard throughout the night in procuring and forwarding ammunition and subsistence to the troops at Westport and in the trenches. General Blunt and staff worked all night, and before day mounted their horses and rode to the front.

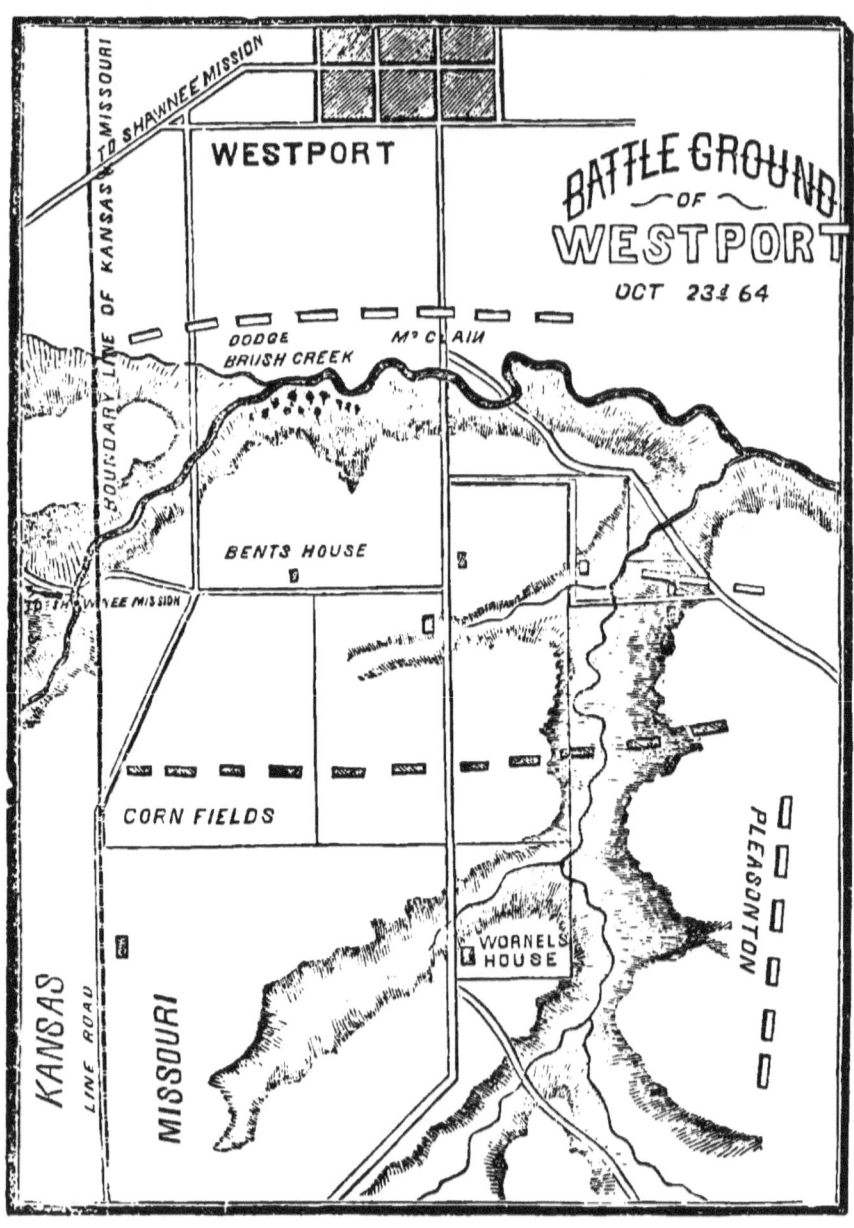

CHAPTER XIII.

BATTLE OF WESTPORT.

The Sabbath dawned upon hostile armies; one intent upon invasion and rapine; the other, sternly moved to resist and defeat the foe. The intense feeling among Kansas troops, as the faint flush of morn lit up the eastern sky, cannot now be realized. All felt they were defending their homes. The artillery of the opening conflict could be plainly heard at many of their firesides. It was a day such as seldom dawns upon a people. Mothers, wives, little ones, were uniting in prayer for protection. An host of implacable foes, in insolent triumph, were thundering at their doors. But no one shrank from the bloody conflict. Each felt here was the hour of manhood; and all were equal to the grand occasion.

The volunteer troops of General Curtis were left watching, during the night, extended lines of camp-fires, which told them the foeman's whereabouts. East of Westport extends the long line of the Big Blue, with its broken country densely covered with timber. Two miles south is Brush creek, a small stream emptying into the Blue, with precipitous banks, densely wooded. It branches about four miles west at the Shawnee Mission, and heads a dozen miles further in Kansas. Four miles north is Kansas City, at the junction of the Kansas and Missouri Rivers. The Kansas is almost due north, with a well-timbered stream, easily defensible—Turkey creek lying between—and emptying into the river near Kansas City. This was an important part of the line adopted by General Curtis, in the event of falling back to Kansas City. North-east lies Independence, distance twelve miles. One road runs directly east from the town to the Blue. The Byrom's Ford road runs south by east from Westport, till it strikes the stream The road to Little Santa Fe, a small village on the State line, about twelve miles south-west, passes directly south across Brush creek. The Byrom's Ford road leaves this just north of the creek, while the Hickman's Mill road crosses it about three miles from Westport. The country south of Brush Creek and east of the Big Blue, is high table land—the summit level between the Big Blue and the Kansas Rivers. For over two miles, contiguous to Brush Creek on the south, the cultivated fields extend, with lines of fences and walls, admirably adapted for sheltering troops. They were freely used by both sides.

Beyond this, for about four miles, swells the open prairie, until you reach the broken country about Indian Creek, where the dense timber, interspersed with occasional fields, offers good cover for a retreating army.

The troops who were to participate in this day's operations, were located in this wise: General Curtis, with the volunteers at Westport as an advance, and the main body of the militia in the intrenchments at Kansas City. Thus his line extended north and south. The rebel army were encamped on the Big Blue, from the vicinity of Byrom's Ford, where their main body bivouacked, westward to beyond Russell's Ford. General Pleasanton, with the four brigades of cavalry under his command, had succeeded on the evening of the 22d, in occupying Independence, and defeating the rebel rear division with some loss. Three brigades, Sanborn, Brown and Winslow's (of the 17th Army Corps), were on the road to Byrom's Ford, following in the direct track of Price's main army; while General McNeil, with the 1st Brigade, was moving from Independence, on a road running north and west towards Hickman's Mill. The Union army was therefore advancing from the north and east; while the rebel army were moving south and west. General Curtis' main purpose would be to prevent them going any further west, and if unable to defeat them fully, to turn them southward. Two roads run in this direction, both of which the rebel army covered;

the State line road already spoken of, north of the Big Blue till you crossed it some miles beyond Little Santa Fe, and the other crossing at the Russell Ford, and passing through Pleasant Hill and Harrisonville, some miles east of the river road. McNeil's movement upon the road from Independence to Hickman's Mill, south of the Blue, was designed to obtain possession of this road at the mill, and so check a movement on that line. In addition to these forces, Major General A. J. Smith, with 10,000 infantry, was moving rapidly from Lexington to Independence, hoping to participate in the final engagement, should we succeed in holding Price.

The earliest dawn found General Blunt with his staff at Westport, and the utmost activity prevailing throughout our lines. The brigade of Colonel Blair, consisting of the 4th, 5th, 6th, 10th and 19th Regiments K. S. M. (Cavalry), with the 9th Wisconsin Battery, and the section belonging to the Colored Battery under Lieutenant Minor, were ordered to march at 3 A. M., from the intrenchments to the front. McLain had already moved. By 5 o'clock, Colonel Blair was on the move.

The 1st, 3rd and 4th Brigades, Colonels Jennison Moonlight and Ford, were already moving out to attack the enemy, who from his position, if allowed, could at his leisure attack us in front, or turn our right flank.

The 1st and 4th Brigades, numbering in all not more than 1,800 men, with McLain's Battery, moved

FORMATION OF OUR LINE.

on the south road, crossed Brush creek and took position, mainly to the right of the road. The north bank of the creek was covered for over a mile with timber and sparse brush. South, the timber extended for half a mile, when the road passed between heavy stone walls for some distance. To the left, the timber was dense, made so by the junction of a small creek with the main one; while to the right were open fields, on the northern edge of which the timber swept to the west in shape like the horn of a crescent. Here then the line was formed. Our left, consisting of the 2d Colorado and 16th Kansas, rested on the lane; the battery in the field near the timber, while the 1st Brigade deployed to the right. General Blunt by this movement sought to gain time for the arrival and deployment of the militia, and to hinder the rebel movements upon our right, toward which it was evident a portion of their lines were moving. From the roof of the hotel at Westport, the rebel army could plainly be seen. In front of our little advance, was deploying a large force, consisting, as afterwards proved, of the Division of Major-General Joe Shelby, with a portion of Fagan's Division. (This latter had fallen back to Byrom's Ford, after being driven by McNeil from Independence.) Further to the south and east could be seen an enormous train moving off under protection of Marmaduke's Division, with a large force of conscripts, &c., most of whom were indifferently armed. The glasses of observant officers showed that this train, enormous in extent, was moving towards the south. This was hailed as an evidence of Price's intention to fight only when necessary to enable him to escape with the immense plunder of his raid.

A small body of the 6th K. S. M. was sent under Colonel Burris, Vol. A. D. C., to scout through the timber to the east, which in that direction came close to the town, and might easily afford a cover to a flanking movement. He soon returned with information that the enemy were all west of the Blue and south of the Byrom's Ford road.

Our troops were barely deployed before being hotly engaged. The fences impeded active operations by cavalry, but afforded protection to skirmishers, who were pushed rapidly forward. McLain was in position at the edge of the timber, half a mile to the rear. At first the firing was entirely artillery, with the exception of a few shots exchanged by the skirmish line. The rebels continued deploying, receiving large reinforcements, and advancing with spirit and vigor. Their long lines pressed forward steadily, displaying as they did so in the centre a fine battle flag. Two guns, under Lieutenant Eayres, were ordered forward, taking position on the hill and overlooking the open prairie across which the enemy was advancing. The guns did excellent work, were double shotted with canister, while the range being short and the firing rapid, every shot told. The enemy's guns replied with vigor, and the ball was opened. Colonel Moonlight, with the 2d Brigade, had not yet taken position. Captain Hinton, General Blunt's Aide, was sent to the Colonel with orders to press forward on the right. He found him deploying his troops, consisting of the 11th Kansas, detachments of the 5th and a battalion of the 12th K. S. M., under Lieutenant-Colonel Woodworth.

Along the line the fighting continued with varying fortune on either side. Lieutenant Beach, of the Colorado Battery, with the left section, was ordered forward to relieve Eayres, whose ammunition was nearly exhausted. Finally the battery took position at the front; centre section occupying the road. On our right a heavy attack was made by a rebel brigade, resulting in the pressing back of that wing. The 15th Kansas cavalry had just previously been compelled to fall back, so that the left of the 2d Brigade was unprotected. A new line was immediately formed two hundred yards in the rear. As the 2d Brigade fell back, the enemy succeeded in raking the exposed flank. Two squadrons of the 11th Artillery and Infantry were immediately wheeled, and returned the fire. By this movement, which was well performed, the enemy were checked. Lieutenant-Colonel Woodworth, of the 12th K. S. M., held the right flank, gallantly charging with his "Tads" upon the rebel skirmishers and driving them back to their main line. While the 2d Brigade was thus retiring, an order was received from General Blunt, directing Colonel Moonlight to withdraw, move towards

Shawnee Mission, and watch the enemy's right flank, following and keeping them out of Kansas.

While this was occurring on our right—the 2d Brigade withdrawing, and the 15th re-forming—the rebels were rapidly forming on our left for a charge down the lane, for the purpose of capturing the guns under Lieut. Birdsall. They had previously succeeded in planting a section of Parrott guns on the line road, and with a raking and rapid fire, rendered our position one of extreme danger. Dobbin's Brigade was formed, and headed by Shelby in person, a bold and dashing charge was made. The lane had been swept by the fire from their guns. Portions of the 4th Brigade were rapidly formed, consisting of the 16th Kansas, and a battalion of the 2d Colorado, under Captain Green. With wild huzzas, our boys led by Col. Sam Walker in person, dashed forward on the charging brigade, which in close column moved on the guns in such dangerous proximity to them, that the men barely had time to run them to the rear by hand, when the galloping squadrons met in the fierce contest. Everywhere could be heard mingling yells and cheers; while still in the advance, Colonel Walker, sabre in hand, dashed into the midst of the rebels. The encounter was brief. Before the wild onset of our counter-charge, the keen edges of the flashing sabres, and the quick crack of their Colts, the rebels broke and fled precipitately to their main columns, which, still a mile to the south, were constantly increasing in numbers. Colonel Walker was severely wounded in the foot. His personal daring was the theme of all who saw or participated. Still the rebels advanced, though thus checked on the left, and finally succeeded in face of a destructive fire from the 1st Brigade, in forcing a heavy column into a small copse, which jutted out from the main line, to the right of Colonel Ford. Our line commenced falling slowly back, forming and fighting on each ridge as it did so.

In the meanwhile, Colonel Blair's Brigade having formed south of Westport, on high ground overlooking a little creek, the southern acclivity of which was covered with dense timber and undergrowth, was dismounted (every sixth man detailed to hold horses), advanced through the timber and across the creek. The militia were deployed to the front and left of the 15th Kansas, occupying the ground left by the 2d Brigade. The enemy were strongly posted behind a stone wall, while we were partly protected by the fence and timber. Firing was kept up rapidly for half an hour. The militia took advantage of every shelter, and like hunters in pursuit of game, did not throw away their powder, but watched the chances of hitting some one. It was not an orderly, but a very effective fire. No advance was attempted, and soon Colonel Blair retired in obedience to orders, with the balance of the division, through the timber across the creek, taking his former position on the north side. Colonel S. J. Crawford, now joined Colonel Blair, and assisted during the balance of the day in the direction of this militia. General W. H. M. Fishback joined his brigade, and with it participated in the action.

The entire division now occupied a position upon the north bank of the creek; the battery upon a commanding point of the ridge, covering the road and timber on south side; the volunteer cavalry on the bottom and near the crossing, while a part of the 2d Colorado, under Captain Green, and the 12th K. S. M., under Colonel Treat, were deployed on foot as skirmishers.

In the rear of this our first position, the activity was general, the enthusiasm thorough, and the spirit of emulation and determination visible on all sides.

General Curtis had arrived between seven and eight at Westport, after giving necessary orders at Kansas City. All the males able to work, were set to work on the entrenchments; Brigadier-General Sherry, K. S. M., being placed in command. The mounted militia force, with the mercantile battery, under Captain Zesch, were moved to Westport, where, under the direction of staff officers, they were dismounted, horses sent to the rear, and the men placed in position preparatory to the final advance.

In the meantime General Blunt had proceeded to the front, now our second line, upon the north side of Brush Creek. The rebel force could be distinctly seen deployed in great numbers. An occasional shot from the skirmish line could be heard, and the sound indicated a gradual advance. The 1st Brigade had formed a second line in rear of the dismounted militia, along whose line could be seen rapidly riding the commanding and staff officers. Colonel Colton, commanding 5th Regiment, was most conspicuous for coolness and courage. McLain had opened from our extreme left, shelling a small body of timber, through which he believed a column of rebels were advancing. The firing ceased, under orders from General Blunt, who believed our own men were endangered. A small body of rebels advanced through the timber, were met and gallantly repulsed by the militia under Colonel Colton. The men stood up to them like veterans, pouring in their volleys as regularly as trained infantry practising. The rebels broke and fled, before a militia force of about equal number. Colonels Colton and Crawford rode along the lines encouraging and directing the men, who, as the rebels turned in disorder, set up a wild cheer.

Meanwhile, Colonel Blair, hearing a rumor to the effect that the rebels were attempting to flank him, without waiting for orders, moved into the dense timber to the right, twice the length of his line, and pushed it steadily forward. A messenger was sent to General Blunt to inform him of his movement. At the same time, Generals Curtis and Blunt, both fearing this flank movement, sent orders to Colonel Blair to carry out the operation he had already commenced. The 19th Regiment, which had been formed and dismounted to the rear of the main force, was moved by a road further to the right, and, as the militia emerged from the timber, formed on Colonel Blair's right. General Curtis himself joined this movement, encouraging the militia by his presence. Dodge's Battery with two howitzers were piloted through a narrow defile to a point where the guns could be admirably placed, by a venerable patriot of seventy-five, who was upon the field ready to do his humble share of the work. The right of the line commenced immediate demonstrations upon the enemy who were posted along the forces to their front. Skirmishers filled the field, poured a destructive fire from the fences and from a large brick house in the orchard just beyond. The right of the brigade was sent forward to clear the house. It was gallantly done. Adjutant James Aikens of the Bourbon county Battalion, was severely wounded in this movement. The left of the line moved forward steadily through a stubble field to their front.

While the right was thus moving under the immediate eye of General Curtis, the left and centre, under direction of General Blunt, had also advanced.

When our line moved, it did so rapidly, regaining its original position, and punishing the enemy with great effect. Our artillery was well served. The rebels fought stubbornly. Hardly had we taken position, when the enemy charged in column upon a section of McLain's, occupying the road; the 15th being to the right in front, with Company "E" deployed as skirmishers, and forming the left of the line. Colonel Jennison rapidly rallied the skirmishers and led, in person, a charge upon the rebels' right flank. Two squadrons of the 2d Colorado, under Captain Green, simultaneously formed and charged upon their left. The dash was irresistable. Short, sharp, but severe; and when it was over the rebel column fled in disorder, leaving one hundred prisoners and a number of killed and wounded. Captain Curtis Johnson, commanding Company "E," 15th, distinguished himself greatly, both in the charge and a personal encounter with Colonel McGee, commanding a regiment of Arkansas rebels, who was killed, while the Captain was severely wounded in the arm.

The enemy fell back upon the road. Our lines were again advanced on the right of the road, driving the enemy at all points. Progress was, however, stubbornly contested, and was for a time but slow. We now presented a formidable appearance; our lines having fairly debouched from the timber, and with a steady, unbroken front were moving forward.

The scene was superb, combining all the wild picturesqueness of a battle field with (for a short time) the regularity of a parade. Another charge, made by Colonel Hoyt and Captain Thompson, with a portion of the 15th and 16th, carried some stone walls to the centre and right centre of our lines. The boys went at it with wild cheers. The rebels fled to the main line, which yet offered a formidable front. The walls cleared by the charge were immediately occupied by our skirmishers. On the main road, near the line first formed at early dawn, was found a broken and dismounted gun. It bore the mark of a Texan foundry, and was evidently an imitation of our Parrotts. We learned afterwards that a shell from the section under Lieutenant Eayres had struck the muzzle of this gun while the charge was being inserted. The gunner's hand was taken off, the gun burst, as our shell exploded, and six men were killed and wounded, as also several horses.

While the lines were thus moving, quite an exciting episode occurred to the rear, on the left of the road. General Blunt had turned back a short distance to give some orders, and while doing so the main body of our troops upon the right swept forward in advance. Returning with a few members of his staff and orderlies, he found a howitzer, which had been stationed in the dooryard of a farm house, a little to the left of the road, and in the edge of the creek timber, seriously threatened by a small column of rebels advancing from the east. The howitzer was without support, but the gallant squad in charge, under direction of a sergeant, were most actively engaged in double-shotting it with canister and firing into the compact rebel column. The General and party dashed forward, and, revolvers in hand, the small party formed themselves to defend the gun. So near was the rebel force that pistol shots were exchanged, when a portion of Company "E," 14th Kansas, Lieutenant Clark commanding, acting as escort to the General, dashed up and charged the rebels, who fled. It was supposed this force had been driven and separated from the main rebel army by the advance of Pleasanton on the Byrom's Ford road, near which they deployed. The gallant activity of the artillerists, as well as the prompt dash of General Blunt, saved the guns.

In the meanwhile we were swarming forward. Behind us to the right the militia still poured. The regiments left at Kansas City had been brought forward, and were now moving through the timber a mile to our rear. The artillery were all in position, and eighteen brass Parrott guns, with thirteen mountain howitzers, were playing briskly on the rebel lines, falling slowly back in admirable order before our advance. Lieutenant Hicks, with two guns of the 9th Wisconsin Battery, and one ten-pound Parrott of the Colored Battery, was placed upon the right wing; Captain Dodge, with three other guns, was on the left. When the rebel column formed for its last charge, Captain Dodge opened on them with spherical case, at a distance of five hundred yards. McLain in the centre, had driven a battery of four guns from the rebel front. Lieutenant Eayre, with the right section, was then ordered to the 1st Brigade, on the right of the line road. General Blunt himself, took direction of the firing on the left and centre, and with Captain

Dodge's guns following him, assumed position after position, opening on the rebel lines. Thundering cheers also burst along our lines, as shell after shell made gaps in the enemy's ranks. The gunners could not see the execution, for the smoke of their guns; but our advancing troops watched the effect, and cheered tremendously as the gaps were made and closed.

It would be impossible with words to paint the scene. The pencil could only give the figures; but imagination cannot furnish memory with the vivid details by which to reproduce the battle scenes of that Sabbath morn.

At the summit of a slight slope, amid the general backward movement of the enemy, a small body seemed determined to stand. Colonel Jennison, with General Blunt's body guard, and a squadron of the 2d Colorado, charged upon them. The rebels fled in disorder, not waiting to feel our sabre's edge, but inclining rather to trust the fleetness of their steeds. Some fled to the timber on the left, which was also occupied by the command repulsed in their attack on the howitzer. A detachment of the charging squadrons was dismounted and formed along a wall skirting the road to the left, and opened a galling fire on them. They left, soon rejoining the main body.

A general charge was now ordered; Generals Curtis, Blunt and Deitzler leading it. The 1st Brigade was formed; Lieutenant-Colonel Hoyt, with six companies of the 15th, on the left of the road; Colonel Jennison, with the 3rd Wisconsin Battalion, two companies of the 2d Colorado, one company of the 15th, and General Blunt's Escort, were rapidly advanced and impetuously charged. The 4th Brigade, under Colonel Ford, also formed, and charged simultaneously, the guns dashing well up to the front (McLain with two sections, finding himself with canister only, had advanced at the top of his horse's speed and took position in front); Dodge and McLain pouring in heavy charges, which told upon the now wavering rebel lines; the little howitzers charging and firing at the front of our skirmishing lines; with the wild huzzas of the volunteer cavalry in the advance, and the thundering cheers of the racing militia to the rear, as they came tearing across the fields; while the bending and wavering rebel lines, falling back in partial disorder, formed a scene never to be forgotten by any who witnessed it. While our artillery was taking this third and final position, Captain Dodge found the rebels were opening with a gun about nine hundred yards to his front, and somewhat to the right. A well directed solid shot from the Parrott, sighted by Captain Dodge, broke this piece at the first trial.

The charge was made, and the rebels broke disordered upon our right and centre. Again our lines were advanced. Everywhere in front, were seen the general officers, cheering and encouraging, greeted with the enthusiastic shouts of the men, while twice the rebel columns had broken and re-formed. Both lines were now deploying upon the open prairie, ours still having the advantage of some fields and fences.

At this time, a heavy column of cavalry could be seen emerging from the timber, and deploying about a mile to the east, and advancing towards the rebel right. Some doubts were felt as to its character, but as the line deployed, the union guidons plainly visible, were hailed with thundering cheers. A battery was opened upon the retreating rebels by this new foe. The enemy's right rapidly formed a new front, and attempted to check their advance. They made a vigorous charge and compelled a portion to fall back hastily. Again was our artillery advanced, pouring in a destructive fire. Again was our cavalry pushed forward, and the rattle of small arms was continuous along the front. Pleasanton's brigades charged simultaneously, and the rebel rear broke before this onset in wild disorder, making their way through the Indian Creek timber, in rapid rout, scattering arms, equipments, etc., as they fled, and leaving their dead and wounded on the field. It had been evident for some time, that the force at our front was fighting only to cover the safe retreat of their train and main army. For miles the ground was strewn with the *debris* of a defeated and routed army, while the dead and wounded told the bloody character of the fray. Shouts that made the heavens ring; a rapid trampling of hurrying squadrons; dense clouds of dust moving swiftly to the South;

a swinging forward into column of the forces on the left; the thundering of the guns dashing down the road; while far in the advance, the yells and cheers of pursued and pursuers, were taken up and echoed by the triumphant pæans which, from the hurrying militia in the rear, again caught up by those at Westport, and travelling on the wings of the wind, were borne jubilantly on to Kansas City, where those who in dread suspense had waited the welcome news, again made the welkin ring, and onward it fled to tell afar that the invaders had been defeated—the traitors driven back—and that the homes of Northern Kansas were saved from desolation.

CHAPTER XIV.

GENERAL PLEASANTON'S OPERATIONS ON THE TWENTY-THIRD.

The night of the 22d found General Pleasanton's force in possession of Independence, and moving in the rear of Fagan's discomfited command towards Byrom's Ford, where, on the previous day, Colonel Jennison had resisted the advance of the rebel army. Clark's Brigade held the rebel rear; while the veteran brigade, commanded by Colonel B. F. Winslow, 4th Iowa Cavalry Volunteers (a brigade which up to this date had marched eight hundred miles, and then had not one man dismounted,) led the advance of the Missouri Cavalry, pushing the enemy until half-past ten P. M., and bivouacking three miles from the Blue. General McNeil, whose daring and activity were mainly instrumental in driving the enemy from Independence, moved at midnight upon the Hickman's Mills road, with orders to reach the junction of the Independence with the State Line road at Little Santa Fe.

ARREST AND ACQUITTAL OF GENERAL BROWN.

Brigadier-General E. B. Brown was ordered forward to relieve Colonel Winslow and open the attack at the morning's earliest hour. At five A. M., troops commenced moving. General Brown had been directed to attack the enemy vigorously, as he would be supported. From some cause, the attack was not made as anticipated, and General Pleasanton riding to the front, relieved General Brown, placed him under arrest, and directed Colonel J. F. Phillips, 7th M. S. M., to take command; Lieutenant Colonel Crittenden assuming command of the 7th.[*] General Sanborn was ordered to support the advance. Colonel Winslow, by request of General Pleasanton, assumed direction of the advanced movements. The enemy were posted in strong force on the west side of the stream; the ford and approaches being obstructed by Colonel Jennison's defences, materially strengthened by the rebels when they occupied his position. Their line was formed in force about a half mile from the stream. Bearing upon the ford, a heavy gun was planted, by which our line, as it formed and advanced was seriously annoyed, and quite a number killed and wounded.

One battalion of the 4th Iowa Cavalry, under command of Captain Dee, one hundred men of the 4th Missouri Cavalry, and the 7th M. S. M., commanded by Lieutenant-Colonel Crittenden, were

---

[*] General Brown was afterwards tried at St. Louis by a Court Martial, under charges preferred by General Pleasanton, for his conduct on this occasion, but was honorably acquitted of all failure to do his duty.

dismounted and formed on the banks of the river. The firing opened sharp and effective. The 4th M. S. M., Major G. W. Kelly commanding, and the 1st M. S. M. Cavalry, commanded by Lieutenant-Colonel B. F. Lazear, were formed in column, directed to cross and charge the enemy beyond the ford. This order was executed in the face of the galling rebel fire and despite the obstacles in the creek. A number of men and horses were killed and wounded in the stream. Nothing daunted, our troops resolutely pushed forward and gained the west bank. In the meanwhile, the 7th M. S. M. crossed, bearing to the right. A furious engagement commenced. Major Kelly forming in the rear of Colonel Crittenden, the latter swung his lines quickly to the left of the road, while Major Kelly made a similar movement to the right. The rebel line was driven back for two hundred yards. They then occupied a range of low hills, extending through an open field to the left, and along a bluff covered with dense wood on our right. It was strengthened very much by high fences and some log buildings, behind which the rebels were posted.

The 4th Missouri State Militia dismounted and formed on the right; the 7th also dismounted, with a battalion of the 4th Iowa Cavalry, while Colonel Phillips took command of the 1st M. S. M., with intent to charge.

The character of the ground was such as to render cavalry movements difficult, and utterly preclude any formation but that of a column of fours. Twice the effort to charge was gallantly made. Twice it failed. The storm of shot and shell howled down that declivity from the armed lines along the brow, sweeping the road and insuring the destruction of horse and rider bold enough to attempt the ascent. The 1st Regiment dismounted, and the Brigade of Colonel Phillips advanced together, supported by part of Colonel Winslow's command. General Sanborn's were moving across the ford at this time; one regiment, the 2d Arkansas Cavalry, Colonel Phelps, Jun., being already engaged. To drive the enemy from his formidable position, became an absolute necessity. A charge was ordered and made. When within one hundred yards of the rebel line, our troops gave way in disorder, unable to stand the terrible fire. By direction of Colonel Winslow, one regiment had been held in reserve. Here the officers, Colonels Phillips, Winslow, Lazear, etc., rallied their repulsed but not disheartened men, gallantly exposing themselves in this duty to the scathing fire from the fences. Colonel Winslow's veterans were brought up and formed. Again both brigades charged. The movement was successful, though the enemy's lines were stubbornly held until the troops met, and the contest became an hand to hand one. Across the field, for one hundred and sixty yards, our troops pushed steadily. They literally moved in face of a shower of lead. Sharpshooters occupied the tree-tops, singling out the officers with fatal effect; Col. Winslow being struck in the left leg. A number of line officers were shot. Captain Blair, of the 4th M. S. M., fell mortally wounded. Van Sickle, Hamilton, Dale, Bryson, Barkley, Christian, Combs and Milner, of Brown's Brigade, fell beneath this leaden tempest.

The movement was pressed with increased vigor, the enemy driven from their shelter, and as they fell back to the timber, were followed and driven still further west in great confusion, leaving their dead and wounded, with a number of prisoners in our hands. Just as they turned to move off, a rifle ball struck Colonel Winslow, and though the latter kept his saddle for over a mile in the pursuit, the command of his brigade devolved upon the young and gallant Lieutenant-Colonel F. T. Benteen, Commanding the 10th Missouri Cavalry. By his direction, the 3rd Iowa Cavalry, under Major B. S. Jones, were dismounted and pushed forward. At the log houses already spoken of, were found about two hundred men of Brown's Brigade, who were sheltering themselves in disorder from a very hot fire the enemy were pouring on them from the woods at the western edge of the field.

They were urged into the open, and with the dismounted men of the veteran brigade, advanced across the open field at the double-quick to the woods beyond. The enemy resisted the advance with great gallantry. We pushed through the timber to the prairie. Here were some guns in position playing furiously on our advance, which moved so rapidly as to induce the rebel commander to withdraw all artillery and cavalry across the prairie, beyond the reach of our own guns now opening on them. The 4th Iowa Cavalry was on the skirmish line.

Our advance rested here for a short time—the enemy having temporarily passed out of range—long enough for the three brigades to concentrate, General Sanborn being on the left, Phillips in the centre, and Winslow on the right. Our loss, owing to the shelter afforded by the timber, was not as great as might have been expected for the stubborn resistance encountered, and the formidable position held by the enemy. Two hundred killed and wounded, will cover it. The fighting had lasted for several hours, and it was noon as we mounted again and moved across the prairie, forming a line nearly at right angles with the army of General Curtis, then most actively pressing the enemy about three miles further north and west.

Colonel Benteen soon after moved into a corn field, with the intention of feeding his exhausted animals. It became evident, in a very few minutes, that a battle was raging at the front. Our line of march had been to the south-west, and the enemy was driven beyond the Harrisonville road.

General Sanborn had followed and driven the rebel rear across the prairie, and as he now came in full sight of the battle-field of Westport, with all its active scenes, he re-formed his brigade, and moved against the front which Price's army had formed to meet him. They opened a galling artillery fire which was responded to by Colonel Cole, with Thurber's Battery. A charge was made by the rebels, which shook the right of Sanborn's Brigade, and drove in a portion with considerable confusion. Our guns were double shotted, and soon checked the desperate onset. They were fighting for the purpose of withdrawing from the field in something like order. In this they succeeded, though at great loss. Generals Curtis and Blunt had seen this advance, and with their whole line were rapidly driving in the rebel front opposed to them, doubling it upon their right flank, which had faced south and north just east of the line road, to meet Pleasanton. Twenty rifled guns opened along the entire line, and making great gaps, drove the enemy in confusion. Colonel Benteen, who had seen Sanborn charged, and the slight confusion produced by it, was moving forward. He swung his leading regiment—10th Missouri Cavalry—into line to the left, and ordered them to make a counter charge, which was done in splendid style. The whole command joined in the rapid and successful movement; the enemy fled, and the two gallant but wearied armies met upon the State line road, pressing forward in pursuit. As they swung into column Generals Pleasanton and Blunt met, hurriedly exchanged congratulations, and pressed forward to Indian Creek, where they, with General Curtis, Generals Deitzler and Fishback,

Governor Carney, General Sanborn, General Lane, and the principal officers with both armies, and citizens who had participated in the battle, stopped at a farm house for consultation and refreshment.

The pursuit of the retreating rebels was maintained by Colonel Jennison with the 1st Brigade, and a battalion of the 2d Colorado, Captain Green, who kept fearlessly on their heels for ten miles, skirmishing to the crossing of the Blue four miles beyond Little Santa Fe, where just at sundown a stand was made by General Fagan, who opened on our daring troopers with three rifled guns, and compelled them to desist from further pursuit. In this charge Major McKenny, and Colonels Crawford and Cloud of Gen. Curtis' staff, were most active. Colonel Jennison, in his published report, says of the former: " During the pursuit I was accompanied " by Major McKenny, of General Curtis' staff, who " is entitled to special mention for assistance rendered " here and elsewhere, as well as for his assured and " courageous bearing upon the field." A consultation was held at Indian Creek. General Pleasanton suggested a movement by his division on the Harrisonville road, urging the exhausted condition of his men and animals,—most of the men had been constantly in the saddle for thirty days; as also the necessity of the Missouri troops being at their several posts in time for the ensuing Presidential election. General Deitzler and Governor Carney urged with great force that the militia of Northern

Kansas be relieved, and presenting the fact of their condition in the field without proper equipments, &c., with the necessities of their families and business pressing upon them, as reasons for the step. Generals Curtis and Blunt both coincided in this view, in which General Pleasanton acquiesced. General Curtis knowing the danger in which Southern Kansas and the posts along the line were placed, as well as the insufficiency of his own force to effectually check the enemy, desired that no deflection should be made from the direct line of march pursued by the enemy. It was finally determined to move to Santa Fe the same evening, and then follow the retreating foe with the combined Volunteers of Kansas and Missouri, and the brigade of militia from Southern Kansas under General Fishback and Colonel Blair. In accordance with this programme the following order was issued:

Head-Quarters in the Field,
On Indian Creek.

General Field Order,
No. ——

So much of General Order No. 54, Head-Quarters Department of Kansas, as proclaims martial law in Northern Kansas is hereby revoked.

The enemy are repelled and driven south. Our success is beyond all anticipation. The General commanding delights to relieve the people North of the Kaw from the burden.

By order of Major General Curtis.

C. S. Charlot, Major and Chief of Staff.

In the meanwhile the whole army moved to Little Santa Fe, at which place, shortly after dark, they

camped for the night. The 4th Brigade, Militia, and the 19th Kansas State Militia continued their march, the balance of the militia returning to Kansas City, whence they moved homewards under the supervision of Governor Carney and their officers. At Little Santa Fe our troops succeeded in obtaining some needed rest, food and forage; most of the animals being now fed for the first time since leaving the Big Blue.

From General McNeil's published report we give his movements on this eventful Sabbath. General Pleasanton severely criticised the action of McNeil, who was afterwards tried on charges made by his commander, and like General Brown, was fully and honorably acquitted of all blame. (See Appendix: Sketch of General McNeil.

At 4 o'clock A. M., October 23rd, I flanked a large camp on the opposite side of the Blue, and near the Byrom Ford. I ascertained it to be the enemy. I sent a detachment of the 2d Missouri Cavalry (Merrill's Horse) to the ford, and halted to feed horses, having marched two days and nearly two nights without forage. At daybreak a heavy fire commenced on my right and in the direction of Westport. I moved on towards Hickman's Mills, expecting to be able to strike Price's flank, moving cautiously about four miles. Firing had ceased for some time, when suddenly I found myself in contact with the entire force of the enemy. I at once formed my brigade in line, advanced my skirmishers, and opened on their column with a section of Captain Montgomery's Battery (three-inch Rodman rifles). The enemy had formed their line of three lines deep, and actually surrounded me on three sides. My skirmishers (7th Kansas and Merrill's Horse) most gallantly pressed up to the main line of the enemy's centre. In the meantime he had placed batteries in three different locations, and opened a well-directed cross-fire upon Montgomery. I was consequently compelled to move him some four hundred yards to the left, recall my skirmish line, and occupy the new position. I determined to hold this position at all hazards, in hope that the remaining brigades would come up. Towards night the enemy retired, leaving about forty of their dead on the field. In the morning (October 24th) I pushed on their trail, passing between Hickman's Mills and Little Santa Fe, where I then learned that the other brigades were pushed on, and met them about twelve miles from Santa Fe, where our lines of march intersected.

Major S. S. Curtis, who, with Captain Kingsbury's Company 2d Colorado, had been sent by General Curtis to Independence, to communicate with General Pleasanton, overtook General McNeil while this artillery duel was progressing, and corroborates the amount of force against which McNeil's had to contend. As the battle of Westport was fought by the Divisions of Shelby and Fagan, it follows that Marmaduke's Division and the new one formed by Price from his conscripts and recruits, were with the train encountered by General McNeil. All data concur in making the rebel army at this time as about 30,000. General McNeil had about 1,800 men. The rebel train was guarded by about 15,000, counting Marmaduke's Division.

While our victorious troops were driving the rebels southwards, Colonel Moonlight with the 2d Brigade and a portion of the 12th K. S. M., was moving down the line, watching, hawk-like, the enemy's march, and ready to swoop upon any detached parties, or resist the main column should it cross into Kansas. Colonel Burris accompanied the column. All the splendid hours of that battle-morn, until the sun dipped far down the meridian, these gallant troops stood at Shawnee Mission, listening to the cannon's sullen boom, the fainter rattle of small arms, and the mingling sound which marked the sway and sense of the struggle. Debarred from direct participation in the glory of its passing phases, they yet well esteemed the important trust delegated to them and their commander. How well it was performed, these pages tell. A small rebel force had crossed the line in falling back from the battle. But Moonlight was on their trail. At Little Santa Fe, Captain Huntoon, with Company "H," 11th Kansas, being in the advance, struck the rear and drove it across the line out of Kansas. The brigade pushed on to Aubrey, and rested till towards morning of the 25th. So lay our forces. The main body near the village of Santa Fe, the 2d Brigade about six miles south, while General McNeil was about four miles to the south-east. The rear of the rebel army camped a little east of Aubrey.

The editor of the Kansas City *Journal of Commerce* thus graphically describes some incidents and scenes on the battle-field:

"The battle-field exhibited evidences of the fiercest contest. The enemy had fled in such haste, that he had been forced to leave his dead and many of his severely wounded. In the field next to the lane, on this side of Wernel's house, there were seven dead rebels lying side by side, and near them an officer, said to be Colonel McGee; around the latter the rebels had built a little pen of rails. A little further on, we saw a dead rebel lying stiff and stark by the road-side, shot through the head. Still further on were the remains of a rebel cannon, broken to pieces by a shot from one of our guns. Striking the open prairie beyond Wernel's, the evidences of the fight were visible all about—dead horses, saddles, blankets, broken guns and dead rebels. A little distance from the forks of the road, on the Harrisonville road, lay a dead rebel, the top of his head shot off by a cannon ball. He was the very image of a bushwhacker, and had on three pairs of pantaloons. On one of his fingers was a large gold ring. One of our soldiers tried to take it off, but the finger was so swollen that it would not come off, and he left it and passed on. Another dead rebel we saw in this part of the field. He was clothed in a fine suit of new clothes, evidently the plunder of some store or house. On the prairie our shells seemed to have done the main execution. About three miles out was a rebel shot through the bowels, and left by his companions by the roadside to die. At a house by the road was one shot through the neck—a mortal wound. Early in the day the rebels took possession of Mr. Wernel's house for a hospital. Here they left about a dozen, too severely wounded to be moved, and three soldiers to take care of them. We interrogated some of these men, and they all were members of Dobbin's brigade of Arkansas troops. With one exception, of those we conversed with, they claimed to have been forced into the service; one, a boy of eighteen, said he volunteered rather than be conscripted. The most of those wounded will die, being shot through the body. The less severely wounded were removed last night to Westport, and are receiving the same attentions as our wounded.

Quite a haul of prisoners was made during the day. Some forty or fifty of them were marshalled in line just at night as we came through Westport, and started off under guard for this place. Many of them were mere boys from sixteen to nineteen years old. Some of them had a bushwhacker look, while some of them looked like " good quiet farmers," who had lately joined the expedition for plunder. One of them remarked that they "had got the joke on Old Pap this time, as they would surely beat him into Kansas City." Another remarked that " He wished Old Pap was along with them."

One thing was to be remarked of all the rebels we saw —dead or alive—the stolid, ignorant, degraded appearance of the whole of them. They seem to belong to a different race from ours, and most certainly an inferior one. In truth, this war is one of intelligence, enlightened and Christian civilization against barbarism. These miserable, degraded, hungry wretches, on their errand of plunder and devastation to our peaceful homes, are fit representatives of the half-civilized power that is endeavoring to overthrow republican institutions on this continent.

Woe would have betided the homes of this hated city had these wretches made good their entrance here. That they did not, we owe, under the good Providence of God, to the brave Kansas boys who helped us beat the invader back. We should certainly have been overpowered had they not crossed the line and helped to fight their own as well as our battle on Missouri soil.

Our wounded, as well as those of the rebel army left on the field, had been carefully and promptly attended to, under the direction of Surgeon S. B Davis, Division Medical Director, who by General Curtis had been announced as Medical Director of the army. He was present at Lexington and at the Little Blue. At Independence, a hospital was organized and placed under charge of Surgeon S. P. Earickson, 16th K. V. C. Thirty-one of the most seriously wounded were left in the town, and were retaken by General McNeil. Arrangements were made at Kansas City for ample hospital accommodations. The severely wounded on the 22d, at Byrom's Ford, Hickman's Mill Crossing, and on the State line, were left on the field. On the morning of the 23rd, Surgeon Davis, with Surgeon Philip Harvey, U. S. V., and the various regimental surgeons, were efficiently engaged with organizing an ambulance corps. The regimental Chaplains were all active and very efficient. Surgeon Davis, with ambulances, proceeded to the front for the purpose of gathering the wounded of the previous day, but as the battle had commenced, this became impossible. Major Davis remained at the front, rendering efficient service as Aide, until the final charge was made. The field was then searched, and all the wounded removed. A number too seriously injured were arranged in a temporary hospital at Westport, to which a number of gallant members of the 2d Regiment K. S. M., who had remained on the field from the 22d unattended, were removed. Assistant Surgeon Graham, 13th K. V. I. (who, being on furlough, had volunteered his services), was placed in charge. The steamer "Tom Morgan" was sent to Independence, and all the rebel and wounded of Kansas regiments removed. Surgeon Harvey was placed in general charge of all the field hospitals now established, and on the 24th Surgeon Davis started to rejoin the army. Surgeons Pollock, 2d Colorado, and Ainsworth, 11th Kansas, and Assistant Surgeons Vance and Aikens, 2d Colorado Volunteers, had preceded him.

CHAPTER XV.

PURSUIT OF PRICE DOWN THE STATE LINE.

At sunrise of the 24th, the troops now comprising the Army of the Border were on the march. The rear of Price's Army had encamped eight or ten miles to the south. The advance, with their immense train and imperfectly armed division of conscripts, volunteers and bushwhackers, under a Brigadier-General Tyler, the prisoners and Provost Guard, and the division under Marmaduke, was at least five miles further. The rebel army moved with great celerity, being all mounted. It marched, as appeared from its broad and massively marked trails, in two columns of companies, one on each side of the Prairie road, with artillery, etc., in the centre.

The 1st Division was under Major-General James G. Blunt, and consisted of the volunteers of the department of Kansas (except Moonlight's Brigade) and the militia from Southern Kansas—the region now threatened. The composition of the 2d Division, under Major-General Alfred Pleasanton, has already been given. Its brigades were led by efficient officers.

The commanding General was accompanied by Company "G," 11th Kansas Cavalry, under Lieutenant Gill, and a detachment of the veteran 2d Kansas Cavalry (about one hundred and fifty), under Major Henry Hopkins, with four howitzers under Sergeant Sloonacker. The 2d Brigade, 1st Division, Colonel Thomas Moonlight, consisting of the 11th Kansas, under Lieutenant Colonel Plumb, and a detachment of the 5th, under Captain Young, with four howitzers, about 700 men, were detached, watching the rebel right flank.

The force now in direct pursuit of Price was about 10,000 men, with three field batteries, and two of mountain howitzers. General Rosecrans left Independence the same morning that the cavalry marched from Little Santa Fe. The infantry division, under Major-General A. J. Smith, from Independence had marched towards Harrisonville, north-west, but too far east to be of service against Price.

As the camp broke, the 1st Division took the lead; the 4th Brigade, Colonel Ford, being in advance. Three squadrons of the 2d Colorado formed the advance, which was commanded by Captain E. W. Kingsbury.

Nothing of importance occurred during the march except the capture of several stragglers and a number of exhausted rebels who were abandoned by their comrades. At the crossing of the Big Blue, was to be seen the marks of Colonel Jennison's presence in stark forms of several bushwhacking looking individuals, who had met their fate during the night. Among these was one clothed in a Federal uniform, who, in obedience to general orders, was hung as a spy.

The day waned, the march continued with unabated vigor, and the road was more thickly strewed with the *debris* of a retreating foe. Hundreds of broken down and abandoned animals could be seen feebly grazing along our line of march. Broken wagons, and, about noon, the limber and caisson of a twenty-four-pound howitzer, captured on the 22d from General M. S. Grant, near the Moccabee farm, were found on the road. The rebel rear kept well in advance, and a dense moving column of dust some miles to the south alone told of their presence. Occasionally small parties might be seen moving from the right in the direction of the main column. As the afternoon waned, evidences of the haste with which the rebels pressed forward were visible on all hands. Large droves of foot-sore cattle were now found, as well as many sick men lying by the road side.

The country through which the march extended was entirely deserted. So far, the main body of neither army had entered Kansas. The State line road runs about a mile from the east border of Kansas. As the troops marched through the hours of that pleasant October day, the western prairies were eagerly scanned by those who hourly expected to see the wreathing smoke arising which would tell of the invaders' torch. But the indomitable Moonlight was pressing on that flank, and until darkness hid the pursuit, no outlying parties of marauders ventured into the State. At Coldwater Grove, about fifteen miles from Santa Fe, the 2d Brigade struck the rebel centre, and skirmished with it for some time. The movement was a bold one, and entirely successful in creating a panic sufficient to induce the rebel commanders to keep their force well in hand and move steadily south. Seeing that they must camp on the Marias des Cygnes, where the road to Fort Scott deflects from the Line road, Colonel Moonlight moved rapidly towards Mound City, which was threatened by this route.

The border of Missouri, through which both armies were passing, was entirely desolate; not with the grand monotony of nature, but with the ruin of civilization and cultivation. Desolation most absolute and appalling; for it told of the savage devastation of partizan warfare, and of the fearful retribution the passions of men had inflicted. The condition of the Missouri border affords a vivid illustration of the solemn warning of the sacred writer: "It must needs be that offences come; but woe unto him by whom offences cometh." The outrages inflicted upon the Free State settlers of Kansas by citizens of Missouri, for and in behalf of human slavery, were fearfully balanced by the woe which had lighted upon their land.

During the fifty miles of this march not an inhabitant was to be seen. Where they had lived was marked by the charred remains of consumed dwellings, the only standing parts of which were brick chimneys, built according to Southern fashion, on the house's exterior. These are familiarly known as "Jennison's Tombstones," from the fact that that partizan, in his campaign of 1861–2, burnt the houses in all districts infested by bushwhackers. Long lines of grey ashes told where fences had stood; while rank crops of unsightly weeds marked where cultivation had once smiled. It was a fair land to look upon. Broad, swelling prairies stretching east and west; well-defined water courses, with dark masses of wood robed in autumnal glory, all combined to make a bright picture of pastoral beauty. Yet it was desolate and dreary, and in spite of the natural advantages, there rested over all a sense of brooding horror.

At sundown the column halted at Westpoint, a deserted and half burnt village upon the State line, about forty miles north of Fort Scott. At this place the evidences of gaining upon the rebel march were more apparent.

Darkness came on. The troops of the 1st Division made such preparations for refreshing themselves as their scant means allowed. The crimson light of many fires gleamed through the gray night mist.

Some of the cattle abandoned by the rebels were slaughtered, and the fresh beef, roasted on sticks over blazing fires, was eagerly eaten by hungry soldiers, in most instances without salt or bread. Thus they rested. The clouds grew darker and a heavy mist began to fall.

In the meanwhile impending operations were of course the subject of discussion between the Generals. It was evident that the retreating rebels could not march further that night. They had traveled sixty miles without rest. Eight miles to the south was the Marais des Cygnes* river, at the Trading Post crossing of which the rebels would probably encamp. They had left the Line road near this place (Westpoint), and were then in Kansas. The Trading Post, a small hamlet on the south side of the stream, was about two miles west of the line, and was surrounded by a populous farming settlement. During the previous summer a company of the 15th Kansas had been stationed there. A large quantity of hay belonging to the Government was stacked there. The stream is wide; the Ford has steep banks; the timber dense and broad, and the approach from the north easily defended from two mounds, between which the road passes.

General Blunt urged that army pass to the west, crossing by a ford four miles above, and thus flanking the enemy, be placed right in its path, compel-

---

* Swamp of the Swans.

ling Price to fight or surrender. This movement was urged with great pertinacity, but was finally rejected by General Curtis, as involving an additional march of fifteen miles without the certainty that the rebel army would not move so easily and rapid as to render it of no avail. He therefore determined that the pursuit be followed on the same line, directing that General Pleasanton's Division now take the right for a night march. Over two hours were consumed in this change. General Sanborn took command of the advance, with his own and Phillips' brigade; Colonel Gravelley, 8th M. S. M., having the front.

While this change was progressing, and the weary 1st Division were taking advantage thereof to rest as well as they could, Captain Kingsbury, with his battalion of Colorado Cavalry, unacquainted with the new order, had pressed close upon the rebel rear, which he struck about four miles from Westpoint.

The malignant fury of the rebel invader was now apparent. They had entered Kansas. The first house across the line was the scene of a dastardly murder. An old, gray-haired minister of the Gospel lay dead, with white locks reddened by his own blood. The woman and children were frantic and crazed with terror and grief. The fence and outhouse were burning. The interior of the cabin presented a woe-begone appearance. A perfect saturnalia of destruction seemed to have reigned. Everything not portable had been broken. On the floor were black and charred marks, where fire had been set. The frightened inmates were stripped of nearly every article of clothing on their persons or in the cabin; and to crown the brutality, in very wantonness, the ruffians had shot one of their exhausted horses and tumbled it into the spring, in order to make the water useless. Such was the first scene witnessed by those of our officers who had pressed on behind the advance. Lieutenant-Colonel Wheeler, 13th Kansas, Captain Young, 5th Kansas, and Captain Hinton, A. D. C. to General Blunt, all rendered the bereaved woman what assistance and consolation they could.

The latter moved on to overtake Captain Kingsbury. At every dwelling the scene thus described was repeated. Fortunately the men had fled or were in the militia regiments halted at Westpoint. Night had fallen, darkness and rain set in, and a cover afforded for marauding which was freely used. This portion of Kansas (Linn county) is the section which suffered most under the rebel march. A writer in the *Border Sentinel* thus describes the condition of the county, and *some* of the brutalities practiced:

"Along the line of retreat of the rebel army every house within reach of the main body or flankers was robbed of everything it contained. All kinds of clothing were taken; even the flannel was in some instances taken from infants. Every morsel of food, cooked and uncooked, was consumed, destroyed or taken along; and all the stock that could be led or driven was taken; in fact, everything valuable and not valuable was taken; so that those men and families whose hard fate it was to be in the way, are left stripped of every comfort and necessary of life. * * * *

"The retreat of the rebel army is marked not only by robbery and desolation of the wildest kind, but the fiends were not content with that. Six miles north of the Trading Post they murdered Samuel A. Long, aged fifty-six years; he was previously robbed of his money. Three miles north of the Trading Post, John Williams, a preacher, aged sixty years, was indecently mutilated and then hung. Five miles north of the Post, Richard B. Vernon was murdered; and in the vicinity of the Post, John Miller, aged sixty-five years, was killed. Many other citizens, all unarmed, as these were, were shot at."

Another writer in the Leavenworth *Times* gives his testimony:

"The rebels sustained their well-earned reputation for savage brutality, which had previously secured for them an infamous place in history. Seven or eight men, aged and unarmed, were murdered near Trading Post. In an extent of six miles wide through which the army passed in Linn county, every house was plundered of all kinds of provisions, blankets, clothing and all articles, valuable or worthless, that could be carried off. Even the flannel was taken from infants, in two instances that have come to my knowledge; and two young ladies were stripped of every article of clothing except one under-garment to each. A woman who was holding a sick baby had the shawl rudely torn from about it. Only one house was burned in this county (Mr. Dowd's store, at Trading Post) and it is said that Price had the man shot who did that."

During the day dispatches had been sent by General Curtis to Lieutenant-Colonel Drake, 17th Kansas, commanding at Paola, after our columns were south of that place, informing him that his post was no longer in danger, and directing that he render all possible assistance to reinforcing Mound City and Fort Scott. Dispatches were also sent to

Fort Scott, and at sundown to Colonel Moonlight at Mound City, directing him to press forward to the former post at all speed, holding it at all hazards until our army reinforced him. The messenger (citizen) sent with this dispatch failed to get through, having been driven back by rebel scouts, and was met several miles from Westpoint by Captain Hinton, who sent him to try again, accompanied by a member of the 15th Kansas, whose family lived in the vicinity, and who knew the country thoroughly. They succeeded in reaching Colonel Moonlight during the night.

Mound City, the county seat of Linn, was eleven miles west of the Trading Post, which the rebel advance reached at four P. M. Messengers were sent to warn Captain Greer, Company "I," 15th Kansas, who with eighty men of that regiment and three companies of militia, exempts and negroes, was holding the place. A detachment, about six hundred strong, was seen moving in that direction. This was believed to be a bushwhacking force, until scouts brought intelligence which proved beyond cavil that it belonged to the rebel army.

Every precaution and preparation was made by Captain Greer. His small force was posted so as to command the approaches. The Government stores were loaded for removal. Information was sent to Fort Scott south and to Paola north of the rebel approach. About this time a dispatch was received from Colonel Moonlight, who was pressing vigorously on to relieve this place. Scouting parties were sent out, one of whom encountered a rebel picket six miles from town. Intelligence was received from Colonel Drake. He was on the march with part of the 17th Kansas. The 11th K. S. M., Colonel Mitchell, had joined Colonel Moonlight. The 19th, Colonel F. W. Potter, was at Paola. About midnight Colonel Moonlight reached Mound City, having marched sixty-five miles without food or forage.

At the Trading Post was encamped the rebel army. Captain Kingsbury attacked and drove in their pickets about eight P. M., immediately sending back messengers to General Blunt, supposed to be close behind. He continued skirmishing slightly for two hours, until relieved by Colonel Gravelley, and ordered to withdraw from the advance by General Sanborn.

The advance of Pleasanton's Division reached the vicinity of the mounds, occupied strongly by the rebel outposts, about 10 A. M. Finding the rebels in force (as General Sanborn believed), and not knowing the topography, by his orders, Colonel Gravelley withdrew our pickets about half a mile, and the troops were ordered to rest. Sanborn established his head-quarters at the house of Elder Williams, three miles north of the Trading Post. The country hereabouts being enclosed, the 1st Division was halted three miles further to the rear, on the open prairie, unable to reach the fields where forage and fuel could be obtained. For hours Colonel Blair's Militia Brigade, still further in the rear, stood by their horses, having no orders to rest, without fire to dry their drenched garments, and without food. About midnight some fires were lighted, but they were shortly extinguished, under apprehension that our position would be seen through them.

General Curtis, whose object was to press the foe, at least keep him aroused and in a state of activity, so as to complete the breaking down of his forces from exhaustion, finding the column halted, and no sound of conflict to be heard, sent Majors Weed, McKenny and Hunt, with Capt. Meeker, to General Sanborn, to ascertain the cause of the halt. They found that officer in his blanket, and were informed that he was satisfied the enemy was in force upon the mounds in front, and that he could not take the responsibility of moving further till daylight. On this being communicated to General Curtis, he ordered that artillery be opened upon the rebel camp. Owing to the darkness and storm, this was not accomplished till near daylight.

In the meanwhile, Major R. H. Hunt, with Captain R. J. Hinton, had moved to our picket lines, aroused the Colorado battalion from its bivouac, and passing Colonel Gravelley's quarters, informed him of their intention, moved out to attack and drive in the rebel pickets, determining to carry the mounds under cover of the rain and darkness.

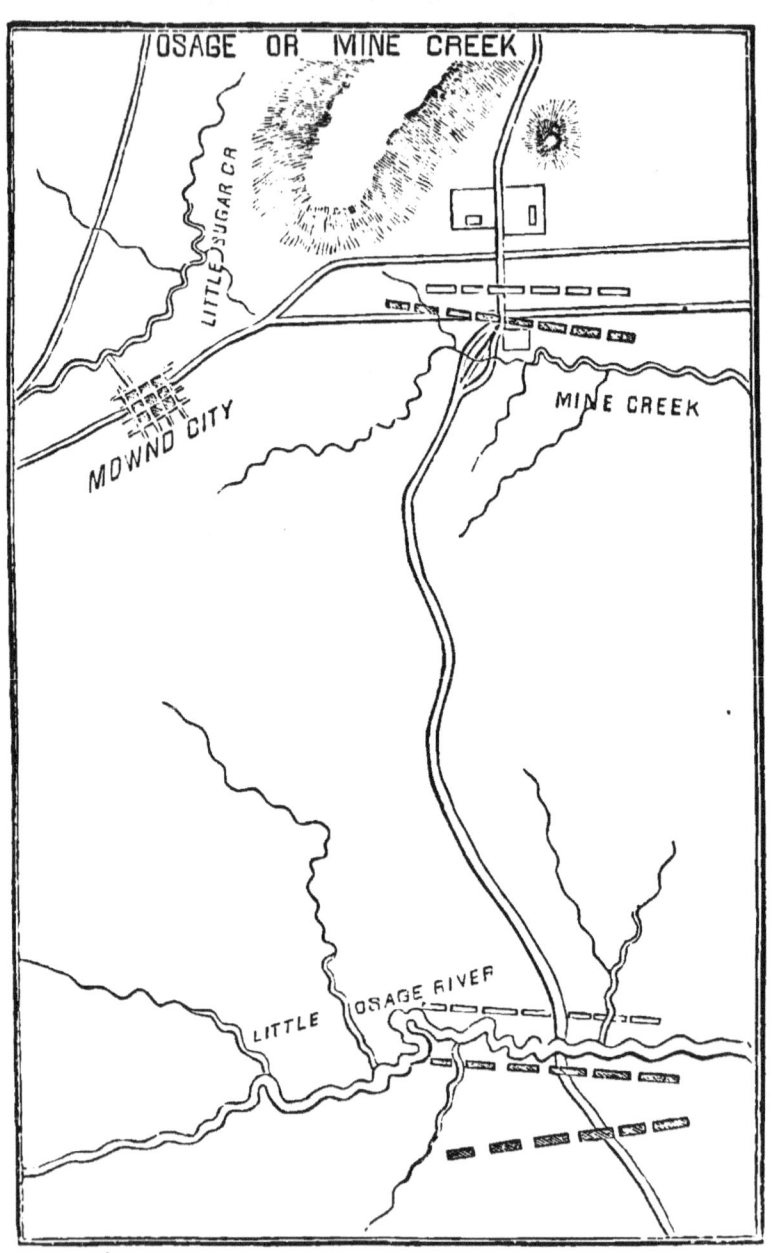

CHAPTER XVI.

ATTACK ON THE MOUND—BATTLES OF MARIAS DES CYGNES AND MINE CREEK.

The Colorado boys moved cheerfully to the work before them. It was a dangerous task, the character of which seemed hightened by the darkness of the night, and the heavy mist soon to change into a tempest of rain. Yet these were favorable assistants; the rain deadened our movements, while darkness covered the approach. Captain Kingsbury believed the rebel force on the mounds comparatively small, and stated his first attack had created alarm; that before withdrawing, the harnessing of animals, the movements of wagons, and other preparations for leaving, were most plainly audible in the rebel camp, which seemed to occupy a large space on both sides of the river. The enemy's exhausted state was evident from their failure to obstruct, as they might have done, the passage of the stream, the road through the timber, and the steep banks beyond.

Our picket line was formed along the main road, and in the open fields about a half mile from the timber's edge. East of the road was a steep mound, with bare sides, looking to the north. West of the road, and a little further to the south, was one higher and more precipitous, covered with brush and trees to the summit. These afforded formidable points of defence, and looming through the flashing lightning and rifted rain-clouds, seemed more difficult to attain than afterwards, when daylight gave a correct idea of the surroundings.

As the Colorado boys advanced, Colonel Gravelley (who accompanied them, having sent for his command), Major R. H. Hunt, Capt. R. J. Hinton, Capt. Kingsbury, Lieut. Hubbard, Signal Officer (who with some of the corps had joined the movement), were joined by a volunteer scout of General Blunt, Marcus, formerly of the 10th Kansas, who some time previously had passed our pickets and succeeded in creeping through the brush and tall grass half way up the eastern mound, listening to the rebels talk, and ascertaining their numbers. He reported this mound held by about three hundred men; that the force north of the stream was a brigade under General Slemmons, with three guns.

The darkness was great, and the heavy rain poured down. The 2d Colorado advanced on the north-west, while Colonel Gravelley's force, now moving up, were placed to their left. The line moved steadily till within a hundred yards of the mound, when clear and sharp through the night rung the rebel challenge, replied to simultaneously by ours: " Who goes there?" and " Who are you?" as quickly answered, "Federal troops," "Confederates." The sound of the challenge had not died away when the hill-side blazed with a long, waving, flashing line of fire, and the sharp ring of musketry gave forth rude alarm. Through the darkness flashed returning blaze. With varying fortune our line moved on steadily up the hill, driving the rebels back. A small squad of Colorado men passed round the western base and looked on the southern side of the mound. They were soon greeted with a blinding flash, the crashing of a hundred bullets, and under so overwhelming a fire, fell back to the main body, having learned of the extent of the force stationed there, through the lightning and musketry flashes.

General Sanborn had been ordered by General Curtis to open with artillery, but so far its sound was not heard. Colonel Gravelley dismounted and most gallantly led his men, in the face of a heavy fire, up the mound, as did Captain Kingsbury also. Major Hunt had returned to see to the artillery. Captain Hinton moved with the advance. Just before day broke, a rebel battery opened, though their shells overshot and did no damage. With a cheer our line advanced and carried the top of the mound and opened a brisk fire upon the rebels formed in line of battle in an open field just south of this mound.

The day broke clear, and the welcome sound of our artillery was heard. The shells fell however in the neighborhood of the men on the mound. General Sanborn was moving forward with his command. Major Hunt riding up, soon caused a cessation of the fire, and the battery was moved to a better position.

From the condition of the roads through the heavy rain, and the passage over them of the rebel army, it became evident that the movements of our troops would necessarily be slow. General Curtis, with his staff, was on horseback at the earliest dawn, and moved to the front. From the summit of the captured mound, about 2,000 rebels could be seen in line of battle on the edge of the timber, from a battery in which, at long intervals, they sent a shell screaming in our direction. After the storm of the night, the clouds had broken away, the sunrise lit the scene with splendor, and all the landscape glowed and twinkled. It was hailed as an omen of success.

Lieutenant-Colonel Benteen, with his brigade, by direction of General Sanborn, had sent one regiment to a ford three miles west, and the 4th Iowa Cavalry to report to Colonel Gravelley, and under his direction they were directed to carry the mound on the right, which about daylight was done without serious opposition.

General Pleasanton, unattended, rode to the summit of the mound, followed by General Sanborn.

STATE OF THE VACATED CAMP.

The troops were then formed in column on the road; the enemy's rear guard falling back rapidly through the timber. Colonel Gravelley, with the 8th and 6th M. S. M. (the latter commanded by Major Plumb), and Kingsbury's Colorado Battalion, moved towards the ford, followed by Colonel Phillip's advance, the 2d Arkansas, Colonel Phelps. Major Hunt and Captain Hinton, reported to General Pleasanton, and by him were requested to assist General Sanborn as Aides.

At the ford a small body of rebels were engaged in felling trees to obstruct the passage. Major Hunt moved rapidly with a detachment of the 2d Colorado, led by Captain Kingsbury, to drive them away. A sharp fusilade ensued, lasting a few minutes, not however before the enemy had succeeded in creating an obstruction which was a serious cause of delay. We passed through the hastily vacated camp. Clothing, blankets, parts of tents, camp utensils, mess chests, etc., all betokened the hasty evacuation. The picture was hideous in its filth. The *debris* of a camp is never a sightly object, but the peculiar features thereof were enhanced by the knee deep mud, the remains of slaughtered cattle, the broken equipments, and the disgusting effluvia which greeted the nostrils. The little hamlet looked woe-begone. A few women, ashen grey with terror, and half naked, poured blessings upon the troops as they moved by. In every house were found sick or wounded rebels. Some stragglers were captured during the morning, and it is believed were hung by our troops in the rear. The passions aroused by the sight of their pillaged homes, their insulted friends, and the knowledge of the base murders committed on old and defenceless men, might afford palliation of such acts of summary retaliation.

At the crossing, the advance was joined by Colonel S. J. Crawford, and Colonel C. W. Blair, Volunteer Aides-de-Camp, who had pressed forward to see the position of affairs. Colonel Blair, knowing that his brigade could not cross till late in the morning, and naturally anxious as to the fate of Fort Scott, which was his post and the residence of his family, had come to the front. General Blunt also joined General Curtis at the ford.

The 2d Arkansas Cavalry were first on the south side, followed immediately by the Colorado Battalion. Detachments of the 5th and 8th M. S. M. came next. The enemy had set fire to a couple of large ricks of hay and some abandoned wagons in a field to our front, and beyond the smoke could be seen moving columns.

Emerging from the timber a body of men were seen drawn up in line of battle, about half a mile distant, and in front of a farm house. It was at first doubted whether these might not be a portion of our own force who had crossed below the main ford. Colonel Blair assured Colonel Phelps that such could not be the case, and also called his attention to the fact, that no guidons were displayed by them. This was undoubted evidence of their hostility.

The charge was sounded, Colonel Phelps heading his regiment, Colonel Crawford and Major Hunt moving with it; while Colonel Blair and Captain Hinton galloped to the right to bring forward troops there forming. The 2d Colorado, under Captain Kingsbury, which had been sent forward by General Sanborn, pressed to the charge as fast as their weary animals would move.

Half way to the enemy's lines we flushed their skirmishers, who were concealed in the rank grass beyond a gentle rise. Firing a hasty volley, they retreated quickly to their main body, which moved off by the left flank at full speed, our squadrons in rapid pursuit. The first line had been formed facing the west. About a mile beyond, another line was now formed, facing to the north, and strengthened by three guns—two rifled and one small smooth-bore—its right resting on a timbered ravine, running from the main stream. The left rested upon a small knoll on the summit of which was a log cabin. Their artillery opened, but principally firing solid shot did no great damage. The whistling of shell was however by no means unfrequent.

Orderlies were sent to hurry forward the artillery, while directions were received from General Sanborn not to press a charge until other troops had been brought forward. Generals Curtis and Pleasanton were then at the ford directing movements there.

Finding that our guns did not come forward as rapidly as was hoped, it was determined, as the fire from the rebel battery was galling our troops, to endeavor to capture them by a combined movement of all the troops now deployed. The 2d Arkansas, led by Colonel Phelps, and the 2d Colorado battalion, under Captain Kingsbury, advanced most gallantly, the men cheering lustily as the charge was sounded. The regiment to the left failed to support them promptly. The small force in front still pressed forward in spite of the heavy fire from the rebel line, and though unable to charge in consequence of their numbers, they compelled the foe to give way, though but slowly.

At this time Major Hunt rode up to Colonel Phelps, informing him that "the General expected him to capture those guns."

"I would have done so five minutes ago," was the Colonel's reply, "had I been properly supported."

With an assurance that he should be, Major Hunt galloped to the left, and the 8th M. S. M. swung into line and forward on the charge. The line, consisting of the 2d Arkansas, three companies of the 2d Colorado, and the Missouri regiment, charged in gallant style; other troops closed up in the rear, while two of Thurber's guns opened, having been brought up on the gallop. As we advanced, the rebels broke to the rear—failing to come to close quarters—leaving their small gun on the field, which we took. Owing to the delay on our left, the enemy were enabled to save their Parrotts, by rapidly limbering to the rear and going off on the gallop.

Another line of battle was seen about two miles south as we pressed forward, but it moved off as we advanced, after firing a few shots from their rifled guns. Three roads met in the main .one leading across the stream; one to our right lead direct to Mound City; another—the centre, over which the main rebel army moved—was the direct road to Fort Scott, Mine Creek and Osage, some five and ten miles south, and entering the military and telegraph road a few miles above Fort Scott. The other, to the left, branched again, one uniting with the Mine Creek road, and the other following the State line.

Phillips' Brigade (M. S. M.) moved forward on the road to the centre. Colonel Cloud, was ordered by General Curtis, to take the 2d Kansas, under Major Hopkins and Captain Cosegrove, and move on the extreme right. The Colonel himself, with a small detachment, moved on the centre. Lieutenant-Colonel Benteen, with the veteran brigade of Colonel Winslow, moved on the road to the left, some distance behind Colonel Phillips. Major Weed, Major Hunt, Colonel Crawford, Colonel Blair, Captain Hinton, and other staff officers, moved to the front to render what assistance could be given. The Colorado Battalion moved on the centre road. Considerable delay, and consequent separation of troops occurred, owing to the difficult passage of the ford. General Pleasanton pressed forward the troops, sending orders to Sanborn and McNeil. General Sanborn had previously halted, and let his men and horses feed.

In the meanwhile the advance brigades moved rapidly across the open prairie. Soon the timber of Mine Creek, about five miles south-east of Mound City, came in sight. As the gallant Missouri and Arkansas troops under Colonel Phillips reached the brow of a long acclivity which overlooked the creek valley beyond, the enemy were discovered in great force formed in line of battle upon the north side of the stream, with their right resting upon the crossing and left extending north-west and resting on the timber of the stream. The open prairie, sweeping away, afforded the grandest possible field for cavalry movements. It became evident that here the battle was to be fought. The rebels, deployed six lines deep in the centre, showed a force of from 12,000 to 15,000 men. As it afterwards appeared, the two divisions of Fagan and Marmaduke, comprising the flower of the rebel army, were thus arranged in battle array under the direction of General Price, who commanded in person. Beyond the creek to the south could be seen a long train and accompanying troops, extending for some miles. This was Shelby's Division and the new one under Tyler, with the plunder and prisoners of the Missouri raid. The rebel artillery, ten pieces, was stationed on the left of their line, an error on the part of the rebel General which our officers were not slow to perceive.

If we succeeded in breaking their centre, there was no possibility of their withdrawing the guns. From our front to the rebel lines, the ground formed a gentle descent. On the right, and a little to our front, was a farm house and fences. To our extreme left and front was a slight swale, the timber and creek, then a rising corn field with a log cabin at the top.

The brigade of Colonel Phillips had halted upon the edge of the table land, with skirmishers well thrown out, about one thousand yards from the enemy. Colonel Benteen was still some distance in the rear. Major Hopkins, with the 2d Kansas and two howitzers, came up on the extreme right. General Pleasanton had been informed of the position of our forces, and was pressing to the front with a section of Rodman's guns, and his escort, accompanied by Major Curtis, who had reported him for duty.

It was apparent the rebel army were determined to fight here, with the expectation of checking our march, and so enabling them to move more leisurely towards Fort Scott. The whole of their line was not visible, the right being behind the brow of the hill, descending into Mine Creek. Their artillery was playing with considerable effect upon the right of the unsupported brigade of Colonel Phillips, still steadily advancing. Majors Weed and Hunt galloped to the left to inform Colonel Benteen of the position of affairs on the right, and desire him to press forward with a view to charge before the rebels had time to do so, a movement which it was evident they were about to execute. The Colonel responded heartily to the suggestion, and the brigade, consisting of the 10th Missouri Cavalry, Major W. H. Lask; the 4th Iowa Cavalry, Major A. R. Pierce; 3rd Iowa Cavalry, Major B. S. Jones; and the 4th Missouri and 7th Indiana Cavalry consolidated, under Major Simmonson, moved in column on the gallop, each regiment forming on the left of Phillips, as they came up.

At this time the rebel guns were firing canister at an enemy they supposed to be advancing on their right, and hidden from view by the rise in front. This alone saved Colonel Phillips, who, if known to be unsupported, would have been swept from the field by a vigorous advance. In the face of this fire, which tore the ground in front, and filled the air with hurtling missiles, Colonel Benteen's Brigade broke from regimental columns, forming into line to the right and left, and moving steadily forward till they reached short range. The rattle of musketry, mingled with the roar of artillery, the shouts of the soldiers, the scream of the shells, the crash of small arms, the hissing sound of canister, and the cries of the wounded as they fell about us, filled the air, forming a picture, when set off by the walls of steel before, and that about and behind us, that can be easier remembered than described. It was evident that a desperate effort was preparing in the rebel lines. A group of officers could be seen in the centre, evidently of high rank, while others were dashing furiously up and down, and fiercely the tiger rebel yell met and mingled with the wild hurras of our men. The long lines of rebels, with crash and fury of raging battle about them; the slender brigades deployed and advancing on their front, while to the north, across the broad prairie, were to be seen the rapidly deploying troops advancing to reinforce our front.

These scenes take longer to describe than to enact. While these troops were pressing to our assistance, deploying to the right and left, forming a second line of battle, and the generals, with their escort and staff were riding hastily forward, Colonel Benteen had, without hesitation, dashed on under a fire so terrible, that even his veteran troops were for a moment staggered. The brigade to the right was showing signs of distress, when, making a right half wheel, and sending to Colonel Phillips to move at the same time, away went Benteen, both brigades precipitating themselves upon the centre and left of the rebel lines.

The gallant staff officers of General Curtis, so soon as the charge sounded, rode to the right and left along the line, cheering and encouraging the troops, charging themselves in the very thick front and foremost of the fight. Colonels Crawford and Cloud were in the centre, Colonel Blair with Majors Weed and Hunt, and Sergeant Sloonacker, 15th Kansas, were on the right; Captain Hinton had moved with the extreme left of Colonel Benteen's command. Major Curtis, with the escort company of General Pleasanton, and two of Thurber's guns, which had now reached the field, opened on the rebel right.

Forward! was shouted along the line. Away it went; at first slowly, and then with a fierce momentum, dashing and crashing through the rebel right and centre. A rush—a scramble—a confused vision of flashing sabres on our right and centre; the wild trample of rushing horses; the frantic shouts of charging combatants; the crash of small arms—not continuous as in line—but rapid and isolated as of individual combat; the cessation of the enemy's artillery fire, and the intermittent fire of our own guns, were the elements which made up a scene worthy of being immortalized in the verse of Tennyson, or by the brush of Horace Vernet.

So rapidly had the centre and right swept forward, that the extreme left, which from the nature of the ground had not been able to charge simultaneously, and was now swinging, half-wheel to the right, with the view of crossing a ravine, clearing the corn field on the south, and attacking the disordered rebel force on the flank as it emerged from the wood;—this force as it swept through the ravine and into the field, was fired upon by our own guns. Supposing these shells to be from the rebel guns, the left went thundering through the field, when they were fired upon by a line of skirmishers. With a cheer our boys dashed forward. The rebels fled; a number lay wounded, and over them went the line amid a volley from those behind the fence at the top of the field. In front of a log cabin stood an old woman, with several children clinging to her skirts, fearless of the leaden shower which ceaselessly pattered against the cabin wall; with dress disordered and grey locks floating in the wind, the old lady shouted, while we whirled past, "God bless you, boys! God bless you boys! Hurra for the Union! Hurra for Kansas! Give it to 'em!" and similar exclamations. The sight was inspiring. The blessing came like a draught of wine, and with a wild shout the troops cleared the fence, swept over the prairie beyond, and attacked the disordered rebels as they emerged from the timber, capturing a Major and a number of men. Several shells had already fallen in our midst, when it became evident that the left was mistaken for rebels, and it fell back across the prairie to the supports which were coming up.

The firing was directed by General Sanborn, who had mistaken these troops for the enemy, but as soon as they fell back, both General Pleasanton and General Sanborn rode up and ordered the fire to cease. Captain Hinton was with the left and participated in the charge.

While this was going on upon the left, the right and centre had completely routed the rebel force, causing them to fall back in wild disorder over Mine Creek and reform upon the south side, about a mile beyond. Colonel Benteen was in hot pursuit, until General Pleasanton, who had reached the field just as our charge was being made, sent an order directing that no further advance be made until the division could concentrate.

When our attack was made, from the capture of so many rebel officers of high rank it would appear that they were all assembled in and about the centre. Brigadier-General Cabell was captured by Sergeant Calvary M. Young, of Company "A," 3rd Iowa Cavalry, and Major-General Marmaduke was captured by Private James Dunleavy, of Company "D." Two stands of colors were taken by Major Pierce, 4th Iowa Cavalry, (who in the engagement cut down eight men with his own hands,) besides a large number of prisoners and four guns. Colonel Jeffards, formerly a Lieutenant-Colonel in the famous Stonewall Brigade, surrendered with a number of men to Colonel Cloud. Among other officers captured was Colonel John Waddell, a nephew of General Frost, of Camp Jackson notoriety. Colonel Crandall, Marmaduke's Adjutant, was taken near his chief, as was his Medical Director. Brigadier-General Slemmon, who commanded the rear attacked by our troops at the Mounds and at the Trading Post, was mortally wounded, and died afterwards at Newtonia. Brigadier-General Graham was killed and left on the field. A large number of field officers of various grades were captured, about eight hundred of the rank and file, and nine guns, which, with the one taken at Marias des Cygnes, made ten. The wounded left on the field numbered over two hundred, while the dead was about the same. A number of our officers were severely wounded, but our actual loss was not more than one hundred and fifty men. The impetuosity of the charge, and its complete success, accounts for this slight loss. Had Colonel Phillips' brigade been armed with sabres and carbines, in place of long rifles, the victory would have been more complete. Yet never was there witnessed a more overwhelming rout than the field of this glorious charge presented. The field was won against 12,000, by two brigades, numbering not more than 2,500. Major-General Fagan was at first reported killed, and the body of an officer, found afterwards to be that of General Graham, mistaken for him. General Cabell informed Colonel Wheeler, that when he was captured, Price himself was within a few feet, and only escaped by the fleetness of his horse, and absence of any distinctive dress which could render him a mark.

Major-General Marmaduke was captured by Corporal James Dunleavy, of Company "D," 3rd Iowa Cavalry. The rebel General was rallying his men, Dunleavy galloping towards him, occasionally firing. Marmaduke mistook him for one of his own men, and started towards him, reproving him for firing on his friends. Dunleavy stopped, waiting coolly till Marmaduke got within twenty or thirty rods of him, then covering him with his revolver, ordered him to dismount and surrender. General Marmaduke did so, and his horse galloped off. Colonel Blair was riding by at this time, and Dunleavy seeing he was an officer, offered to him the prisoner. The Colonel declined the trouble, when Marmaduke said: "Sir, you are an officer; I claim protection at your hands; I am General Marmaduke." Taking charge, Colonel Blair said he would protect him until delivered to General Curtis as a prisoner. Marmaduke at this seemed much relieved. Dunleavy then said, "Colonel, remember I took him prisoner. I am James Dunleavy, Corporal of Company "D," 3rd Iowa Cavalry." Colonel Blair told the Corporal (who was severely wounded in the right fore arm, but still held his revolver vigorously) to come along, and he should have the honor of being introduced to General Curtis as the captor of General Marmaduke. Colonel Blair moved to the rear with his prisoner, passing Generals Pleasanton and Sanborn. A led horse was taken from a soldier, and Marmaduke mounted, as he complained greatly of fatigue. Colonel Blair found Generals Curtis and Blunt, with Senator Lane, and other staff officers at the house of Mrs. Reagins, about a half mile from the field of our successful charge. The prisoner was introduced, as also his captor, whom the General found afterwards to be a son of an old Iowa friend. He directed the Corporal to retain Marmaduke's revolver. An amusing incident occurred at this time.

When the rebel line was forming, Marmaduke's Division was on the right. Its commander rode a very fine mare, which he called "Miss Mary Price.'

After performing some equestrian feats, and extolling the qualities of his steed, he asked the old lady whose blessing had saluted us as we charged by her door, "what she thought of Miss Mary"—adding, boastingly, of riding over the Kansas Jayhawkers. After the battle, the old lady went to Mrs. Reagin's, and seeing Marmaduke, saluted him with, "How are you, General, and how's Miss Mary Price, and where's the Kansas Jayhawkers now?" The General answered not. Majors Weed and Curtis, with Colonel Cloud, were busy in collecting the prisoners, scattered all over the field. General Curtis placed them in charge of Lieutenant-Colonel J. J. Sears, 18th U. S. C. I., Acting Provost Marshal, detailing a Missouri Regiment to guard them. The captured guns were brought up to Mrs. Reagin's and turned over to Colonel Sears. The charge upon these guns, surrendered by Colonel Jeffards to Colonel Cloud, was made by a portion of the 10th Missouri Volunteer Cavalry, and a detachment of the 2d Kansas Cavalry acting with Colonel Cloud. General Sanborn, who had now come up, was directed to move his brigade to the right of the line, and take the advance. The troops on the skirmish line being completely worn out, Colonel Cloud was directed to take their place with the 2d Kansas.

These movements following the rebel defeat, had transpired while Colonel Benteen and Colonel Phillips were still pressing the enemy across Mine Creek. A formidable line of battle had been again formed by them on a prairie ridge about one mile to the south. This they soon abandoned, and our skirmishers pursued them beyond the dividing ridge of Mine Creek and Little Osage. The rear of our troops (General McNeil and General Blunt) were still far behind. General Pleasanton complained of the former as not showing willingness to move forward. Major Charlot, General Curtis' Adjutant, was sent to bring his brigade forward, and to arrest General McNeil if hesitation was evinced. His brigade being in advance of the 1st Division, delayed General Blunt at the crossing. Some wagons had broken down and obstructed the ford, causing delay. General McNeil stated that no order for an advance had been received by him. He came up on the gallop upon receipt of the order. As the Major was *en route* to General McNeil, he passed Mrs. Reagin's, where our prisoners and wounded were being gathered, and found Captain Gates and Major Suess, of General Pleasanton's staff, disputing with Colonel Sears for custody of the prisoners, claiming them as "General Pleasanton's prisoners." They were informed that, as General Curtis, the senior officer present, had placed them in charge of Colonel Sears, they would be retained by that officer till relieved.

Our dead and wounded were left on the field to the kindly care of the citizens; so also were the rebel wounded. Our movements were still onward. Fort Scott lay in the direction of the enemy's march. Stores to the value of two millions, belonging to the

Government were there. Hence the necessity of pressing after the shaken, but not yet beaten, rebel army.

To the early attack on the Mounds, and the vigorous driving of the enemy at the Trading Post Ford, and in the valley beyond, is to be attributed the engagement and consequent victory at Mine Creek. Had not the Colorado Battalion carried the Mounds, and so opened the ball before daylight, the important Post at Fort Scott, and the whole of South-east Kansas, would have fallen a prey to the rebel army.

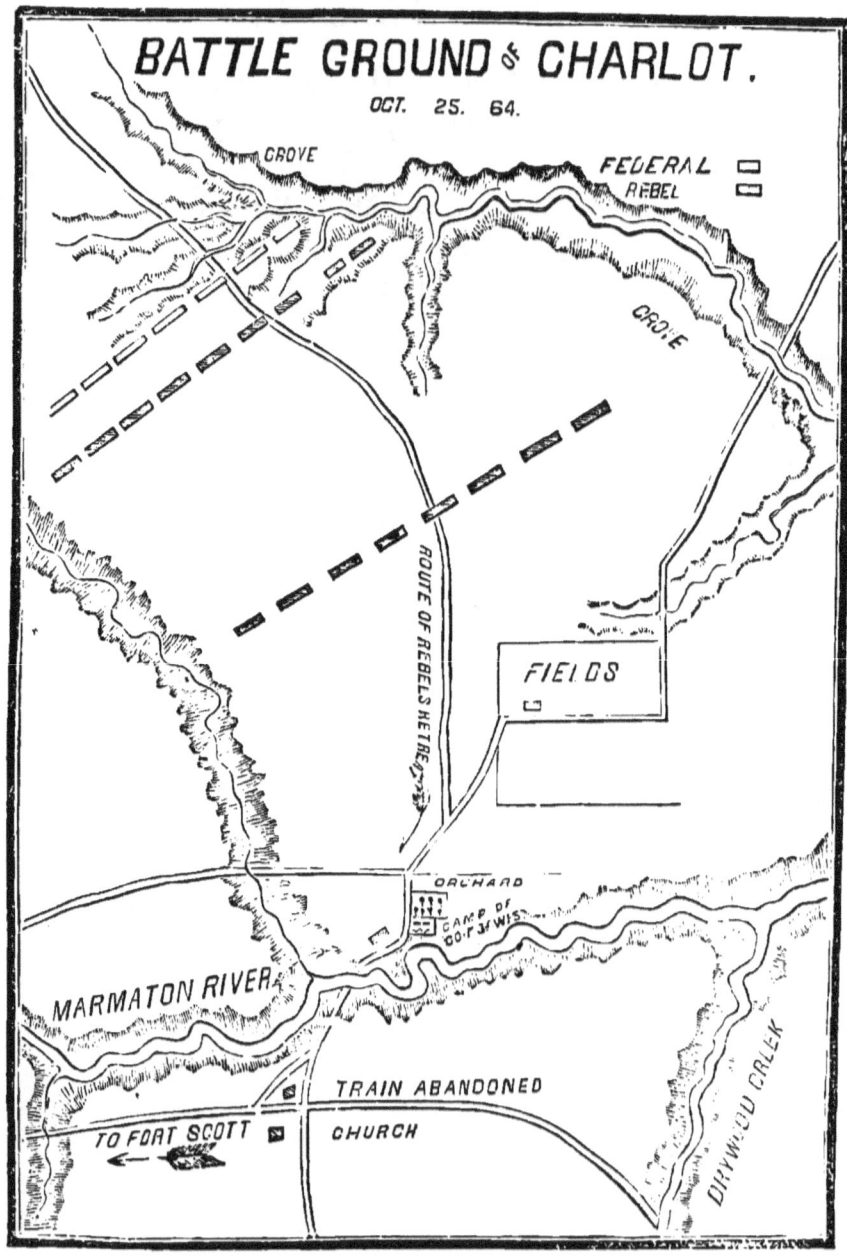

CHAPTER XVII.

ENGAGEMENTS AT THE LITTLE OSAGE AND CHARLOT—MARCH OF MOONLIGHT—ENGAGEMENTS AT MOUND CITY AND FORT LINCOLN—REBEL CAMP ON DRYWOOD CREEK—OURS AT FORT SCOTT AND MARMATON.

WHILE the prisoners were being gathered in, the captured guns and trophies taken care of, and messengers sent in haste to hurry forward McNeil's Brigade and the 1st Division, the two brigades of Benteen and Phillips which so gallantly reaped the harvest now being secured on Mine Creek, were, under orders from General Pleasanton, reforming their lines and awaiting the forward movement. Benteen's veterans, indeed, had pressed onward in hot haste, and when directed to halt were reforming for another charge upon a line presenting itself along a ridge about a mile south of the stream. This was evidently intended to cover the retreat and recovery from disorder into which our impetuous charge had thrown the divisions of Marmaduke and Fagan. As the veteran 2d Kansas, one hundred and fifty strong, took the skirmish line (having reported to General Sanborn, now moving his troops upon the right for that purpose), and moved steadily forward, this line melted away, and when the ridge was reached were seen joining the main column.

The scene was most striking. Seldom, if ever, has "the pomp and circumstance of glorious war" had so broad a field whereon to display its attractions. The battle-field with its hideous concomitants of death and suffering was veiled by the intervening timber. Beyond the valley, bodies of troops, dimly discernible, were pressing forward to join the pursuit. Thin columns of smoke, wreathing upward in the soft Indian summer haze, told of the desolation which the invader had wrought behind us. Before were rising denser and fresher the same black tokens, and the van of their march was plainly distinguishable by ruddy masses of cloud which told of burning prairie, hay ricks and buildings. To the straining eyes on the halted skirmish line it was still certain that they were moving direct towards Fort Scott. Colonel Charles W. Blair, who, accompanied by Captain Hinton, had moved to the extreme advance, scanned the horizon eagerly with his glass, and grew restless at the delay, which, however, was necessary to concentrate and reform our troops, broken and disorganized by the rapid pursuit and subsequent charge. About a half mile to the rear of the skirmishers, a fine display of extensive cavalry movements were visible. Three brigades were forming in column of regiments. Colonel Benteen on the left, Phillips in the centre, and General Sanborn moving to the right. The formation was perfect, and the level prairie to their front allowed the whole extended line to move unbroken. In the front and centre rode the two Generals, Curtis and Pleasanton, with their respective staffs and escort, forming themselves an attractive feature of the pageant thus unconsciously exhibited to the observant eye. General Blunt had returned from Mine Creek to endeavor to hurry forward his own division.

As the bugles along the line blared forth the advance, the division moved in the direction of the Little Osage, near which, some four miles distant, the enemy's main advance could be seen. Half way upon the prairie fresh smoke was rising densely, telling of some new horror. When our skirmishers moved past the house, the bloody form of a young man, just shot down, was to be seen at the threshold. It was a well-cultivated farm. The extensive ricks of hay and corn stalks which were stacked in the barn-yard were burning, while all the adjoining prairie was fast blackening with the flames which ran along its swells. The house had been stripped. The young man was a member of the Linn county militia, who knowing the enemy's march would be by his dwelling, had left his command and reached it, only in time to be murdered. Further to the west some miles, a heavy volume of smoke could be seen rising from a dense body of timber, which was known to be in the vicinity of Fort Lincoln. A small column of mounted men could be seen moving therefrom towards the main body of rebels. Further to the north, and moving to the west, by the aid of glasses, could be distinguished another body of cavalry, which it was believed was the gallant 2d Brigade, under Colonel Moonlight.

As afterwards appeared, Colonel Moonlight, with the 11th Kansas volunteers and Lyon county militia, under Colonel Mitchell, had reached Mound City about one P. M., having marched sixty-five miles without rest or food, accomplishing the last thirty miles in five hours. Here the messenger sent by General Blunt, directing him to move on to Fort Scott and hold the place at all hazards, was received. Captain Greer with the force at his command had already given a small body of rebels, the evening before, a taste of his quality. Towards morning, Lieutenant-Colonel Samuel A. Drake, with two companies of the 17th Kansas, arrived. Colonel Drake was in command at Paola, and immediately on learning of the safety of that important post, had, leaving the 18th K. S. M., Colonel Potter commanding, moved with the balance of his force to Mound City, making a night march, arriving in time to aid in the defence, by checking a force then moving up Sugar Creek. As day broke, scouts arrived with the intelligence that the enemy's advance, eight hundred strong, were moving direct towards the post. Moonlight formed a line of battle to the north-east of town, and a sharp skirmish ensued, which resulted in the rapid withdrawal of the foe—our cavalry pursuing for two miles in the direction of Price's main army. Manlove, a member of the militia under Captain Greer, was killed, and Mr. Williams was severely wounded, during this fight. From the high prairie, where the 2d Brigade withdrew and moved towards Fort Scott, they had an opportunity to witness the magnificent charge made by Benteen and Phillips at Mine Creek. Moving on the Telegraph road, Moonlight again encountered the enemy at Fort Lincoln. They held the heavy timber, were apparently in force, and after some sharp skirmishing the 2d Brigade was withdrawn, its commander leaving a battalion of the 11th Kansas to watch the enemy, while he moved up the stream and flanked them to the west, marching rapidly to Fort Scott, which he reached at four P. M. The rebels burned the buildings at Fort Lincoln, and several houses, robbed the post-office and store, murdering one of the citizens. At Mound City, another brush was had with a straggling force. About 10 A. M., a body of one hundred and fifty advanced within a half mile of the public square. Captain Greer sent the militia to meet them. The rebels took possession of a corn field. Lieutenant Parks was severely wounded in this movement. Colonel Drake, with his command, then advanced into the field, and succeeded in dislodging the enemy, who fled, leaving some wounded and six prisoners in our hands. Captain Greer, with a portion of the militia, by a flank movement succeeded in capturing several. Eighteen prisoners were taken. The danger to the people in and around Mound City was over; their work however, had only just begun. Our march down the line had been so rapid, and work from the previous three day's fighting so great, that but few of the surgeons were with the pursuing troops. Surgeons Ashmore and Twiss, of the 11th and 15th Kansas, were left to take care of the wounded. The resident practitioners, Doctors Bender and Hiatt, heartily co-operated. Every suitable building at Mound City was converted into hospitals for our own and the rebel wounded. About two hundred rebel dead were buried by the citizens on the field at Mine Creek. For days after, bodies were found in the long grass and brush fringing the stream, where, when wounded, they had dragged themselves. Sixty wounded rebels were conveyed to Mound City, and there received every attention that humanity demanded. A number of our own wounded were also moved hither, as afterwards others were taken to Fort Scott. The noble women of Linn county labored unremittingly in full gratitude for their rescue. The wanton burning of the prairie, in which the rebels indulged, was in the end mainly injurious to themselves. These fires swept the fields on Mine Creek and the Osage, burning the bodies of their wounded and charring the remains of their dead. At Mine Creek, many of their wounded were burned to death.

The 1st Division found many of the charred bodies as they passed. In one instance, a man was lying on his face, and his clothes had all been consumed except his pockets, which were protected by his body. In the pockets were found some Confederate scrip, a few dollars in specie, and a pass which the soldier had at some time received from his commanding officer, allowing him to visit home for a week. This proved afterwards the means of recognizing the dead man. At Fort Scott, where the rebel prisoners were collected, and a good deal of inquiry was being made by them concerning the fate of various comrades, the Union soldier who had taken this pass from the pockets of the dead rebel, walked up to the line and inquired if any of them knew of such a man, calling the name found on the pass. "Yes," eagerly replied one of the rebels coming forward, "was he taken prisoner?" "Why, what do you want to know for?" "He was my brother," was the quick response. "Well," said the Union soldier, "all I can say is, that you have burned your own brother to death; I found this in his pocket."

We left our troops moving towards the Little Osage; the 2d Kansas, under Major Hopkins and Captain Cosgrove, being still in the advance. Colonel Cloud commanded the skirmish line. About two miles from the stream, we again flushed the rebel rear, which was driven rapidly towards the timber. The movement was active and continuous, and under it both men and animals gave way, many of the latter falling exhausted. The timber swarmed with rebel skirmishers, as our advance halted for rest and reinforcement. In the meanwhile, General McNeil, under the stimulus of imperative orders, had galloped to the front, assuming the left as he reached the line, midway between the two streams. Reporting to General Pleasanton, sharp words passed between them; General McNeil exonerating himself from the charge of intentional delay, by a declaration that no orders had been received by him prior to those borne by the Assistant Adjutant General, Major Charlot. He was imperatively directed to take the advance, which he did, and maintained with the utmost alacrity.

The skirmish line was reinforced by the 2d Arkansas Cavalry under Colonel Phelps, Jun., which had been foremost in the fray since sunrise. Though the woods were alive, and the foeman's force unknown, Colonel Phelps rapidly charged across the bottom and into the timber, driving the rebel skirmishers before him. In this movement, he was supported by the 2d Kansas. General McNeil now arrived. His brigade (unsupported by artillery, which by orders had been left with Colonel Benteen's command, and did not report to McNeil again during the expedition) moved rapidly down the stream, crossing at the ford some distance below, accompanied also by the Kansas and Arkansas Cavalry, under Colonel

Phelps and Major Hopkins. Just as the head of our column emerged from the timber, it was fired on by the enemy's skirmishers. They were soon dislodged. Again we pushed forward toward a cornfield on the left of the road and beyond a little stream. Here the movement was checked by a heavy fire from the field. It was apparent that another battle had to be fought. The enemy were visible in great force at our front. Extending on the south side of the Little Osage, about one mile, is a smaller stream emptying into the Osage just east of the crossing. One half mile south, are two small farms, one rather southwest of the other, nearest to the timber, with a small strip of prairie between the fields. Beyond this, three hundred yards, was a smaller stream, quite narrow and deep, running parallel with the Osage. In crossing this, our horses were compelled to swim. Just south was the large cornfield, within which the enemy was in force.

Here another throw was to be made in the game of war. McNeil rapidly formed his little brigade into column of companies, dismounted the 5th M. S. M., ordered it to take down the fence, which was done gallantly in the face of a galling fire, and then in clear, sharp tones, addressed the brigade as it was formed, telling them "that it made no difference whether there were one or ten thousand men in that field, he wanted them to ride right over them."

The response was a wild cheer, and almost before the order to charge was given, the impatient troops swept through it like a tornado. Nothing could have withstood that wild rush, and the enemy melted away. Beyond the field, and to the left, the enemy had formed another strong line of battle. Behind this some distance, and to the right, so that the two were *en echelon*, was a still stronger line. Catherwood, who was in the advance, was now beyond the field, and as yet unsupported. His command, the 13th Missouri Cavalry, swept into line as it left the field of the charge. General Pleasanton who was directing the movements, requested Major McKenny to order Catherwood to charge. Between the two rebel lines was a road. The Major, after giving the order, detached a squadron from our right, to see that no attempt was made to flank Catherwood. The line in the latter's front was strong. General McNeil was hurrying forward, when General Pleasanton sent an order through one of his staff, Major Suess, directing the brigade to move "by fours right on the road, and not hazard the charge." Catherwood was moving forward in obedience to orders conveyed by Major McKenny, who was now riding towards the squadron stationed on the road. The officer last sent, rode up to the Major, and complaining that his horse was worn out, asked him to convey the order. McKenny promptly declined, giving as a reason, that he had just conveyed a different order, which he believed would be executed successfully. Instead of delivering the order, Major Suess rode off diagonally from Catherwood, and neither Catherwood nor

McNeil received it. Gen. McNeil was now moving on the gallop with the balance of his brigade in support of Catherwood, when General Pleasanton rode forward and very angrily accused McNeil of disobeying his orders to move "by fours right on the road." An explanation was given that no such orders had been received; but General Pleasanton imperatively said they had been, and ordered McNeil forward. The latter pushed on; the charge was made and the enemy gave way, slowly falling back to the third line already mentioned. Here a stubborn resistance was made. The line was formed in a low basin, evidently being used for a temporary halting place. It was surrounded by a semi-circular swell of prairie, along the brow of which the rebels were strongly posted.

For twenty minutes they held us at bay under a severe fire, until the brigade, which had become somewhat scattered in these impetuous charges and pursuit, again reformed, and in the line of battle charged, driving the enemy in confusion, and following in rapid and continuous pursuit for two miles. The effect of their charge was of course aided by the rapid advance and deployment of the other brigades which had as fast as possible crossed the Osage, moved to the front, and were now getting into position.

Passing through their temporary resting place, every evidence of the haste with which they retreated was to be seen. Scattered over the ground, were arms, clothing, blankets, equipments, mess utensils and food. Their killed and wounded were left as they fell. Quite a number of wagons were found half consumed. Large quantities of fixed ammunition, both for large and small arms, was scattered for miles along the line of retreat. Hundreds of broken down and wounded animals were seen on the prairie. It now became evident that the enemy's flight no longer endangered Fort Scott, the direction of his march being turned east of that place for the first time during the day's operations. The credit of the gallant movements at the Osage, is due to General McNeil and the troops under him; especially for the rapid pressing of the advantages gained.

The brigades of Colonel Benteen, Phillips and General Sanborn, followed as fast as their jaded horses would permit, in support of McNeil, who continued to pursue the foe, till he again turned in force nearer the Marmaton River, a few miles east of Fort Scott.

Nothing is more surprising in the history of this day's successes, than the small force by which they were won. At Mine Creek, not more than twenty-five hundred were engaged, and at Little Osage less than two thousand of our gallant troopers, drove a foe outnumbering them more than five to one, having also the advantage of chosen position and the shelter of timber and fences. It was most unfortunate for the complete success of our arms, that the delay at the crossing of the Marias des Cygnes, the condition of the roads and of their animals, rendered it impossible for the gallant 1st Division to reach the front till after sundown—too late for assistance; this, too, in spite of the unwearied exertion of General Blunt and his Brigade Commanders, who had each felt themselves in a measure deprived of their right to defend their own State, by the result of the change in the line of march made the previous night.

With General McNeil rode several of the volunteer and staff officers of General Curtis, among whom were Senator James H. Lane and Colonel Crawford, now Governor of Kansas. Captain Hinton, of General Blunt's staff, was also with the advance. Among the troops under McNeil was the veteran 7th Kansas Cavalry, under Major Malone, much of which had been originally recruited in this section. They, as always, behaved with the utmost spirit, but escaped with only two men wounded.

In the long and disjointed line of march which our forces now made across the wide prairie dividing the Osage and Marmaton waters, General McNeil held the advance, at least two miles ahead of the next brigade, which was Colonel Benteen's. Following were the brigades of General Sanborn and Colonel Phillips, with whom rode the Generals. Several miles to the rear was the 1st Division, while scattered all between were the jaded stragglers seeking to keep up with their commanders. The condition of the artillery was of the worst character.

The little mountain howitzers managed to keep well up to the front, but Colonel Cole's rifled guns were dragged wearily far in the rear by the jaded stock, over roads broken by ruts, and fetlock deep with mud.

At last the enemy approached the Marmaton. He was again compelled to fight. At this point it is quite a considerable stream, with wide bottom prairie, dense timber and swift rocky ford to cross. Being encumbered with his train, Price turned to resist for its passage, and McNeil it seemed likely, would pay dearly for his temerity. The entire rebel army was drawn up in line of battle (four lines deep) about two miles from the stream. As we afterwards learned, even his partially armed recruits being used to swell the strength and add to its formidable appearance. The point for resistance was well selected. They formed their line of battle along the edge of a swell where the plateau dipped to the river valley. A slight rise was of advantage in concealing a flank movement from their left. Their main centre was protected from charging by a strong stone wall, behind which, and in rear of a fighting division, was placed their raw troops. The right extended till it rested on some trees and undergrowth jutting out from the main stream, the timber of which could not be seen from our lines. The movements and extent of our forces were plainly visible to them. A small creek and farm, called after the proprietor, gave the name of Charlott to this engagement.

McNeil did not hesitate, but promptly formed in line of battle to resist, and, if possible, drive the foe. His slender lines looked like a pigmy in the face of the rebels, whose flanks extended three-quarters of a mile beyond our own. A brisk fire of small arms was opened on both sides. General Lane hastened, at the request of McNeil, to hurry forward reinforcements. Generals Curtis and Pleasanton were informed by him of the position of affairs at the front, and his apprehension that McNeil could not hold the ground until more forces were brought up. Major McKenny was requested by General Pleasanton to order McNeil to advance his right, and assure him of support. The order was given, and McNeil responded, "I obey the order with pleasure: it is the most joyful news I have heard to-day." Colonel Crawford and Captain Hinton galloped along the line of our advancing forces with the view of hurrying troops and guns to his assistance. Two howitzers were sent to the front. Major Suess, of General Pleasanton's staff, brought up a couple of Rodman guns, which were immediately opened upon their right and centre, causing it to retire hastily after a few rounds. The enemy's wings continued to advance, under a heavy fire from our exposed brigade. The two howitzers were opened on their right with considerable effect, finally causing it to fall back on the centre. Our right was still threatened by a heavy column, when the howitzers and Rodman guns were turned in that direction, and after rapid firing the movement was checked. The lines of both armies on our right were in extremely low ground, and as a consequence the shells from the howitzers fell at our own front causing considerable confusion. Major McKenny rode back to remedy this, when the guns were advanced. Colonel Benteen's Brigade came up on a trot, and, by direction of General McNeil, forming a second line of battle, both advanced towards the enemy at a walk, all exertions being unavailing to move the horses to either trot or gallop. Before this steady movement the enemy retired, gradually massing his wings on their centre, and then abandoning the field in haste, as the sun sunk below the horizon. Our loss was but small. Colonel Benteen had several wounded, among whom was the gallant Major Pierce, of the 4th Veteran Iowa Cavalry, who was shot in the foot. Here, then, was the golden occasion to once more precipitate a ruinous flight upon the invaders. Had all of our forces within reach, jaded though they were, been moved to the assistance of McNeil and Benteen (who of themselves had borne the brunt of this day's work) until the enemy were reached at the Marmaton, the result must have been to them complete confusion and overwhelming disaster.

General McNeil moved steadily on as the enemy fell back to protect the crossing. Again the rebel lines deployed in great force and threatened to flank our forces on the right and left with heavy columns. He sent a courier in hot haste to General Pleasanton, asking for assistance. This message arrived while Pleasanton was discussing the idea of falling back to camp at the Osage, some six or seven miles to the rear. Major McKenny urged the General to push forward to the Marmaton, a much shorter distance to our front, where wood and water could be had. While discussing this, as before stated, McNeil's message arrived. His dangerous position could be readily seen, as the great array of the enemy was fully visible about a mile distant. General Pleasanton sent word to McNeil to hold his position until reinforced. At this time a courier from Fort Scott arrived, who stated that that post was distant but two and a half miles. By General Pleasanton's order, the head of the column was turned to that place, and General McNeil was left to the chance of the 1st Division reaching him in time. Fortunately for McNeil and Benteen, the enemy were too busy in making good their own retreat to attack them.

General Curtis had ridden rapidly forward till in sight of the field of Charlott, and at the moment when the enemy were just falling back, when his attention was attracted to a column moving off to the right, which he supposed a flanking movement. Seeing however that it passed beyond the enemy's lines and still moved away, leaving the slender force at the front unsupported, he rode hastily to the head of the column, where he found General Pleasanton, who informed him that being advised by Lieutenant Ehle, 3rd Wisconsin Cavalry, who with a couple of scouts had just reached the field from Fort Scott, that they were within two and a-half miles of that post, he had determined to take his exhausted troops there for rest and subsistence. General Curtis remonstrated at leaving McNeil unsupported, and against any loss of distance in the march, urging that the troops bivouac on the prairies, and supplies be sent for. He also stated emphatically; that so far as the troops of his department were concerned, the campaign would be over only when Price had surrendered, or was driven across the Arkansas. General Sanborn, however, still continued to lead the column to the right, and the exhausted condition of both men and animals was so great, while the demands of nature for food and rest were so imperative, that the General reluctantly acquiesced.

Instead of two and a-half miles, as General Pleasanton had been informed, it was at least six miles to Fort Scott. Major Curtis and Major McKenny arrived in advance, and immediately exerted themselves to have supplies forwarded to Generals Blunt and McNeil, to whom orders had been sent to bivouac. General McNeil had already done so, when General Blunt reached the front, and misunderstanding, or not receiving the order, moved his Division to Fort Scott. Meeting the supply train for himself and McNeil, by a further blunder, the wagon master turned back, and thus the gallant troops of the 2d and 3rd Brigades were again left without food, which McNeil's did not obtain till the next morning.

It was a busy night at Fort Scott, every one attached to the post being engaged in supplying the exhausted soldiery. All night long troops were arriving, the prisoners of Mine Creek with their escort bringing up the rear towards morning. The citizens exerted themselves to the utmost, what few remained at home. One lady, Mrs. Emmert, the wife of the editor, deserves especial credit for her unwearied hospitality which, during many hours, never flagged, and seemed exhaustless in abundant cheer and pleasant welcome to all.

The enemy continued to fall back across the Marmaton, whence their camp extended to the Drywood, six miles south. The bold, vigorous and successful pursuit, the great disasters of the days, and the bivouac fires, which, hazy and afar, told them of their enemy's presence, had greatly disheartened and almost utterly demoralized them. Had General Curtis' plans been followed, troops bivouacked when evening fell, supplies been brought from Fort Scott, and the 1st Division pushed to the front before daylight to attack them, their defeat would have been overwhelming. No better evidence of this could be given than the fact, that during the night nearly four hundred wagons were burned by Price's own orders, with a large amount of ordnance and stores of all kinds. The noise of bursting shells, and the light of the burning train, which was with the advance at Drywood, was heard and seen by McNeil at Fort Scott. It was believed at both points, that a renewed attack had been made, and rumors of the capture of guns, etc., floated in on the sunrise. Their utter demoralization was made evident from an incident which occurred at a camp on the Little Drywood. Not knowing the cause of the explosion, a wild commotion ensued, in the midst of which a general officer rode up, exclaiming, "The Yankees are on us, boys! the Yankees are on us! save yourselves as best you can!" That brigade fled in utter disorder. At three in the morning, the rebels broke camp and resumed their retreat. At least forty wagons were left uninjured by the enemy, which, with their contents, were secured by McNeil next morning. A large flock of sheep were gathered up, that also had been abandoned. Among the spoils, were several wagon loads of small arms and ammunition, a twenty-four pound gun carriage, and a large quantity of arms, mess utensils, equipments, etc., were gathered along the first ten miles of their march. The fords on the Drywood were heavily obstructed by Price, and several hours were consumed by McNeil in removing them. Benteen with the 4th Brigade moved to Fort Scott, for supplies. McNeil pushed on towards Lamar, camping at Shanghai, twenty-seven miles from Fort Scott, that night.

CHAPTER XVIII.

FORT SCOTT DURING THE INVASION AND THE BATTLES OF THE 25TH—MARTIAL LAW ABOLISHED, AND MILITIA DISBANDED—PROCLAMATIONS OF THE GOVERNOR.

NEXT to Leavenworth, the post of Fort Scott is the most important in Kansas. It was in greater danger than any other point on the border during the invasion of Price. To insure its safety was the cause of most strenuous exertions; while its capture was evidently one of Price's main objects in his southward movement. The scenes in and around this place, form, therefore, no inconsiderable addition to the history of the campaign.

Owing to the foresight of Colonel Blair the people of Bourbon county found themselves in an organized condition when it was evident that a rebel army threatened them. In Fort Scott, four well drilled companies of militia responded to the call. Two belonged to the business community, one were the Quartermaster's employees, and one composed of colored men. Companies were also organized in the surrounding townships. On the 10th of October, a regiment of militia encamped about the post. Colonel Blair, having turned the command of his sub-district over to Captain Vittum, 3rd Wisconsin Cavalry, took with him a battalion of militia under Lieutenant-Colonel Eves, with other troops, and marched to Hickman's Mills. Captain Vittum had with him about two hundred regular volunteers, belong to different Kansas regiments, awaiting at this depot an opportunity to rejoin their regiments in the Department of Arkansas. There was also a small squad of colored artillerists, recruiting under First Lieutenant Wm. D. Mathews, colored, who was placed in command of all colored men called out there under proclamation of martial law.

On Saturday night, the force at Fort Scott was augmented by the arrival of several companies from Allen county, under Colonel Twiss, and a battalion from Woodson county, under Major Goss. Brigadier-General John B. Scott arrived and took command of the militia.

The first alarm occurred on Monday morning, October 24th. About one o'clock A. M., one of the siege guns on Fort Blair gave forth its warning; the drums beat to arms, and in a few moments all was in readiness. It was soon discovered that no immediate danger threatened Fort Scott; but the occasion of the alarm was one that filled many hearts with sadness, for its nearest neighbor had met the dreaded fate. Marmaton had fallen before the common enemy. Soon after twelve o'clock on the morning of October 23rd, about one hundred and fifty rebels, under the command of a Major I. Piercy, attacked that town. The only force to oppose them was forty poorly armed citizens. The rebels approached so quietly that our men had barely time to get into line when they were fired upon. The fire was returned, and two bushwhackers wounded. The others fell back a short distance, but soon returned to the attack, driving the defenders out in disorder.

The village was then sacked, and fire was set to the Methodist church, the stores of Aitken & Knowles, and of Cobb & Jones. The house of Mrs. Schaen, widow of an officer of the 10th Kansas, was also burned, Mrs. S. being savagely maltreated and robbed. Ten prisoners were taken, stripped nearly naked, and shortly afterwards marched a short distance, and, unarmed and defenceless, were fired upon. Six were killed, four escaped by running to the woods after the first fire. Those killed were Lieutenant-Colonel Knowles, late of the 2d Kansas Colored Volunteers, Doctor L. M. Shadwick, who had also served, D. M. Bowen, Joseph Stout, Warren Hawkins and A. McGonigle.

Upon receipt of this news, Captain Vittum immediately sent out what cavalry he had, in hopes of intercepting the gang, but failed to do so, and nothing more was heard until the news arrived that it had attacked a train on Cow Creek, coming north, burned several wagons, and robbed a large number of refugees of most of their money.

Monday came, and with it increased anxiety. Those who lived in towns on the line of the enemy's retreat, not knowing but that the next hour would find their homes in ashes, and all they held dear, impoverished, dead or dying, can imagine the feeling that existed; one not so much that of anxiety for their own personal safety, as for that of their helpless families.

During that day, innumerable rumors—some of them of the wildest character—were in circulation. The news had arrived of the defeat of the enemy at Westport, and of his retreat down the line. Telegrams were received announcing this fact, and indicating, that unless our already wearied troops could flank them on the right, and turn them to the east, Fort Scott would be in great danger. In the morning, some of the citizens imagined they heard artillery firing in the east, and about noon it was reported that General A. J. Smith had attacked the enemy's advance train at Pappinsville. It was also reported that the rebel Generals, Cooper and Gano, were coming up from the south with a large force, and marching in the direction of Fort Scott. These were samples only, and subsequently proved to be without foundation.

In the meantime, the fortifications of the city were greatly strengthened. In addition to the substantial works erected by General Curtis in the winter of '62-3, long lines of rifle pits were dug, temporary breastworks of sandbags made at the crossing of the Marmaton and elsewhere, blockhouses put in repair, and every possible preparation made for a desperate resistance. Night came—the night before the battles which decided the fate of South-east Kansas. Its visible gloom was but typical of that which gathered within the hearts of all. Every one slept on their arms, in the place assigned them. Sleepless vigils were kept in homes made heavy by the dread of the coming morn.

During the night, dispatches were received from General Blunt and Colonel Blair, announcing the approach of the enemy, and bidding us be watchful. It had been confidently expected that Colonel Moonlight, with his brigade, would be able to reach Fort Scott that night, but the following dispatch dispelled that hope:

"The enemy encamped six miles south-east of Mound City. I cannot reach you early in the morning. THOS. MOONLIGHT."

Lieutenant-Colonel Campbell, of the 6th Kansas Cavalry arrived from Fort Smith that evening, and he being the ranking officer at the Post, Captain Vittum turned the command over to him.

Colonel Campbell had been in command of a train from Fort Smith, which was attacked by the guerrillas who had already sacked Marmaton, on their retreat from that place. The following dispatch announces the result:

EXPECTATIONS OF ATTACK.   245

FORT SCOTT, Oct. 24.

CAPTAIN JOHN WILLIAMS, A. A. General:

Refugee's train from Fort Smith, escorted by detachment of 6th K. V. C., under Lieutenant-Colonel Campbell, was attacked at Cow Creek by a party of Bushwhackers, and sixteen men killed, and part of the train burned.

CAPTAIN VITTUM, Fort Scott.

As soon as the day dawned, the house-tops and different elevations were crowded with anxious men and women, gazing at the hills north of the city, expecting each moment to see the enemy. Bodies of cavalry could be seen, and for a time it was believed the desperate hour had arrived, and that the force then in view was the advance of the enemy. Men grasped their weapons and prepared for defence. Women and children made ready for departure to a place of safety, in case the city was shelled. But fortunately, the alarm was groundless, the force in view being the Allen and Woodson County Cavalry, who had been stationed there the night before.

The hours passed by, the day wore on, noon came, and still no enemy; but his approach seemed certain, for our scouts brought information that he had passed south from the Marias des Cygnes that morning. It was only a question of time, which was the more oppressive from its uncertainty.

Nothing was yet known of the victories at the Marias des Cygnes, Osage and Mine Creek, and but little doubt existed that our army had failed to turn the retreating foe from his line of march. The very fact of his being on the retreat, instead of being a guarantee of safety, made (to those who recollected the history of such events) the fate of the city seem more terrible, unless he were pressed too closely, to make a stand long enough to attack where any resistance was made.

It should have been stated before that the Government stores had been sent out under escort of the Quartermaster's employees. Small trains, however, had been detained, and the wagons used to barricade the streets.

The hours of the afternoon wore on more and more terribly. Up to noon our telegraphic communication had been kept open. But it was then kept severed, after the rebels had sent several confused dispatches, which succeeded only in awakening suspicion. Most of the women and children had been removed. A few ladies, however, determined to stay till the last moment, in hopes of being of use to the wounded, as they were in encouraging the defenders.

The sun moved towards the west. Several scouting parties were out, one of whom captured and brought into town three prisoners. About four o'clock, Colonel Blair arrived, and was greeted with the most earnest demonstrations of esteem and gladness; for not only had they confidence in him as a soldier, but the news he brought of Price having turned east ended a most painful suspense.

Shortly after, Colonel Moonlight arrived with his wearied but indomitable command. Every preparation was then made to get supplies for the exhausted army, by whose valor the post and people had been saved.

Soon the following dispatch was received, thus giving the first authentic intelligence of the victory at Mine Creek and Little Osage. Colonel Cloud, after the latter engagement, had withdrawn from the pursuit, and proceeded to repair the telegraph in the vicinity of Fort Lincoln and Mound City.

BATTLE-FIELD, NEAR MOUND CITY, Oct. 25.

To Commanding Officer at Fort Scott:

A battle and a victory near Mound City. We captured five guns. Generals Marmaduke and Caball captured; also many prisoners. We are still pursuing. The rebels are retreating towards Fort Scott. We hope to keep them from reaching you.

(By permission) W. F. CLOUD,
Colonel & A. D. C.

General Scott, of the State militia, had withdrawn the militia from the place previous to Colonel Moonlight's arrival. They returned after learning the news.

As soon as General Curtis reached the post, anxious to relieve the people of Kansas from the toil and sacrifice they had borne for fifteen days, the following order was issued:

HEAD-QUARTERS, DEPARTMENT OF KANSAS, }
IN THE FIELD, FORT SCOTT, October 25, 1864. }

GENERAL ORDER, }
No. 57. }

Fifteen days ago, apprehending an assault upon my Department by Major-General Sterling Price, commanding a force of 20 to 30,000 rebels, intent upon a devastation and plundering of the State of Kansas, I deemed it necessary to proclaim martial law within this State, and in the country occupied by my forces, in order to secure a sufficient force, with the aid of the Governor, to avert disasters and maintain the honor and power of the Federal Government within my Department. The enemy having been beaten in several battles, driven below the settlements of Kansas, all danger of the State from that invasion, which seems to have ended, and the restrictions and burthens incident to martial law no longer necessary in my command; General Order No. 54 is therefore rescinded.

(Signed) S. R. CURTIS, Major-General.

The militia were then relieved. Brigadier-General Fishback, who had accompanied the 4th Brigade, was directed to return to his head-quarters at Paola, holding his command in readiness to repel raids, &c. General Davies was placed in temporary command of the District of South Kansas, while General Blunt pursued the enemy. Colonel Sears was directed to remove the prisoners to Leavenworth. No *resume* of events occurring at this post would be complete without some detail of the operations of the Quartermaster Depot, under charge of Captain M. H. Insley, U. S. A.

With all his transportation in constant use, Capt. Insley was sorely pressed, and was often unable to meet the demands made upon him, constantly increasing and urgent, for supplies. This was especially the case after the rebel retreat south of Fort Scott.

The danger to the depot and supplies were so great, that Captain Insley was directed by the Commanding General to have everything in readiness for evacuation, and to remove at once all heavy articles. This movement would have aroused and completed a panic among the citizens. Captain Insley, in the exercise of a wise discretion allowed him, retained the Government property till the last moment, and by this act and his presence, keep the citizens quiet, and hastened on preparations for defense, inciting all to hold out to the last. When the alarm was given on the night of the 24th, it was quite evident that

necessity for prompt action existed. Everything had been for sometime in readiness. Only a handful of men, less than eight hundred, were at the post, and it was determined to get the Government property away without delay. Through the night of rain and storm, every one worked cheerfully, and the morning saw long trains wending their way to the North-west, into the interior of the State. Two million dollars of Government property, was thus transported to a place of safety. The train remained absent till the 3rd of November.

This removal, naturally and largely, increased the onerous labors imposed upon Captain Insley, after the pursuit was resumed by General Curtis. Without teams, wagons, or employees, for nearly all were off with the stores, Captain Insley pressed all the citizens' teams that could be found, and giving them half loads, sent them after the rapidly moving army, under escort of Lieutenant Ehle, 3rd Wisconsin, Captain Young, 5th Kansas, and others. His energy greatly reduced the suffering of our troops, though from the rapidity of our march, the insufficiency of transportation, and the impoverished condition of the country through which we passed, it was impossible to entirely supply them.

As we again take up the pursuit, the Proclamation and Order of the Governor, and of Major-General Deitzler, are here inserted. They belong to this phase of the narrative, and fitly close the record of the militia and its services :

EXECUTIVE DEPARTMENT,
Topeka, Kansas, Oct. 27, 1864.

No invader's foot treads the soil of Kansas. Price and his robber horde have fled ingloriously before our gallant soldiery. I congratulate you. It is cause for congratulation to the State and to the country, for the defeat of the marauders is sweeping and complete.

Commanders of brigades, regiments, battalions and companies, will march with their respective commands to the counties to which their respective commands belong, and there disband them, making a careful record of the term of service of each man, and see to it especially that proper receipts are given for all property taken or received, while in the field, or on their march homeward, so that each man may obtain pay for all service rendered, or means furnished, during the time the militia of the State have been in active service. I cannot, however, direct this order to be issued, without paying an earnest tribute to you, citizens of Kansas. The call upon the militia of the State was written on Saturday night, the 8th, and published on Monday, the 10th of October. You answered it with alacrity. You left business, the farm, the shop, the office, the pulpit, at a season of the year when every material interest called upon you to remain at home, and self-support almost demanded it.

Seizing your arms and securing your ammunition, you marched to the border, and in less than three days presented a defiant front, full fifteen thousand strong, to the rebel foe. You stood together ready to hurl him back. Never did citizen soldiers show greater promptness, or spring to arms with sterner will. The fire and spirit of the heroic blazed out in all your conduct. It will be an example to arouse the courageous and stimulate the daring. Citizen soldiers of Kansas, the present will remember, and the future cherish, your gallant, your self-sacrificing action.

THOS. CARNEY, Governor.

PROCLAMATION.

EXECUTIVE DEPARTMENT,
Topeka, October 27, 1864.

By the combined courage and energy of Kansas and of Federal troops, under Divine Providence, the State has been saved from a devastating raid. If the foe has trod our soil, it has been only as a routed enemy. Defeat and disaster have followed his steps, and he has fallen and failed before the dashing gallantry and heroic action of our brave men. Now, therefore, I, Thomas Carney, Governor of the State of Kansas, do recommend, that Sunday, the 30th of October, be observed as a day of Thanksgiving and Prayer.

Let praise be given to Almighty God, because He has turned aside the marauder and the murderer; because He has saved the sacking of our cities and the plundering of our people; because, above all, He has preserved them from bloody hands and a traitorous foe.

Let prayers be offered to Him for the recovery of the wounded, and the afflicted of the martyred dead who fell nobly doing a soldier's and a patriot's duty. Let prayers go up to Him, that the hands of the evil doers may be smitten, and they no longer be permitted to rend a free people, and wet this once happy land further with human blood.

Let all the people beseech Him whose breath is our life, and whose will is our law, that peace may soon bless the Republic, one and undivided, upon the benign and christian basis of universal freedom.

THOS. CARNEY, Governor.

GENERAL ORDERS.

HEAD-QUARTERS KANSAS STATE MILITIA, }
TOPEKA, KANSAS, October 29, 1864. }

I. Commanders of regiments and detachments called into active service by the proclamation of the Governor and Commander-in-Chief, of the 8th of October, will cause to be made out and fowarded to these head-quarters, immediately, a complete and accurate report, showing the number of men that turned out and are entitled to pay, and the number of animals and the amount of transportation actually used in the service under said proclamation.

They will also muster for pay, at as early a day as practicable, the militia thus called out, making a separate roll of such persons, including negroes, as are not liable to military duty under the militia laws of Kansas, but were ordered into the service by proclamation of Major-General Curtis, declaring martial law. Blank muster and pay-rolls will be furnished, upon application at these head-quarters.

II. All claims for subsistence, forage, fuel and transportation, will be made out in proper form and forwarded, as directed by the Governor, to Major-General Geo. W. Deitzler, at Lawrence. Persons presenting such claims will be required to furnish the receipt of the regimental or battalion quarter-master, by whom the supplies or transportation were taken or employed, or make affidavit to the correctness of the claims, and that the articles were really taken by militia, giving, if possible, the number of the regiment, or the name of its commander.

III. Claims for horses lost in the service, must be sustained by the certificate, under oath, of at least three credible and disinterested persons, setting forth the value of the animal lost in the service.

IV. Vouchers will be given for all claims allowed, and will be paid by the General Government upon the approval of Major-General Curtis.

The General Commanding, desires to tender his tribute of praise and express his pride to the citizen soldiery of Kansas, who, at the first signal of alarm, marched to the scene of threatened danger, with an alacrity and enthusiasm, which has no parallel in history, leaving homes and occupations to the care of the women and children, the decrepid and infirm, in the holy zeal for the welfare of the State, and who bore themselves, almost without a murmur, through the fearful crisis, suffering all the hardships and privations incident to the season, without tents or a sufficient supply of blankets, and camp and garrison equipage, with a virtuous gallantry, and who, when victory had crowned our cause, returned quietly to their homes to enjoy the deliverance purchased, under the guidance of God, by their self-sacrificing and noble action.

The conduct of the people of Kansas in the campaign just ended, challenges the admiration of every loyal and patriotic mind, and furnishes an example which, if followed, a similar outpouring of the people of the Northern States, would certainly, effectually and speedily crush this wicked rebellion, together with its cause.

While we mourn the loss of the gallant dead, who sleep quietly in honored graves, and deeply sympathize with the wounded and the bereaved, we have cause to congratulate ourselves that our casualties are so light, and also, that the threatened invasion is not entirely without compensating benefits.

It has developed the military spirit of our people, and inspired full confidence in our power and ability to successfully defend the State. It has given arms and equipments complete, to nearly every man in Kansas, and to-day we can safely boast that we have a better militia establishment than any State in the Union. The enemy is not ignorant of these acts, and it is confidently believed, he will not again venture an attempt to overrun Kansas It is gratifying to observe, too, that large portions of two classes of notorious and peace disturbing characters—bushwhackers, and the wives and families of rebel officers and soldiers—have accompanied Price to Texas. The removal of so large a number of rebel women, whose influence was vastly more pernicious than that of twice the same number of men, will tend to lessen the danger of another invasion, confederate soldiers having no longer the inducement to make annual visits to their families in Missouri.

The expenses incurred by the campaign, though amounting to millions in the aggregate, will not prove a heavy burthen on the State. By direction of Major-General Curtis—to whose kind co-operation and well directed energy in furnishing arms and other supplies, without which our efforts would necessarily have been feeble, we should cheerfully accord a full measure of our triumphant success—the General Government will assume the largest item of expense, such as subsistence, forage, fuel and transportation, and it is more than probable that the General Government will re-imburse the State for the pay proper of the militia.

By order of

GEO. W. DEITZLER,
Major-General K. S. M.

JOHN T. MORTON, A. A. G.

That the exertions of General Curtis were fully and gratefully appreciated by the State authorities, in spite of the misunderstanding at the beginning, is evident from the following extracts from the reports of various officers. The State Adjutant General says:

"The Commanding General of the Department, with due appreciation and proper feeling, held the militia, as far as possible, in reserve, and in guarding such defensive positions, as would probably lead to the least sacrifice of life; using his regular troops for those decisive movements in battle upon which great issues depend, and in which large fatality may be expected. In this he was celebrated—first, by the military consideration that his veteran and experienced troops were more to be depended upon in the moment of peril than the militia; and secondly, from the humane consideration, that owing to the peculiar relationship sustained by the militia to their families and the State, he would preserve them as far as possible from the dangers of the battle field, and would only rush them into the deadly conflict, when the fortunes of the day demanded every sacrifice. The militia of our State will duly appreciate the consideration of the General, and while he must honor them for the alacrity with which they sprang to his support, they will honor him that he did not inconsiderately, or needlessly, jeopardize their lives."

General Deitzler thus expresses his thanks:

"I cannot close my report without expressing, in behalf of the people of Kansas, my grateful acknowledgements for the distinguished services rendered in the campaign against Price's plundering and marauding army, by that noble patriot and gallant chieftain, Major-General S. R. Curtis.

Always at his post, and ever watchful of the interests entrusted to his care, he saw the threatened danger, even before the invaders appeared at Pilot Knob, and was the first to sound the tocsin of alarm. * * * Turning a deaf ear to the schemes of politicians and office seekers who followed the army, he manifested a singleness of purpose, and a devotion to duty, rarely witnessed.

"To the knowledge and ripe experience in military affairs, the vigilance and energy of Major-General Curtis, and his kind co-operation in furnishing arms and ammunition, and the necessary supplies to the militia, Kansas owes in a great measure her preservation from the devastating hands of a ruthless foe; and to him we tender our sincere thanks."

General James H. Lane, who served to the night of the 26th, with General Curtis, thus speaks on the same subject:

"I cannot close this report, without expressing the thanks of the people of Kansas for the gallant defense made of our State.

"Devastation, ruin and rapine, threatened our border towns; an insolent and hopeful foe had placed himself without interruption within a day's march of our chief city; his avowed purpose was to sack and burn wherever he touched our soil. He was met, checked, beaten back and finally put to rout by the skill and energy of the Commanding General, and the indomitable, persistent and dogged fighting of our volunteers and militia.

"It would be impossible to mention particular instances of meritorious conduct, where all did so well, without seeming injustice to some, and I therefore reluctantly refrain from doing so.

"The States of the great North-west, whose troops participated in this brief but important campaign, have added another to the long list of brilliant achievements won by them during the war.

"To the militia of my own State, who sprung to arms with the alacrity of other days, at the approach of the foe, I will be permitted to tender special thanks. Going out without the hope of fee or reward, some have fallen, others have been maimed for life, while all have testified their devotion to the common cause, and their love for our gallant young State. To one and all of these, let us be ever grateful."

The arrival of the large number of rebel prisoners in Fort Scott, excited both citizens and soldiers to a high degree. The former, especially, were greatly wrought up by the outrages committed in Linn and Bourbon counties. Especially were the general officers objects of curiosity and denunciation. Marmaduke had made himself peculiarly infamous by his daring raids, and the atrocities which accompanied them. General Curtis having ordered them to Fort Leavenworth, where new prison buildings had been erected, gave directions also to retain the General and field officers in the same custody and treatment as that received by the rank and file. Also not to permit any violence or discourtesy to be offered them.

Marmaduke complained of this treatment. After General Curtis resumed the pursuit, General Pleasanton removed the principal prisoners, Generals Marmaduke and Cabell, Colonel Jeffards, and others, to the hotel where he himself was staying. This excited much feeling and indignation, it being charged that Federal officers were dispossessed of their rooms to accommodate the rebel prisoners. Captain Hall, 2d Colorado, was in immediate charge of the prisoners. He had orders from General Curtis to march immediately. General Pleasanton ordered him to remain in Fort Scott until he could hear from General Rosecrans, reported on his way there. That officer being senior, his orders would supersede those of General Curtis. The latter, finding General Rosecrans did not reach the front, assumed command of General Pleasanton's force. General Curtis had directed all the previous movements, but had not assumed direct command. General Pleasanton, taking ground that, so far as he was concerned, the campaign was over, necessitated the formal assumption by General Curtis, as he would have to take the responsibility. General Pleasanton sent a dispatch on the 27th, acquiescing in this arrangement, informing General Curtis that he had ordered Sanborn and Benteen to move in pursuit, and stating that his health prevented him keeping the field, and a surgeon's certificate to that effect. He also reported that the prisoners would be removed to Fort Leavenworth. General Curtis' motive in directing this removal was founded on a wish to effect an exchange with Price at an early day. Leavenworth would be more convenient than St. Louis.

The latter was then in communication with General Rosecrans, and urged and obtained an order from him directing himself (Pleasanton) to proceed to St. Louis, *via* Warrensburg, Mo., with prisoners and captured guns.

General Rosecrans had followed closely in the rear of Pleasanton, reaching the neighborhood of Little Santa Fe the day of the battles in Kansas. Here he was overtaken by Lieutenant Robinson, Chief Engineer on Department Staff, who, accompanied by Colonel Ellithorpe, editor of the Leavenworth *Conservative*, and an escort, was pushing forward to rejoin General Curtis. They had been delayed in gathering the entrenching tools, etc., used at Big Blue and Kansas City. General Rosecrans desired that they would travel with him. The Engineer party did so that day (the 25th). General Rosecrans had a cavalry escort of about one thousand men, and camped early in the afternoon. Next morning the march was not resumed till seven A. M., and the command went into camp after making twelve miles. Lieutenant Robinson, finding that at this rate he would not overtake troops following an enemy marching sixty miles per day, left Rosecrans' camp and pushed forward to Fort Scott, camping on Mine Creek that night, the 26th. General Rosecrans was very coarse in his criticisms of General Curtis' movements, saying in the hearing of Colonel Ellithorpe, among other things, that "old Curtis appeared to be driving Price back again into Missouri." This criticism could have come only from a jealous nature, as the folly of allowing a rebel army to ravage Kansas was too plain to be disputed. He also declared that his method of marching was the thing; that such racing as Price's could not be kept up, and that his infantry would have to come up and finish the job. He also designated the Kansas troops as Border ruffians, and said he understood that Jim Lane was running the machine. Finding, however, that the "racing" was kept up, General Rosecrans turned back in disgust, returning to St. Louis; on his way there, however, withdrawing his troops from the face of the enemy, as will be seen hereafter.

General A. J. Smith, of the 17th Army Corps, who with the infantry division had pressed closely behind Pleasanton, reaching Independence the morning of the 24th, was by General Rosecrans directed to move in pursuit by way of Harrisonville, thus throwing him out of the direct line of pursuit, and by moving east preventing General Smith from rendering any service in the defeat of Price, a result which must have greatly chagrined that sturdy old fighter.

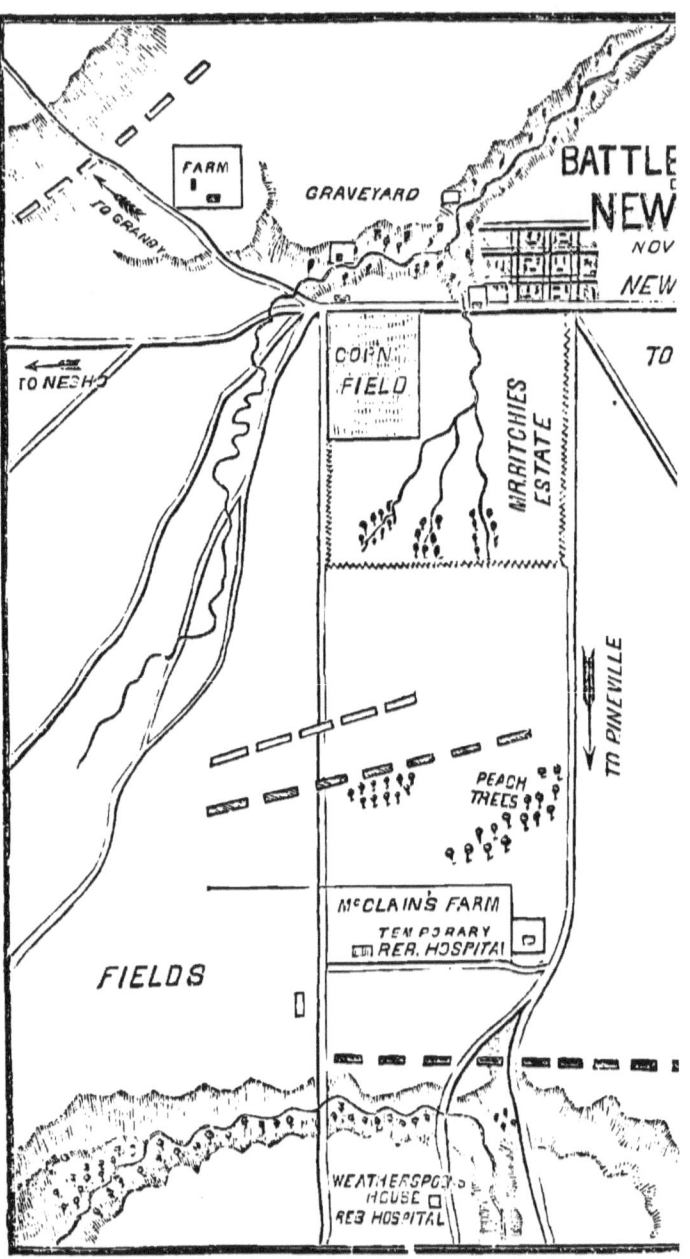

CHAPTER XIX.

PURSUIT FROM FORT SCOTT—BATTLE OF NEWTONIA—GENERAL ROSECRANS' ORDERS—CONSEQUENT ABANDONMENT OF THE PURSUIT.

GENERAL CURTIS left Fort Scott at an early hour on the morning of the 26th, accompanied by the Brigade of Colonel Moonlight, taking the direct road to Lamar and Carthage.

General Blunt followed soon after, accompanied by the Brigades of Colonels Jennison and Ford. The 1st Division was reduced in numbers, but rendered more effective for its work by leaving behind all worn out men and animals. But four guns of the Colorado Battery were taken; horses in good condition being had for that number and the guns of the 9th Wisconsin Battery. Captain Dodge reported all the men of his command fit for field duty. The section of the Colored Battery, Lieutenant Minor, was relieved. Captain Insley, A. Q. M., was ordered to forward, in all, 50,000 rations for the troops, and the same amount of corn for the animals. In pursuance of this order, an extensive foray was made upon the farmers and owners of teams, who were incontinently pressed into service and sent with the supplies.

General McNeil, as before stated, had followed close upon the track of the retreating foe. He crossed at Adamson's Ford of the Drywood, eight miles east of Fort Scott. His progress was here delayed several hours by the obstructions made by the enemy. The demoralization of the enemy was most plainly visible, from the ruined and abandoned material everywhere scattered around. The exhausted troops of General McNeil, who had then been without supplies for three days, marched that day twenty-seven miles, bivouacking at Shanghai, where General Curtis camped. Arriving there at nine P. M., their exhaustion was so complete and utter, that much excitement was manifested when it was found that the general subsistence train had not arrived. Major Hunt, of the general staff, finding that a train belonging to head-quarters had arrived in the night, took upon himself the responsibility of issuing these supplies to the famished troops.

The rebel trail was struck at this point. The troops now assembled, and in direct pursuit, were the Division of General Blunt, consisting of the Brigades of Colonels Jennison, Ford and Moonlight, and the Brigade of General McNeil. Colonel Blair's militia had been relieved by the order abolishing martial law, and he resumed the command of his post. General Lane, Colonel Crawford, Colonel Cloud,

Colonel Ritchie, with other members of the Volunteer Staff, were relieved here and returned to Kansas to resume the active political canvass, which the call "To arms" had suspended.

The Brigade of Colonel Benteen had moved to Fort Scott, and, with that of General Sanborn, resumed the pursuit on the 27th. The latter moved direct towards Newtonia; Colonel Benteen on the Neosho, or Line road.

Nothing of special importance occurred on the 27th, except increasing evidence of the hasty retreat of the rebels. We marched from Shanghai to Coon Creek, where the command halted for several hours, then made a night march to Carthage, marching this day forty miles.

Escaped prisoners came into our lines during the day, and reported that the Kansas militia and others were being marched without proper food and treatment, so that many were almost demented from famine, and liable at any moment to fall from utter exhaustion. This fact, and reported cases of cruelty, determined General Curtis to send a flag of truce to the rebel commander, demanding a release of all prisoners, on the ground that his march prevented that humane treatment and care of them required by the laws of war. Major McKenny was ordered with an escort on this duty. From the condition of the enemy, as reported by those captured on the road and their escaped prisoners, it was believed that Price might be induced to surrender.

Carthage has become a name famous in Missouri. Among the first victories of the war, was that gained here by Sigel. Other encounters have lent their interest to this point. The village, formerly handsome and well built, is now but a mass of charred ruins; some few remaining buildings having been fired by the enemy the previous day. Quite a number of their sick and wounded were left here, and at every house between it and Newtonia, one or more were found abandoned by their comrades. Instances of barbarous cruelty were not unfrequent. After leaving Carthage, among the first objects that met the eye, was the form of a negro, with his skull half blown off, evidently by a gun placed so near as to singe the hair in the discharge. It was acts such as these, as well as charges of murdering their comrades after being wounded, that induced the hanging of a couple of wounded rebels found in a house a few miles from Carthage, where the advanced brigade (Colonel Jennison's) had halted for camp. The act was cowardly and dastardly, whoever was guilty thereof. Yet with rude men, whose passions were aroused by such sights and acts, some palliation may be offered. For the officers who encouraged it, none can be given. This act, and others, were afterwards made the subject of investigation. As we proceeded, the poverty and even destitution of the inhabitants became daily more evident.

General Blunt's Division held the advance. The advance guard was composed of the 16th Kansas, under Major Ketner. Major McKenny, with the flag of truce party, after a ride of some ten or twelve miles, came in sight of the enemy's rear. This was five miles from Granby, famous as the centre of the South-west Missouri Lead mines.

A courier reached the front at this time, with orders from General Blunt to take down the flag, which was done. Major McKenny with his escort, in conjunction with Companies "G," Captain Hall, "A" and "B," Captains Ames and Wright, moved forward rapidly, Major Ketner in command. The enemy appeared to be about two hundred strong, and were strongly posted on a hill and near a small belt of timber. Skirmishers were thrown forward to develop the enemy's strength and intentions. They immediately fell back, and were briskly pursued, until beyond the town of Granby, when Major Ketner halted till the arrival of Colonel Ford, with the balance of brigade. This, and the brigade of Jennison (then under the command of Lieutenant-Colonel Hoyt) were all the troops in advance. Colonel Moonlight had obtained permission to feed at a field near the line of march. Subsequently, General McNeil halted and fed his brigade, by direction of General Curtis, who believing at first the whole division was halted, countenanced the delay. General Sanborn came up while these troops were halted, and by direction of General Curtis, pushed forward on the trot to the assistance of General Blunt.

To return to the movements in front. At Granby we learned that the entire rebel army was then at Newtonia, a few miles to the south. General Price had left this village only a short time before our advance entered. The women and children reported him as defiant, leaving a message, that we could have all the fighting we wanted at Newtonia.

As this was the last point on the line of retreat where grain could be obtained, it was evident that the rebel commander had determined to make a stand here for the purpose of obtaining supplies and resting his exhausted stock. He still had a considerable army, over 20,000 strong, though evidence of depletion was quite strong in our rear. Numerous trails in the direction of Cow Creek and Spring River, showed that guerrillas were falling off and seeking their haunts.

With the ready instinct of a genuine fighter, General Blunt determined to push forward with the small force at his disposal, and engage the enemy, trusting to the arrival of other troops to complete the rout which he predetermined upon. The little column, less than a thousand strong, with McLain's four guns and Patterson's mountain howitzers, was moved forward at the trot.

The road was hilly, and bordered by scrub oaks and undergrowth. At last we reached the brow of a precipitous bluff, where the road *dips* into the extensive plain, on which the town of Newtonia is situated. This plain or valley, is almost enclosed.

South, the land rises abruptly, as in the direction we were moving. West, the road to Neosho winds along the foot of the Ozark Spurs. In the eastern portion of the valley is the town of Newtonia, whose streets we could see filled with men. The smoke rising from the steam flouring mill told that the enemy were at work. South and west of the village could be seen extensive camps and trains, at a distance of from two to three miles.

The guns of the Colorado Battery were brought to the front, placed in position on the brow of the bluff, and opened on the enemy, who could now be seen formed in line of battle in the open valley directly west of the town, and of a large corn-field enclosed by a stone wall.

The 16th Kansas and 2d Colorado, in all less than six hundred men, were formed in line of battle, and at a gallop descended into the valley, moving on the enemy with unwavering front, General Blunt with his staff and small escort taking the lead. Major Charlot, Assistant Adjutant General of the army, reported for duty on the field, and did gallant and efficient service as Aide.

As the slender line plunged into the valley, the 1st Brigade, under Colonel Hoyt, came up and formed in support of the battery, which continued to fire with good effect upon the rebel lines. When we first moved, the enemy appeared in small force at our front, but as our little force deployed, the 16th Kansas advancing as skirmishers, it became very evident that we were in for a struggle with the entire fighting strength of the rebel army.

General Blunt, revolver in hand, with the members of his personal staff and volunteer aides, animated the men with his dauntless courage. Riding to the very front of our skirmish line, now briskly engaged, he personally superintended the movements. Sergeant Patterson, with four howitzers, was placed on our extreme right, in advance, and did most excellent service, pouring canister into a heavy flanking column, with which the rebel commander was seeking to turn our right. The engagement became general and severe. Our men had the advantage, though the disparity of numbers was so great, in superior arms. Our breech-loaders, with the perfect coolness of men and officers, for a time fully compensated the other deficiency. The only purpose now was to hold the tide of battle at its full until the balance of the Division and McNeil should arrive. General Blunt had expected when his advance was made to be quickly supported by McNeil, who was supposed to be close in his rear.

The battery left on the bluff had maintained a rapid fire until our line was endangered. Captain McLain then reported to Colonel Hoyt, who, without waiting for orders, moved to the support of Ford's Brigade. The effective strength of both brigades had been greatly reduced by the rapidity of the movement after the enemy. One-third of the force were unable to keep up, and came straggling to the field for the next hour or more.

The 1st Brigade formed on right of Colonel Ford, with the battery in the centre. The execution of the Parrotts was here quite indifferent, overshooting as they did, the force with which we were engaged. Much damage was however done the rebels scattered through the timber to the south.

From the first moment of our appearance on the bluff, the enemy commenced hasty preparations for leaving. General Shelby, who was in command on the field, seeing very clearly that the rapidity of the pursuit had scattered and weakened our force, believed that he could give us a severe check, raise the spirits of the dejected army, and secure a safe and uninterrupted retreat. But, great as were the odds in his favor, he reckoned without his host. The personal courage of the Union commander on this day was equivalent to a whole brigade. General Blunt never faltered or doubted. Upon this very field had he won his first laurels as a General, and here he was determined they should be renewed. His example was contagious. That little line of nine hundred men met and beat back every attempt to defeat it made by the rebel force of eight or ten thousand now concentrated at its front. Men and horses fell thick and fast. Still the deadly storm continued. The rebels had early opened a well directed fire from a couple of rifled guns on their left, and replied to our plunging howitzer fire, by one almost as effective. The integrity of our line was as much insured by the skill and energy of Sergeant Patterson and his light artillery, as by the cool audacity of all on the field.

The afternoon waned; the sun sunk towards the west; no assistance arrived. Our first line of battle had been formed beyond and to the west of the northern portion of the town and corn-field before mentioned. The flanking movement on our right had been checked by the heavy fire from the howitzers of Colonel Hoyt's command. It now became certain that we were in imminent danger of being flanked by columns through the corn-field and town, when General Blunt sent orders to Captain McLain to fall back about three hundred yards, to a position near some lone trees, whence opening on the rebel right, he was to cover the falling back of our force, and the formation of a second line of battle. This movement was finally accomplished, and the flanking operations of the rebels checked. It was not done however, without some confusion and loss. Captain McLain moving his guns at a gallop to the position assigned, came nearly creating a panic in a battalion of the 15th, at the time of falling back in pursuance of orders. For the first time in the campaign, a line of stragglers could be seen making their way towards the rear. Major Charlot, Colonel Burris, Captain Hinton, and Captain Tough, Chief Scout, exerted themselves efficiently to stay this movement. Most of those who retired were wounded, and many of these returned to the field. The formidable array at the front, and the failure of support from the brigades behind, might well have made the most dauntless quail.

In the ranks of the enemy, the utmost exertions were made by the leading officers, to bring their men to a charge. So overwhelming was their force, that such an event must have produced disaster to us. Among the most conspicuous in these efforts, was an officer of splendid proportions, finely mounted on a white horse, who, bareheaded, and sabre in hand, rode furiously up and down the rebel lines, cheering on the men and exposing himself heedlessly to the utmost peril of the strife. We afterwards learned this was Lieutenant-Colonel Reefe, of Fayetteville, commanding Munroe's Arkansas Regiment. At last he succeeded in shaming his men into an effort. As the 2d Colorado was slowly moving back to the second position, whence McLain was now belching forth his thunders, the quick eye of Captain Green detected a suspicious formation and movements. Without waiting for orders, he brought two companies by "fours right about," and made a counter-charge, before which the rebels flew precipitately, in spite of the orders and denunciations of their commanders. The exploits performed by our troops at preceding engagements, had lent an wholesome dread of their prowess. Colonel Reefe received many complimentary volleys from our line, but seemed to bear a charmed life.

The rebel fire slackened somewhat, as we became well established in our second position. We had now been on the field—holding it with but a handful of men, yet defiant and confident—for over two hours. The sunset's crimson tints were lighting the western horizon; the evening damps began to chill the combatants. The enemy, it was evident, were preparing for another attempt at flanking our left. In this event General Blunt determined to retire to the bluff, whence he knew the enemy could not drive him, and there await reinforcements.

At this juncture, General Sanborn, in advance of his command, was met at the foot of the bluff, by Captain Hinton, General Blunt's Aid, and hastily informed of the position of affairs. It was suggested to General Sanborn to bring his brigade in upon our left, and resist the movement through the corn-field. The General immediately returned to execute this movement. The information was conveyed to General Blunt. It was received by the troops at the front with enthusiastic cheers. At this time, one half of the line was out of carbine ammunition, the firing had been so rapid and exhaustive. The howitzers were yet well out to the front. Captain McLain had retired with his guns to the foot of the bluff, a movement made without orders, and as alleged by the Captain, in consequence of the utter exhaustion of men and horses.

General Sanborn now moved down the bluff and into the valley on the gallop; the 6th M. S. M. and the 2d Arkansas Cavalry, Colonel Phelps, jun., being in the advance. As they neared the field through which the enemy were moving, these regiments dismounted, formed line of battle, driving the rebels through the field. A section of Rodman guns, under Lieutenant Montgomery, was opened on the rebel centre from our left. General Blunt's force again moved forward on a line with Sanborn's. A few volleys were fired, and then some scattering shots terminated the hard fought battle of Newtonia, the enemy abandoning the field.

While General Sanborn was moving into position, General Curtis with his staff and escort arrived. Finding that Blunt had engaged the enemy, the commanding General pushed on with Sanborn to his assistance. The latter deserves great credit for the promptness of his movement, and celerity of his march from Fort Scott. In his published report, General Sanborn says:

"I marched sixty-two (62) miles that day, keeping the artillery and teams along, and reached Newtonia on the 28th, about four P. M., having marched one hundred and four miles, with artillery and train, in thirty-six hours.

"I found General Blunt heavily engaged with the enemy, his line slowly receding, and the enemy's line extending much beyond his on both flanks, advancing rapidly upon the right and left.

"General Blunt directed me to form upon his left, and, if possible, to turn the enemy's right.

"The horses being exhausted, and the field intersected with stones, walls and other obstacles, I was induced to dismount my command, and the regiments were ordered to advance as fast as they could dismount and form. The 6th Cavalry, M. S. M., was the first to meet the advancing force of the enemy. This regiment advanced most gallantly, and had fired two or three volleys in rapid succession, when a triumphant cheer from the line announced that the enemy had turned and was falling back."

It is impossible to record all the incidents of this day. The vigorous attack with a handful of men by General Blunt, is almost unparalleled for audacity during the war; not more so than the severe punishment given to the enemy, and the tenacity with which our position was held, in spite of failure of supports, and the large force of the enemy against which we were pitted. The results of the conflict were most disastrous to them, much more so than to us, though our loss was not inconsiderable. According to reports, our loss was as follows: 15th Kansas, ten killed, twenty-nine wounded and one missing; 16th Kansas, two killed and thirteen wounded; 3rd Wisconsin (Lieutenant Pond commanding) eleven wounded; 2d Colorado Battery, one killed, five wounded; in all ninety-five wounded, eighteen killed and one missing; total, one hundred and fourteen; not more than twenty were seriously wounded. About one hundred horses were killed and wounded. Captain Moses, 2d Colorado, was wounded twice. The enemy lost two hundred and seventy-five wounded, thirty-five seriously. Two colonels were killed. They also buried General Slemmons, who was wounded on Mine Creek, three days previous.

In the first onset, 16th Kansas, Major Ketner commanding, drove the enemy for some distance. He had two horses shot under him. Captain Tough had a narrow escape, a ball passing through the rim of his felt hat. Captain Hinton was partially stunned by the explosion of a shell within a few feet of him. Colonel Burris, Volunteer Aide, deserves the greatest credit for coolness and usefulness. Next to General

Blunt, in perfect and audacious courage, comes Colonel Ford, of the 2d Colorado. The regiment commanded by him were model soldiers throughout the campaign, and won the highest encomiums. Two companies became famous on account of their gray horses. Everywhere in front they were to the rebels as is Death on the pale horse to the wicked.

Newtonia was garrisoned by a small battalion of enrolled militia, under Major Johnson, who retired on the approach of the enemy. Moving towards Mount Vernon, he encountered about four hundred rebels, who were out foraging. A skirmish ensued, in which the rebels were defeated. Lieutenant Christenson, a member of the militia, residing in Newtonia, was taken prisoner, and in the presence of his wife and mother was inhumanly butchered. He was a German, but lately married, and had been for a long time a scourge to the bushwhackers of this vicinity. His body was recovered next morning from the woods, where it had been thrown, brutally mutilated.

Colonel Jennison, in his published report of the campaign, says of Newtonia:

"On the morning of the 28th, the march was resumed, the brigade being then under command of Lieutenant-Colonel Hoyt, passing the Granby lead mines, Newton county, about 2 o'clock P. M., the Colorado 2d being in the advance, with the Colorado Battery. When within about three miles of Newtonia, messengers passed along the lines from the front, with the intelligence that our advance had overtaken the rebel army at the latter place, and was then engaged. The command "Forward—trot—gallop—march!" was given, and never with more hearty alacrity obeyed, and the brigade swept on through almost impenetrable clouds of dust to the open ground north of the town, where our artillery were already posted, and had opened fire with shell upon the enemy's lines, then distant more than a mile, and evidently striving to get into the timber on the Pineville road with the train.

Reaching the crest of the hill upon which the battery was posted, the order was given, and the 1st Brigade moved rapidly towards the enemy, by this time engaged by Colonel Ford's Brigade. The 1st Brigade was immediately formed, by direction of the General Commanding, on the right of the line. Commencing a spirited and determined fire at a range of about five hundred yards, the howitzers, under Sergeant Patterson, doing more efficient execution than at any previous action during the campaign. In this connection, I would mention with particular recommendations to favor, Sergeant Patterson, 14th K. V. C., an experienced and capable artillerist of long service in the Army of the Potomac and elsewhere. During the whole of the campaign, he remained in the faithful discharge of his duties as Sergeant of the howitzer battery, which fired the first gun at Lexington, and almost the last at Newtonia.

For further details of the battle, permit me to extract from the report of Lieutenant-Colonel Hoyt, 15th K. V. C., as follows, he being at that time in command of the Brigade, by reason of the temporary disability of myself, caused by an accident:

"HEAD-QUARTERS 15th K. V. C., IN THE FIELD,
CHEROKEE NATION, NOV. 9, 1864.

* * * * "On the 28th of October, Price was attacked by General Blunt, with the brigades of yourself and Colonel Ford, 2d Colorado Cavalry, at Newtonia, Mo. In this engagement, it was my privilege to lead your brigade, of which I can only say, none could have fought more nobly, or with greater determination, standing under fire a long time without a cartridge to return the galling fire of the enemy, having expended eighty rounds to the man, the alacrity of our movements rendering it impossible for the ammunition train to keep up.

"I desire to mention Lieut. Jos. Mackle, A. A. A. G., 1st Brigade, and Lieutenant W. H. Bisbee, Company "E," 15th Kansas Volunteer Cavalry, acting Regimental Adjutant, for their praiseworthy conduct in the last named, and in fact all the engagements in which this regiment was employed. Of the officers of my command and their men, it is not possible for me to specify particular names, for all were brave, and none were either cowardly or incompetent. "GEO. H. HOYT,
"Lieutenant-Colonel Commanding."

"Maintaining its line of battle unbroken until some time after dark, the 1st Brigade, in obedience to orders from the General Commanding, encamped for the night in the town of Newtonia, having brought in all its wounded, who were properly cared for, and bestowed in the houses of the town."

In the same report, the Colonel mentions the 3rd Wisconsin Cavalry, and quotes from Lieutenant Pond's report:

"Of the battle of Newtonia, Lieutenant Pond reports that his command, reduced to thirty-four effective men, was placed on the left of the 2d Colorado, and took part in the charge led, as at Westport, by General Blunt in person, against an enemy so vastly superior, that the audacity of the charge must have been as auspicious as its valor. That we held that position until our ammunition was exhausted, and afterwards until succor came, history will tell and truly; but *how*, seems a miracle. In this contest, Lieutenant Pond's command lost four men, seriously wounded, and eleven horses killed. The Lieutenant concludes his report as follows:

"It affords me pleasure, in connection herewith, to notice the conspicuous gallantry and heroism of Lieutenant John Crites, Company "D." His coolness and self-possession, under the most terrific fire, gave to his recruits the full assurance of veterans. He was the only commissioned officer in the battalion with me when we entered the battle of Newtonia:

The remaining prisoners of the 2d Kansas State Militia, under Captain Huntoon, came into camp on the 29th, having been paroled by General Price at Granby. They were in a most pitiable condition; starved, half naked, worn out and barefoot, having been robbed by their captors of all decent articles of clothing. Everything possible was done for their comfort.

That night the enemy retired in hasty disorder, leaving their wounded in our lines, and their dead unburied where they fell. The condition of their wounded was frightful. An assistant surgeon of Munroe's Arkansas Regiment, and a medical student recruited at Lexington, were left in charge of the hospital. One sack of flour and a scant supply of a few common drugs, were all that the rebel medical and commissariat stores could furnish. The surgeon came in under a flag of truce, and, announcing their condition, asked such medical stores as humanity demanded should be at his disposal. On arrival of our medical train, their wants were supplied.

Every preparation was made for an early resumption of the pursuit, which General Curtis was now sure would result in the surrender of the rebel army. This was the main purpose of his campaign, and with efficient co-operation after the battle of Newtonia, could have been brought about. Our horses and men, exhausted though they were, were in better condition than the enemy's. Below this point, he passed beyond the range of mills and grain. By a vigorous pursuit, he could be prevented from menacing our posts in Western Arkansas and on the river, while they would be enabled to prevent him crossing that stream.

Even if not successful in forcing a surrender, immediate and unremitting pursuit must exhaust the rebels, deplete his army by constant desertion, and finally compel him to flee only as a mob retires, disordered, demobilized and demoralized utterly.

Such was undoubtedly the reasoning on the night of the 28th. General McNeil and Colonel Moonlight came in after dark. The first was ordered to take the advance next day, moving at three A. M.

Just as the troops were moving out, a courier arrived from General Pleasanton, with orders from General Rosecrans, directing all the troops of his department to return to their respective districts. This of course prohibited any further pursuit, as General Curtis had with him less than 1,500 men, properly belonging to his command. Generals Sanborn and McNeil moved towards Springfield, while the 1st Division was ordered to return to Kansas by way of Neosho. Major Murphy, of M. S. M., was left in command of Newtonia, and every possible preparation made for taking care of the wounded. Subsistence and medical train arrived during the forenoon of the 29th.

The indignation of all was intense. It was felt that General Rosecrans could not have known or appreciated the position. Misinformed as to the campaign, by those whose duty it was to have told the truth, the order recalling was without doubt issued on the idea that the campaign was practically over, and further pursuit was useless. The Lieutenant-General did not, as will be hereafter seen, agree with this view.

The following account of the conflict at Newtonia was sent by General Blunt to Senator Lane, and by the latter published in the papers of the State:

NEOSHO, October 30, 1864,
IN THE FIELD.

TO GENERAL J. H. LANE:

On the 28th instant, at 3 o'clock P. M., after marching all day and night previously, I came up with Price at Newtonia, with Ford's and Jennison's Brigades of my Division. Price had gone into camp in the timber south of the town, thinking that we had quit the pursuit.

Upon discovering our advance, he formed one line of battle in the edge of the timber, another in front on the prairie, developing almost ten thousand men. I moved forward rapidly and attacked him with vigor. The fight lasted from 3 o'clock until dark, and was the warmest contested field we have had in the campaign. With the two brigades, I held the field, without support, until nearly sundown, when Sanborn came up just in time to form on my left and repulse a flanking column of the enemy. We then drove them from the field in confusion.

They retreated hastily, and moved all night on the Cassville road. My loss in killed and wounded, was about one hundred and eighteen, and about one hundred and seventy-five horses killed.

A rebel surgeon, who came in with a flag of truce, reports the enemy's loss at over two hundred. Among their killed were two Colonels.

A spy of ours, who has been with them for several days past and during the battle of the 28th, has come in, and reports that Price has 16,000 men armed, and 10,000 unarmed; that he has still about four hundred wagons, mostly loaded with goods plundered, and that he has burned large amounts of his transportation. He says Price will not fight unless compelled to, to save his train and unarmed conscripts, but will move as rapidly as possible to Red River. He also says Price intended, if possible, to make his headquarters this winter at Kansas City. This is also corroborated by most of the prisoners we have taken.

Price told the Missouri recruits that Kansas could not raise force enough to disturb him in carrying out his programme.

General Curtis ordered the troops to march yesterday morning at 3 o'clock, and vigorously follow up the pursuit, but before the hour arrived, an order came from General Rosecrans for all the forces of Pleasanton to abandon the pursuit and return to the head-quarters of their respective districts. Yesterday I removed to this point to recruit the stock and rest the men, and be within supporting distance of Forts Gibson and Smith.

Orders have just arrived from Lieutenant-General Grant, which will, I hope, enable us to yet do the enemy more damage.

Of the Shawnee county militia, one hundred have come in paroled. They have suffered much for food and from hard travel. All say they were well treated as prisoners. They speak well of General Shelby. I will keep you advised as proper.

Truly yours,

JAS. G. BLUNT.

CHAPTER XX.

RESUMPTION OF PURSUIT—ROUTE OF THE REBELS—THE PEA RIDGE BATTLE-FIELD—ATTACK ON FAYETTEVILLE—GALLANT DEFENSE.

The troops under General Curtis rested at Neosho, on the night of the 29th. Early on the morning of the 30th, a courier arrived with dispatches, enclosing an order, through General Halleck, from Lieutenant-General Grant, bearing date the 28th, desiring the pursuit of Price to be continued to the Arkansas River, or until he encountered General Steele or General Reynolds.

Acting on this, General Curtis immediately issued orders for a continuance of the march, and considering that this overruled the orders of General Rosecrans, received twenty-two hours before at Newtonia, sent dispatches to Generals Sanborn and McNeil, Colonel Phillips and Colonel Benteen. The courier found the latter a few miles north of Neosho; the others were not reached till after arrival at Springfield. They were ordered to move by way of Cassville, Mo. General McNeil used great exertions to overtake General Curtis. When the order was received, he was busily engaged in shoeing his horses, and the time necessarily occupied in the work upon a thousand animals, delayed his march. He however pushed after the 1st Division, and after leaving Cassville, taking with him the best mounted men of the brigade, followed with all speed, and missing the trail, marched direct to Fort Smith.

Colonel Benteen joined General Curtis on the morning of November 1st, at the camp near Pea Ridge. General Sanborn followed to Cassville, whence he issued an order directing Colonel Benteen's movements. That officer returned answer, that being only temporarily in the Department of Missouri, and having received orders from General Grant, through General Curtis, he held himself bound to obey them, and when relieved, to rejoin as speedily as might be, his proper corp command.

A wide difference of opinion existed between the Commanding Generals in Missouri, and General Curtis, as to the policy of pursuing the enemy below Newtonia. The order of General Rosecrans is one evidence, and the following communication to Pleasanton from General Sanborn, is another. As this letter is a good statement of this difference, it is given entire:

HEAD-QUARTERS, DISTRICT OF S. W. MISSOURI,
Springfield, Nov. 12, 1864.

To MAJOR-GENERAL PLEASANTON:

I have just returned from Cassville, and will forward my official report of the campaign in a few days. No one has fired a shot at the enemy since the battle of Newtonia, where the enemy gained great advantage over Blunt at first, but my command got up in time to turn the enemy's right, and the tide of things.

The enemy lost very largely in men and horses in North-west Arkansas, and the border.

My idea was, and is now, that when we got him below Newtonia and the region of grain mills and cattle, we should not crowd him any more, but rather make an effort to hold him in this land of starvation, as we would a garrison out of supplies, until his army broke up and divided. Deserters were very numerous while Price was in this section, but I have seen none that have left him since he was pushed off towards his supplies.

My own view is, that all the efforts of General Curtis to drive the enemy, and they have been great, and entitle him to credit, have been to our detriment and the enemy's advantage, for I believe one-half of his army would have deserted north of the Arkansas, had it not been for the fear of the pursuing foe, and the pursuit has been expensive; but the enemy has suffered badly, and all should be satisfied, I suppose. My dispatches from General Thayer indicate that the troops on the Arkansas will not attack Price.

JOHN B. SANBORN,
Brigadier-General Commanding.

An obvious criticism on this is that the Lieutenant-General and the Secretary of War did not agree with General Sanborn or his immediate commander. An order from General Grant has already been given. To anticipate somewhat, it is here stated, that on the 7th of November, the Secretary of War directed General Curtis to assume command of all troops on his line of march in pursuit of Price, returning them to their proper commanders after its close.

As to the criticism upon the wisdom of General Curtis' policy, a sufficient answer is found in the fact, that an abandonment of the pursuit at the point named, would have flooded the district which General Sanborn commanded, with the worst of bushwhackers. Again, the sagacity shown by General Curtis, is exhibited in the fact that in all probability, not only Fayetteville would have fallen, but that, strengthened by a junction with Generals

Cooper and Gano, Price would have made a comparatively easy capture of Forts Smith and Gibson, and thus replaced his great losses by equally as valuable gains.

After leaving Cassville, it was found that the main force of the enemy had moved to Pineville, and thence by way of Maysville down the State Line. It was determined to push on direct to Fayetteville, as that post being exposed, might fall an easy prey to any superior rebel force. We camped near the old battle-field of Pea Ridge, remaining there two days, awaiting the arrival of the subsistence train, which reached us the morning of the 3rd. Breaking camp in the midst of a severe snow storm, the Army of the Border, now about three thousand strong, marched to Sugar Creek. On this day's march, General Curtis passed across the historic ground made famous by the victory he won over the combined armies of Price, McIntosh and McCullough, under Van Dorn, in March, 1862. Again was he pursuing his old antagonist, but under somewhat different circumstances. Giving that formidable foe the first effectual rebuff of the war, it must have been a source of great satisfaction to the gallant old soldier commanding our troops, to know that he was again driving this same chieftain, and under circumstances which warranted a belief in its being a final and fatal blow to the rebel power west of the Mississippi.

Dispatches were received from General Thayer at

Fort Smith, and Colonel Harrison at Fayetteville, urging a close pursuit of Price as the only means of saving those posts. Three days of unremitting rain and snow, as well as the delay necessary for the arrival of our trains, had impeded our movements. It became evident no assistance could be expected from General Rosecrans' troops. Major Melton, 2d Arkansas Cavalry, commanding post at Cassville, reported with fifty men, and was sent forward to Fayetteville.

About midnight on the 3rd, while encamped at Cross Hollows, in the midst of a heavy storm of rain and snow, dispatches arrived from Colonel Harrison, announcing an attack by Fagan on that post, and requesting assistance. It was then held against great odds, but must fall if not soon relieved.

Fayetteville, eighteen miles in advance of our camp, was strongly fortified by substantial earthworks, garrisoned by a force of 1,100 troops and citizens, commanded by Colonel M. La Rue Harrison, 1st Cavalry, Arkansas Volunteers. It was a place of considerable importance, and contained valuable stores. The 1st Arkansas had been stationed there since the spring of '63. After the disastrous campaign of General Steele, in the spring of '64, bands of guerrillas reappeared in North-western Arkansas, harassing the Union citizens and soldiers, breaking up the mail and telegraphic route, and constantly harassing our trains and forces. They were led by a noted partizan, Major Buck Brown. Afterwards

Colonel Brooks, of the rebel army, appeared in the district with three hundred men. Having authority to raise a rebel brigade, he immediately commenced recruiting and conscripting. Colonel Harrison's force, nominally cavalry, was but indifferently mounted, and as he was compelled to guard and hold open the route north to Cassville, and south to Van Buren, his troops and stock were greatly overworked. At Fayetteville, eleven companies were stationed, of whom only two hundred were mounted. As Price moved north, the rebels became bolder. October 20th, while Colonel Harrison was escorting a subsistence train from Cassville, with one hundred and seventy men, he encountered Buck Brown in Benton county, with some six hundred men, and had a severe fight, which, lasting two hours, resulted in the defeat of Brown, who retreated, leaving several killed and wounded. Learning that Brooks was at Fitzgerald Mountain with eight hundred men, waiting in ambush for the arrival of the train, Colonel Harrison made a detour, passing four miles to the east, at midnight of the 21st, and arrived safely at Fayetteville on the 25th.

The rebels under Colonel Brooks then invested Fayetteville, with the intention of starving the garrison out. The investment was so complete as to prevent foraging other than by sending out well armed parties of mounted men, with sacks for corn, to be brought back on their animals. On the 27th, Captain D. C. Hopkins, one of the most dashing officers the Arkansas loyalists have furnished, while thus foraging, was attacked by Buck Brown with five hundred men. Captain Hopkins forced his way through the enemy, skirmishing with him for several miles, and after a narrow escape from being cut off by Brooks, reached Fayetteville in safety.

On the 28th Brooks occupied East Mountain, a prominent elevation near the post. With two guns, which he succeeded in planting thereon, he annoyed the garrison, shelling the outer intrenchments. Captains Hopkins and E. B. Harrison, with their respective companies, dismounted, were ordered to clear the mountain side. Twice they charged up the precipitous sides; twice were they repulsed. On the third attempt they succeeded in attacking and dislodging the foe, driving him from the summit. In this attempt, our force had, at various portions of the ascent, to pull themselves up the steep sides by means of the bushes and vines, being all the time exposed to the enemy's fire. We captured a number of small arms and a quantity of forage. Several killed and wounded were left in our hands. One of their guns burst in the assault. At ten A. M., Brooks made a desperate and vigorous attack upon the works at the west side. After two hours' severe fighting he was driven off, with the loss of twelve killed and twenty-five wounded, several of these mortally. Buck Brown lost eleven killed and wounded. Our loss was two seriously wounded, one of whom died afterwards, and four slightly wounded.

The enemy still continued in the vicinity of the post, but made no further demonstrations until the 3rd of November. Early that morning, Colonel Harrison's scouts reported 8,000 rebels with two guns, marching under Fagan from Cane Hill. Price had moved continuously to Cane Hill, a village about thirty miles south-west of Fayetteville, known as the head-quarters of a strong rebel community. Here, while engaged in recruiting his command, caring for the wounded, &c., he detached Fagan's Division, 5,000 strong, with two guns, to capture Fayetteville. The rebel General was joined by Brooks and Brown with 1,500 men. At eleven A. M., our works were attacked, the pickets driven in, and without any warning or time allowed to move the women and children, the shelling commenced. During the bombardment, a number of shells entered houses where families were living. One shell passed through the wall of Mrs. Steele's house, exploding in the bedroom of her daughter, the wife of a Federal officer, who had but a moment before left the room. Other shells entered the building used for hospital purposes. Though the hospital flag was flying over the building, the rebel fire was directed there without discrimination. One of their wounded men in our hands was killed by a rifle ball from their lines. The guns used by Fagan were one six pound rifle and one twelve pound howitzer. Three times were the rebels drawn up in line to charge our works; three times was the order given, but each time, under the deadly fire of our rifles, they failed to move forward and attempt the perilous task. At sunset the force was withdrawn, retreating towards Cane Hill with the guns, till only six hundred remained, who left early on the 4th, moving east.

The rebel loss is reported at seventy-five killed and wounded. Ours was nine wounded, one mortally. Our intrenchments protected the men. The garrison numbered 1,128, one hundred and seventy-five of whom were citizens.

A small party sent by General Curtis succeeded in reaching Fayetteville during the night. Before daylight our little army was on its march. Fayetteville was reached at eleven o'clock. The enemy had already retired. The movement was doubtless accelerated by our approach. A small body of rebels under Colonel Freeman, separated from Fagan's command and moved eastward towards White River. They left a broken and dismounted gun. It was afterwards reported that on arrival near Huntsville, this force disbanded in disgust. The main force joined Price, who was collecting cattle and supplies, preparatory to crossing the Arkansas.

Our troops remained at Fayetteville till the morning of the 5th. This delay was owing to the difficulty of ascertaining Price's main line of march. The troops under Colonel Harrison now joined the pursuing army, excepting sufficient garrison to hold the place. Captain Dodge's 9th Wisconsin Battery was also left here, the animals being unfit for further travel. Colonel Moonlight, who, with the 2d Brigade, had been sent from Leesburg, on Pea Ridge, towards Bentonville, arrived in the course of the day. He had encountered a small band of guerrillas, killing two in the pursuit. Colonel Jennison's Brigade had also made a detour to a flouring mill east of the line of march, and drove off a band of rebels who were running the mill. Everything behind us had been cleaned out. At no time during the war had South-east Missouri and North-west Arkansas been so free from bushwhackers.

The condition of the country was poor indeed. The people were utterly impoverished. Very few persons were at home except women and children. Few of these had food sufficient for the ensuing winter, and barely one was decently clad, while most had not sufficient clothing to hide their nakedness. Whatever part these inhabitants might have originally taken, they were, it was evident, sufficiently punished, and in a condition to excite commiseration. The passage of two armies through their midst did not tend to better their condition.

CHAPTER XXI.

FROM FAYETTEVILLE TO THE ARKANSAS RIVER—TERMINATION OF THE PURSUIT—STORM ON THE ARKANSAS—GENERAL ORDERS.

On the 5th, the army camped upon the battle-field of Prairie Grove. General Blunt occupied the house used by him for his conference with the rebel General Hindman, who received so complete a defeat at the hands of Blunt and Herron in November, '62. Cattle were found in sufficient abundance for the use of the troops. This comprised nearly all the subsistence obtained by them. The pursuers lived mainly on the *debris* of the retreating army. Forage was scarce. After leaving this point it became more so.

On the 6th, we reached Cane Hill. Our advance drove out some small bands, and found the town full of rebel wounded, left there by the retreating foe. Nearly one hundred were paroled. Among them was a Major Parrott, Assistant Adjutant-General on Price's staff, who stated to General Blunt that the rebel loss since leaving Lexington on the 20th of October, a period of seventeen days, was, as appeared by the consolidated returns made on the morning before, 10,056. This included killed, wounded, captured and deserters. Large numbers of the latter scattered along their line of march, and for weeks afterwards reported at their homes in Missouri, claiming to have been conscripted. At Cane Hill it was evident that Price had expected to remain some time, his troops having commenced to build huts. Large droves of cattle gathered by him, were left behind. Colonel Benteen's scouts had several brisk skirmishes with the rebel rear guard and scouting parties. Some half dozen were killed. We lost one man, a bugler. Quite an interesting relic was recaptured. It was the flag presented to General Blunt at Leavenworth, in October, 1863, and captured from him by Quantrill, at the Baxter's Springs massacre, shortly afterwards. The flag was in pieces, and packed in an old traveling bag. It was nearly perfect, and when sewn together, only a small portion of the inscription was found missing.

About sundown, we camped near the ground occupied by Price the previous night. The trail was broad and well marked, and headed direct to the Arkansas River. His camp-fires had extended for miles on each side of the road, and the remains of slaughtered cattle showed that large quantities of meat must have been distributed to his men. We pressed forward on the direct trail, having entered the Cherokee country on the previous day, and now moved up the beautiful valley of the Salisan River. On the east the flanks of the Boston mountains sloped to the valley; their summits, lined and softened by the hazy mist of distance, bounded the horizon miles away. Westward rolled the undulating prairies. The valley was dotted with farms, buildings and fields; before the war the abodes of a prosperous and civilized people; now deserted and desolate; the fields covered with rank and unsightly weeds; the dwellings and out-houses falling in ruins.

The order of march was arranged with a view to probable battle, as it became evident that we were close upon the enemy once more. Colonel Benteen's Veteran Brigade was in front; the 1st Division followed; Colonel Harrison closed the column, and Major Ketner with the army train brought up the rear.

We camped late at night, and started early on the 7th, marching in a south-west direction, mainly through woods. The character of the retreat was plainly discernible. By these indications, we were encouraged to push on, as it was evident that the rebels were making for the river in such haste as becomes a panic stricken mob, held together only by their necessities and the instinct of self-preservation. Horses and mules, lean, hungry looking, and worn out, were in every direction to be seen, feebly picking a scanty meal from the prairie. Broken wagons and vehicles of all kinds were scattered along the trail.

Heavy stores, fixed ammunition, shell, shot, etc., were thrown broadcast, as if the fugitives desired to plant the broad swells with cadmean seed. The carriage said to have been used by Price himself, was found broken by the wayside. The advance pushed forward, and about dark came upon a small iron piece abandoned by the foe. At last the condition of the road, the darkness of the night, and the necessity of closing up our column, compelled a halt and some hours' rest. We bivouacked some miles from the Arkansas River, though uncertain of our whereabouts.

The march was resumed early on the 8th. The morning opened in gloom. A rain storm soon set in. Colonel Harrison took the advance. The prairie burning in our front, and the abandoned animals, whose backs still bore marks of saddle and harness, gave proof of the rebels' proximity. Across the prairie, as far as the eye could reach, were seen dark, heavy masses of timber, which proved, as we neared them, to be that covering the Arkansas River bottoms. The trail was fresh. It was evident that a large force had passed within a short period. We pressed through the timber to the bank of the river, and thence by a road newly cut to a point where it was apparent that Price's entire army had crossed.

A few of the stragglers fled as our advance rode up, and the enemy's rear could be seen in the timber on the south side. McLain's guns were brought up, and the rebel retreat accelerated by the thundering echoes of their discharge. With a view of warning the garrisons at Forts Gibson and Smith, between which posts it was evident the enemy had crossed; in honor also of the day whereon, while we stood watching the flight of a lately insolent foe, the lovers of Liberty and Union throughout the loyal States were casting the ballots which silently, yet surely, marked the people's determination to preserve the Union and maintain the Government, as well as to drive out of the opposite woods any straggling foe that might be there, General Curtis directed Captain McLain to fire (with shell) a national salute of thirty-four guns.

Returning to the edge of the prairie, the Army of the Border went into camp. As the day waned, the storm which, with rain and mist, had threatened through all its hours, now broke out in grandeur. The rain poured down in torrents. The forked lightnings flashed, and the thunders rolled heavily and continuously. It was as if the entire aerial artillery, and all voidless forms and forces of the worlds of spirit and space, had been brought together for a grand field day. The scene was truly sublime, vastly magnificent in scale, and wildly tumultuous in its uproar. Great trees fell crashing in the forest, waking echoes which vied with the thunder in their report. The roar of the river came like the distant rush of a cataract, or the wash of the ocean waves on a storm-lashed beach. The heavens over head were blacker than fabled Erebus, except when riven by the lurid lightning flame.

Yet with wild song and shout our troopers made the woods echo and the welkin ring. Their fires were quenched as fast as lighted. Not a tent, house or shelter was to be had. In the midst of the wild scene, and amid the howling of the storm, half fed and almost worn out, the irrepressible gaiety of conquerors broke jubilantly forth.

About ten at night the storm began to subside, and the rifted masses of black clouds moved slowly across the heavens, making visible the deep blue above, which, veiled though it was, still smiled serenely with majestic and awe-inspiring sense of calm repose.

From an account given by the Rev. Mr. Willets, a missionary residing at Dwight's Mission, who was taken prisoner and held until the night of the 7th, the destitution and demoralization of the rebels was most complete. Their whole line passed by him several times, and never therein did he perceive any attempt at organization. They marched as it pleased them, and seemed only intent on putting the Arkansas river between themselves and pursuers. Thirty-two wagons, common farmer teams at that, comprised the train as seen by him. Two guns were all their artillery. In other respects the same appearance of defeat was visible. All with whom he conversed acknowledged openly their complete overthrow. This is borne out by the following, from the Galveston (Texas) *News*, copied from the diary of an officer of General Fagan's Division of Price's Army. The latter is the conclusion of it, including the battle of Newtonia:

OCTOBER 28.—Moved eight miles, and camped one south of Newtonia. The enemy attacked us and were repulsed by Cabell's and Slemmon's Brigades, and a small part of Shelby's Division, with heavy loss; our loss about eight hundred killed and wounded.

OCTOBER 29.—Marched twenty-five miles south-west, and camped on Cowskin Creek; no forage.

OCTOBER 30.—Marched to Magnolia, forty-five miles, and camped; no forage.

OCTOBER 31.—Marched twenty miles and camped on the Illinois River; no forage.

NOVEMBER 1.—Moved to Cane Hill; the weather very cold and wet. We got a little forage, about one-half ration.

NOVEMBER 2.—Remained at Cane Hill. Fagan's Division made a demonstration on Fayetteville, to let McRay's and Dobbin's Brigades pass to north-east Kansas; no forage.

NOVEMBER 3.—Remained encamped at Cane Hill; weather very cold, with heavy snow. Without food or forage.

NOVEMBER 4.—Moved south-west twelve miles and camped without forage. We now abandon wagons every day, the teams having entirely given out.

NOVEMBER 5.—Marched down the Salisan twenty miles and camped. No forage.

NOVEMBER 6.—Reached the Arkansas River, near Pleasant Bluff. We have got plenty of beef, but no forage.

NOVEMBER 7.—Crossed the Arkansas River and marched four miles. No forage.

NOVEMBER 8.—Moved eight miles west and camped; rained all night and snowing at daylight. The sick and wounded suffer terribly. No food or forage. Some of the commands succeeded in getting a little beef, but Cabell's Brigade have none.

NOVEMBER 9.—Moved fifteen miles west, and encamped near the Canadan. The weather very cold, and horses and mules dying by hundreds. I noticed to-day, that several men died on the road from illness and exhaustion, and were left unburied. We had no means of burying them. To-day, General Fagan might have been seen trudging along through the mud and rain, and a sick soldier riding his horse—an act that, I believe, few Generals are accused of now-a-days—but his kindness to his men does not make them love him any the less.

NOVEMBER 10.—The remnants of Cabell's and Slemmon's Brigades were directed to make the best of their way to Arkansas, and report at a given time, at points assigned in the orders. With them the writer came, and after much suffering, we reached Arkansas.

The following dispatch was sent to General Davies, and to Department Head-Quarters at Fort Leavenworth:

HEAD-QUARTERS, ARMY OF THE BORDER,
CAMP ARKANSAS, November 8th,
via FORT SCOTT, November 15.

TO GENERAL DAVIES:

We have just concluded the pursuit of Price, whose rear guard crossed the Arkansas River under fire of our guns. He left another of his guns and his own carriage, which, with other arms and equipments have fallen into our hands. We are now rid of 20,000 or 30,000 half starved bushwhackers and half starved vagabonds, who, I hope, may never return to disturb the peaceful inhabitants north of the Arkansas river. He is also beyond our posts of Fayetteville, Fort Smith and Fort Gibson, which are now safe.

(Signed) S. R. CURTIS, Major-General.

General Curtis and General Blunt issued and promulgated the following congratulatory orders to the troops:

HEAD-QUARTERS, ARMY OF THE BORDER,
CAMP ARKANSAS, November 8th, 1864.

GENERAL FIELD ORDER:

The object of this organization and campaign is accomplished. The rebel army under General Sterling Price has been confronted, beaten in several conflicts, and pursued and driven over three hundred and fifty miles, from the Missouri to the Arkansas. This has been the work of fourteen days. Your marches have been incessant, sometimes for days and nights in rain and snow, and generally on short rations, gathered from the herds lost by the enemy. Your privations, toil and gallantry, deserve the highest commendation; and the success of the campaign in which you have so gloriously participated, most of you from the beginning to the end, must entitle you to the thanks of your Government, and the gratitude of the loyal people of our Country. Your losses are considerable, but nothing in comparison with those of the enemy, who admits a loss in killed, wounded and missing, of eight or ten thousand. All his cannon but two, a large portion of his small arms, his vast wagon train loaded with spoils, and herds of cattle and horses have been left, burned and scattered in the way of your pursuit. His army of twenty or thirty thousand is converted into an unarmed, unorganized mob, destitute of everything, starving with hunger, and far from supplies. Their condition is indeed so desperate as to excite pity more than exultation.

But the greatest achievements of this campaign are the driving a desperate class of vagrant associates of the rebels so far from your homes and the State you defend. Besides this, your stern resistance and close pursuit, saved the towns and garrisons of Kansas City, Olathe, Paola, Fort Scott, Fayetteville, Fort Gibson and Fort Smith, and the valuable public stores of those places; besides checking ulterior purposes of slaughter and desolation, contemplated by the invasion of Kansas.

But it would tarnish the brilliancy of your achievements to claim this for yourselves alone, without acknowledging with gratitude, the share borne in the brunt of the contest, by the troops of Missouri and the militia of Kansas, who shared our dangers, and because of their greater numbers, especially deserve more of the honors due to the conflicts of the 24th, 25th and 28th of October. But to you, including the brigade of Colonel Benteen, who have shared in most of these battles, and continued throughout the long, weary pursuit, to the dark and turbid waters of the Arkansas, where your guns thundered in the rear of the starving, terrified enemy, must be accorded the special commendation of the Commanding General, and the generous approval of your Country.

The special honors due to distinguished comrades in the campaign, will be carefully presented by the Commanding General, in his proper report to Head-quarters at Washington, and to secure the most exact justice to so many deserving commendation, Commanders of Divisions, Brigades, Detachments and Staff Officers, will make full reports, directed to Head-quarters, Fort Leavenworth, at their earliest convenience.

In parting, the General tenders his thanks to the officers and soldiers, for their generous support and prompt obedience to orders, and to his Staff for their unceasing efforts to share the toil incident to the campaign. The pursuit of Price in 1864, and the battles of Lexington, Little Blue, Big Blue, Westport, Marias des Cygnes, Osage, Charlot and Newtonia, will be borne on the banners of regiments who shared in them; and the States of Missouri, Iowa, Kansas, Colorado, Illinois, Indiana, Wisconsin and Arkansas, may glory in the achievement of her sons in this short, but eventful campaign.

The First Division, commanded by General Blunt, will move from this camp according to special instructions.

The brigade of Colonel Benteen will return to his proper corps command by such route as he may consider most economical and advantageous to the Government.

Colonel Harrison will report to Major-General Steele at his earliest convenience.

Colonel Ford, with his command, will accompany the Commanding General to Head-Quarters, Fort Leavenworth.

By Command of Major-General Curtis:
C. S. CHARLOT,
Assistant Adjutant-General.

Head-Quarters, First Division, Army of the Border,
Camp on the Arkansas River, 30 miles West of Fort Smith, Nov. 8, '64.

General Field Orders.
No. 6.

I. The pursuit of the rebel army under Gen. Price having been abandoned and the Army of the Border disbanded by direction of superior authority, the General Commanding the First Division desires to express his thanks and admiration to the officers and soldiers of his command, for their noble conduct and gallantry, displayed throughout one of the most memorable campaigns of the West.

On the 16th of October, the Brigades of Colonel Jennison and Colonel Moonlight, numbering in all but two thousand men, marched from Hickman's Mills, Mo., to Pleasant Hill, Holden and Lexington, to make a reconnoisance and develop the position, force and movements of the enemy.

On the 19th of October, at 11 A. M., we were attacked at Lexington by the enemy 26,000 strong, and held the position until their entire army was developed, when our little force retired fighting and in good order, until the darkness of the night put an end to the contest.

Thus we were enabled to give the first reliable information of Price's force and movements that was known since he had crossed the Arkansas River on his route into Missouri.

On the 21st, the Brigades of Colonels Jennison, Ford and Moonlight, numbering only 3,500 men, fought the battle of the Little Blue, contesting stubbornly every foot of ground with an enemy five to one against them, with the most glorious results. In this contest the 2d Brigade, under Colonel Moonlight, is entitled to special commendation for the gallant manner in which they fought the enemy's advancing columns until reinforcements arrived.

On the 22d, the Brigades of Colonels Jennison and Moonlight stubbornly contested the advance of the enemy at the crossing of the Big Blue; and at the State Line (after the enemy had forced a passage at Byrom's Ford) checking his right flank and punishing him severely.

Thus, by striking the enemy in front, and by three days' severe fighting, he was firmly held in check, until the command of Major-General Pleasanton was enabled to overtake and attack his rear at Independence, and co-operate with us in obtaining the glorious results of the battle of Westport on the 23rd, when the entire Division (including Colonel C. W. Blair's Brigade of Kansas State Militia) attacked the enemy's front, and after a severe conflict turned his right flank, which resulted in his complete defeat and rout.

In this day's contest, credit is due to several regiments of Kansas State Militia for the gallant part they bore, which will be appropriately noticed in official reports.

In the battles of the Osage on the 25th (excepting Companies G, I and K, 2d Colorado Cavalry Volunteers, commanded by Captains Green, Kingsbury and Elmer) you were prevented from participating as you desired, because by the orders of superior officers, the advance was taken from you, after earning and obtaining it by hard fighting; but we cannot but admire the conspicuous courage displayed on that day by our comrades in arms of General Pleasanton's Division, who did their duty so gallantly.

In this day's operations, credit is due to the 2d Brigade, under Colonel Moonlight (who was directed, after the battle of Westport, to move on the right flank of the enemy) for the protection given to the border of Kansas, and especially Mound City, where they fought and defeated a superior rebel force, and saved the town from destruction.

At the battle of Newtonia, on the 28th ult. (participated in by the Brigades of Colonels Jennison and Ford) where you fought and defeated a force ten times your number, a courage and heroism was displayed unparalleled in the history of the war.

To recapitulate: In twenty-three days you have marched over five hundred miles, day and night, through rain and snow, and fought five battles with an enemy greatly your superior in numbers. You have suffered fatigue, hunger and every privation incidental to a soldier's life. The result of your heroic labors (in conjunction with your comrades of the Army of Missouri) is the complete defeat and rout of a formidable rebel army, pursuing them across the Arkansas River, disorganized and reduced to a mob; and the saving of Kansas from premeditated invasion and devastation. For this you are entitled to, and will receive, the plaudits of a grateful country. While we drop the tear of sympathy over the graves of comrades who fell by our sides, we will ever remember that their death was a noble sacrifice for their country.

II. The First Brigade, commanded by Colonel Jennison, is authorized to inscribe upon their banners, *Lexington, Little Blue, Big Blue, Westport* and *Newtonia*.

The Second Brigade, commanded by Colonel Moonlight—*Lexington, Little Blue, Big Blue, Westport* and *Mound City*.

The Third Brigade, K. S. M., commanded by Colonel Blair, the 19th Regiment, K. S. M., commanded by Colonel Hogan, and the 11th Regiment, K. S. M., commanded by Lieutenant-Colonel Woodworth—*Westport*.

The Fourth Brigade, commanded by Colonel Ford—*Little Blue*, *Westport* and *Newtonia:* Companies G, I and K, 2d Colorado Cavalry Volunteers, will inscribe *Osage* on their guidons.

JAMES G. BLUNT, Major-General.

General Rosecrans also issued a General Order at St. Louis, bearing date December 8th, congratulating his troops, and summing up the results of the campaign. The material portions are given. It will be seen that no credit is given to others; no honor accorded to the operations of Generals Curtis and Blunt, or to the gallant soldiers under them. The tone of this order of General Rosecrans is in strong contrast with the generous eulogisms passed on the Missouri troops by both General Curtis and General Blunt.

"On the 8th of October, when General Pleasanton assumed command at Jefferson City, he sent Sanborn, with all his mounted force, four thousand one hundred strong, to follow the rebel track and harrass them until all our remaining cavalry could join you, and the infantry supports came up. You drove the enemy's rear guard upon their main force in line of battle near Boonville, and bearded them in position with a force of only 5,500 men. Pursuing their retreat westward, and keeping them between you and the Missouri River, without an opportunity to double on their track, you waited the arrival of Winslow's command, 1,500 strong, which had followed the enemy from Arkansas, and when, on the 19th, it joined, forming the Provisional Cavalry Division of 6,500 men, exclusive of escort guards, under General Pleasanton, you moved on the foe for battle and victory, overtook and gave them the first sweet taste of your sabres on the 22d, at Independence, where you routed Fagan and captured two of his guns. On the 23rd, you passed the Big Blue, fought them from seven in the morning until one P. M. Their advance quitting Curtis then fell upon you, when, by the combined use of Thuber's double-shotted canister and the sabre, you routed their main force, and by dark had thrown them beyond Little Santa Fe.

"On the 24th, at midnight, after marching some sixty miles, with little water except the rain on your backs, and less food for men or horses, you again overtook them at Marias des Cygnes, began skirmishing, and at four A. M., on the 25th, opening with artillery, routed them with loss, capturing mules, horses, &c., &c. Thence, in a running fight, you pursued them to the Little Osage Crossing, where two advanced brigades, under Benteen and Phillips, charged two rebel divisions, routed them, captured eight pieces of artillery and nearly one thousand prisoners, including Generals Marmaduke and Cabell. Sanborn's Brigade again led in pursuit, overtook them and made two more brilliant charges, driving everything before it, across the Marmaton, whence the enemy fled, under cover of night, towards the Arkansas. After thus marching two hundred and four miles in six days, and beating the enemy, his flying columns were pursued towards the Arkansas by the Kansas troops and Benteen's Brigade, while Sanborn, following, marched one hundred and four miles in thirty-six hours, and on the 28th reached Newtonia, where the enemy made his last stand, in time to turn the tide of battle, which was going on against General Blunt, again routing the enemy, and giving the final blow to the greatest cavalry raid of the war.

"The substantial results of this brilliant series of operations are, that while our infantry and dismounted men nobly performed their share of the work by fighting at Pilot Knob and Glasgow, holding the depots and important points, and backing your hazards; the enemy, entering the State with a mounted force of veteran troops, variously estimated at from 15,000 to 25,000, and eighteen pieces of artillery, with vast expectations of revolutionizing the State, destroying Kansas, and operating on the 'Presidential election,' after having added to his force 6,000 Missourians, which General Marmaduke told General Pleasanton were armed and formed into a division, has been defeated in all his schemes, his mischief confined to the narrow belt of country over which he passed and routed by you in four engagements, he has lost ten pieces of artillery, a large number of small arms, nearly all his trains and plunder, and, besides his killed, wounded and deserters, 1,958 prisoners, which we have now in possession; and the atest reports confirm the statement that when the enemy's forces re-crossed the Arkansas, demoralization, desertion and losses had reduced their strength to less than 5,000, but partially armed and mounted, with three pieces of artillery, and their horses in the most wretched condition; all this has been accomplished by less than 7,000 cavalry, most of whom never before saw a great battle; and your entire loss in killed, wounded and missing, is only three hundred and forty-six, officers and men. The records of this war furnish no more brilliant and decisive results."

This order of General Rosecrans was written at St. Louis a month after the campaign had closed. Its value as an impartial historical document may be appreciated, when it is remembered that the officer by whom it was issued never got within fifty miles of the front, never heard the sound of the guns, and obtained his whole impressions from the reports of subordinates.

There are some misstatements, amounting to misrepresentations of the facts, which require noticing.

From General Rosecrans' summing up, the public would be led to believe that at the battle of Westport, October 23rd, the victory there gained was due entirely to the exertions of General Pleasanton. Without detracting from his merits, or belittling of the splendid fighting done by his division at the Big Blue on that morning; it is most emphatically true, that a handful of volunteer troops, and a few regiments of raw militia, had, after several hours severe fighting, defeated the divisions of Shelby and Marmaduke, and that, when General Pleasanton moved up on the left, General Curtis in the advance, was steadily driving the foe. The arrival of the Missouri troops turned an orderly retreat into a rout, and for that, credit is due equally to both commands. It is said in the foregoing, "you (the Missouri Division) routed their main force, and by dark had thrown them (the enemy) beyond Little Santa Fe." As Gen. Pleasanton's Division formed on the left, when the troops deployed from line of battle into column, and the division of General Blunt held the right or advance, it is not easy to see how General Pleasanton could have driven them "beyond Little Santa Fe." The truth is, that the Brigade of Colonel Jennison, accompanied by a portion of the 2d Colorado, were far in advance of the main column, and at night camped close upon the enemy's rear, four miles beyond Little Santa Fe.

Again, a person unacquainted with the details of the campaign, would not suppose, from the foregoing order, that either General Curtis, or any of the troops under him, were engaged in the pursuit that followed Westport, or aided in the splendid victories which were gathered by our arms on the 25th. Yet it is true that General Curtis directed those operations; that a portion of his troops opened the ball on the 25th of October; that other portions participated in the victorious charges at the Marias des Cygnes, Mine Creek and Little Osage; and that, under his direction, those victories were in a great measure due to the dash, courage and activity of his personal and volunteer staff.

So it is, as relates to the statement that General Sanborn's arrival at Newtonia, prevented the defeat of General Blunt. The report of the former, already quoted in these pages, makes no such claim. Great credit is due him for the splendid march from Fort Scott, and for his promptness on the field. But General Sanborn did not give the "final blow to the greatest cavalry raid of the war." The modest report of the subordinate (Sanborn) is in strange contrast with the claim thus put forth by General Rosecrans.

In fine, the whole order is an adroit specimen of special pleading. It is of a piece with other reports etc., published at St. Louis, while General Curtis, General Blunt and Colonel Benteen, were pursuing the enemy. It was intended and designed to counteract a damaging effect on the public mind, as to the conduct of the campaign against Price, by the Commander of the Department of Missouri, and was put forth to break the force of the implied censure of his superiors, given in the orders directing

General Curtis to assume command of all troops in his (Rosecrans') Department, who might be available to carry forward a pursuit which their immediate commanders had ordered to cease.

CHAPTER XXII.

THE HOMEWARD MARCH—INCIDENTS—RESULTS OF CAMPAIGN.

On the morning of the 9th of November, the various portions of the army proceeded homeward, by routes designated in the order of General Curtis.

The General himself, accompanied by his staff, escort and the 2d Colorado, marched to Fort Gibson, and thence northward to Fort Scott, arriving there on the 15th of the month. The weather was very cold, and the exhausted condition of the stock compelled all to walk a large portion of the route. Nothing of interest occurred. Provisions were exceedingly scant, and the arrival in a land of plenty was gladly hailed by all.

General Blunt, with the brigade of Colonel Moonlight, moved to Fort Smith. General Thayer in command there, esteemed himself compelled to obey the letter of his instructions, and not risk the safety of this important post by weakening the garrison; otherwise, he would have endeavored to have impeded Price's crossing the river.

The ford used by the rebel army, is about four miles above the mouth of the Salisaw, about twenty-five miles from Gibson on the west, and thirty from Smith on the east. It was not generally known, and had only been used hitherto by the Indians.

Major-General Herron being at Fort Smith, on a visit of inspection, and determining to return to New Orleans by way of Leavenworth and St. Louis, General Blunt accompanied him, moving to Fort Gibson, and thence North to Fort Scott.

The only incident of note occurred near Cabin Creek, six miles from Fort Gibson, where, just before the appearance of the small escort of the Generals, a party of seven persons, officers and others of regiments at Fort Smith, on their way to rejoin their commands, were pursued and overpowered by a band of guerrillas. They were driven, before being murdered, a short distance from the road traveled by the troops. As a consequence, the bodies were not seen by them, though traces of a struggle were plainly visible. This was made the basis of a charge against General Blunt, of having left these bodies without burial. The charge called forth a reply from Captain Hinton, his Aide, published in the *Conservative*, Leavenworth, Kansas, which, as it gives the facts in relation thereto, is here inserted. The Captain says:

"As I happened to be one among others with General Blunt, when some of our officers were murdered near Cabin Creek, perhaps the matter may be of sufficient public interest to warrant you in giving place to an account of the transaction, at least in so far as General Blunt is concerned.

"On the 19th of November, Major-Generals Blunt and Herron broke camp at Cabin Creek, about 7 A. M. Some delay occurred, which caused the lateness of the march. The force with these officers consisted of less than one hundred and fifty men, about one hundred of whom were General Herron's escort. Our animals were broken down and half-starved, and quite a number of the men were afoot. The advance guard was from General Herron's escort, strangers to the country and character of the bushwhackers who infest the route.

"About four miles north of the stockade on Cabin Creek, are some abandoned buildings, formerly used for stores, post-offices, etc. To the west of the road about two miles, is a heavy body of timber on Cabin Creek; east of and parallel to the road is the timber of Grand River. On the morning I speak of, when about half way between the creek and the post-office buildings, a faint report of small arms was heard apparently to the left of the road, in the direction of the timber spoken of, by the officers and main portion of the escort. Soon after, word was brought from the advance guard, that a party of about twenty men had crossed the road north of them and in full sight, moving towards the Grand River timber. Of course they were believed to be bushwhackers. By the time our main body had reached the post-office, the bushwhackers had gained the timber. The escort was halted for the purpose of enabling the dismounted men to close up. Neither General Blunt, General Herron, or any officer of their staffs, was then informed by the non-commissioned officer commanding the advance guard, of any further bushwhacking signs, or of any appearance of a party having been pursued by them. A report was made of two horses and a mule being found near the road, with fresh saddle marks on them. These were turned over to three of the dismounted men.

"The escort moved on, passed the timber hills, three miles further, and traveled at least six miles before the evidences of a party having been pursued by the bushwhackers were laid before either of the Major-Generals. It was then too late for us to retrace our steps, even if we had had horses fit to travel.

"It is an unmitigated falsehood to say that we passed in plain view of the bodies of our friends. No one of our party saw the bodies of our murdered comrades. On the contrary, there was no visible evidence to General Blunt, or any other officer, of any friend having been there. If any one was culpable, it was the advance guard in not reporting the signs they saw. These were the evidences before alluded to: the finding of a couple of Enfield rifles (new); of a plain blue vest, bloody, and having a bullet hole in the back, found near the road close to the post office; an invoice of clothing drawn from Captain Insley by Captain Martin Welsh, 1st Kansas Colored Volunteers, bearing date Fort Scott, Nov. 15—also bloody, and an Express receipt dated at St. Louis, made out to "Gardner," supposed to be Chaplain Gardner of the 13th Kansas; of the tracks of a light vehicle turning off the road near where the vest, &c., were found; nor of the signs of the camp of this party at the Timber Hills, seen just off the road by some of the advance.

"None of these facts were made known to General Blunt, nor to any other officer, until after the command had passed some six miles north of the post-office building, and when it was manifestly improper to turn back with our small command and broken down animals.

"The party consisted of Captain Welsh, Captain Thrasher and Lieutenant Macy, of the 1st Colored Kansas; Chaplain Gardner, of the 13th, and three soldiers of Kansas Regiments, returning to Fort Smith. Captain Thrasher and two soldiers escaped; the others were murdered. Since then the loyal Pin Indians have killed six of the bushwhackers who murdered our friends."

* * * * * * *

Captain Thrasher, who escaped, sent the following letter to the father of Lieutenant Macy, which more definitely gives the names of the unfortunate victims. It corrects some mistakes of Captain Hinton:

FORT SMITH, ARKANSAS, Dec. 15, 1864.

To Dr. E. G. Macy, Bloomington, Kansas:

DOCTOR:—I have to communicate the sad intelligence of the death of your son, Lieutenant E. L. Macy. He fell in a fight with bushwhackers, six miles north of Cabin Creek, C. N., on the 19th of November last. Our party of seven—Captain Welch, Lieutenant Macy, Chaplain Gardner, Harbin, Collins, citizen Jones, and myself—were attacked by one hundred bushwhackers. A desperate struggle ensued. Captain Welch, your son, and Harbin, are known to have been killed. Gardner was wounded and captured, and was probably killed after capture. These three fought like brave men, and died as became the true soldier.

Most truly your friend,
L. A. THRASHER.

Colonel Moonlight, with his brigade, had been left at Fort Smith, to prepare for the homeward march. At Fort Gibson, General Blunt found a battalion of the Indian Brigade, under Major Phillips, proceeding to Cabin Creek, for the purpose of strengthening the escort of a subsistence train, then expected. The garrison and Indian refugees had been for some time on quarter rations, and unless supplies soon arrived would be completely out. General Gano, with a brigade of Texans, and Stan Waite's Cherokee Brigade, had kept our troops cooped up at Gibson, and interrupted communications as it pleased them. A short time before, a train had been attacked at Cow Creek. Major Foreman, of the 3rd Indian Regiment, was then in pursuit of the marauders. Gano was reported as moving north of the Arkansas again. These reports compelled vigilance on the part of troops traveling north. The subsistence train was found in the vicinity of Fort Scott, just moving out. Colonel Moonlight, who was several days behind General Blunt, met it at the Neosho, and, under orders from General Curtis, turned back to Cabin Creek, acting as escort until it was beyond danger. He then resumed his march to Paola, where the 2d Brigade arrived early in December. General Blunt reached Fort Scott about November 20th.

Colonel Jennison, with his own Brigade, the 16th Kansas, and the Brigade of Colonel Benteen, moved by way of Cane Hill, Fayetteville and Bentonville. In his published report he gives this account of his return march, which, as presenting one view thereof, is here inserted:

"In this camp, November 8th, was received the order of the General commanding, dissolving the Army of the Border, and attaching to it the 1st Brigade for the homeward march, the 16th Kansas Volunteer Cavalry, 1st Colorado and 9th Wisconsin Batteries, with nearly the entire transportation of the army, and in pursuance of which order the brigade, on the morning of the 9th, took up its return line of march, proceeding very slowly, however, on account of the nature of the roads, rendered almost impassable by the frequent rains experienced for several days previous, and continuing after our arrival at the river.

"From the difficulty of procuring forage, and the total exhaustion of rations, the march northward was necessarily very much retarded, it requiring eight days to reach Fayetteville, which post we reached on the 16th of November.

"But before proceeding farther, it becomes my most painful duty to record the loss of two of the most efficient and faithful officers of my command—Captain Ordoff Norton, Company L, 15th Kansas Cavalry, and First Lieutenant Emmit Goss, Company M, 15th Kansas Cavalry, who were undoubtedly killed while in charge of foraging parties in the vicinity of Cane Hill, on the 12th of November, as all search for them has proven fruitless, and when last heard from they were closely pursued by a large force o. guerrillas, said to be under command of "Lieutenant Incks, C. S. A." Always faithful in the discharge of their duties, never hesitating in the execution of any order, however hazardous, Captain Norton and Lieutenant Goss had endeared themselves to the entire command, by their uniform kindness and affability towards all. Their loss is one which can be illy sustained by the regiment, and their memory will ever be cherished by all whose good fortune it was to be associated with them.

"On the same day (12th) First Lieutenant J. J. Smith, commanding Company E, 15th Kansas Volunteer Cavalry, in charge of another party, was attacked by an overwhelming force of bushwhackers, and in the fight which ensued, Lieutenant Smith was very seriously, if not fatally wounded, he having been left in a critical situation at the hospital in Fayetteville, Arkansas. He was struck in the back and thigh, the former shot going through the body and coming out below the left breast. The latter was a severe and painful flesh wound. Lieut. Smith will probably be permanently disabled for active service, if indeed he recovers from the effects of his wounds at all. I take pleasure, however, in mentioning him here as one of the most deserving officers of the 15th regiment, and one whose determined bravery, throughout the several actions in which the brigade was engaged, entitle him to the highest praise.

"Leaving Fayetteville, we continued the march northward through Keitsville and Bentonville, Arkansas and Sarcoxie, and Lamar, Missouri, arriving at this post on Wednesday P. M., the 23rd of November, 1864, having marched, since leaving Hickman's Mills, on the 16th day of October, about twelve hundred miles, during the most inclement season of the year, without adequate transportation or supplies, subsisting mainly upon the country through which we passed. The loss in horses has been heavy, owing to the want of proper care and forage, and the exposure to which they have been subjected, as well as the numbers killed or wounded in action, all of which loss will, of course, be properly accounted for in the various returns to the respective departments entitled to receive them. Government property of other kinds has been abandoned from the absolute impossibility of transportation, which will also be fully explained in the proper manner."

Out of the conduct of the troops, or a portion of them, on this march has grown a series of accusations, resulting in the court-martialing and dismissal of several officers of the 15th Kansas Cavalry, among them being the Colonel himself. The charges were made not only by the inhabitants of the section through which they passed, but by some of the best officers serving in the Department of Kansas. The charges made involved killing of prisoners, robbery of non-combatants, general burning, destruction and spoilation of property.

A communication in the Arkansas *Journal*, a radical and loyal paper published at Little Rock, the organ of the Free State Government, says, under date of June 7th, 1865, of the condition of affairs in

North-western Arkansas, and of the actions thus charged. The italics are not in the original:

"After the defeat of Fagan at Fayetteville, on the 3rd of November last, and the retreat of the rebel army south of the Arkansas river, large numbers of union people who had, during the fall campaign, fled to that post for protection against rebel persecution, were left entirely destitute of the means of support, and the long continued investment of the place, and the subsequent almost impassable condition of the roads, had rendered it impossible for the government to keep up a sufficient supply of subsistence stores to feed both troops and citizens. In addition to this, the order for the abandonment of Western Arkansas in December last, caused for a time the stopping of southward bound trains, and prevented the importation of provisions by citizens.

"For the three months of August, September and October, 1864, the presence in the country of an average number of fifteen hundred well mounted rebels, under command of Colonel W. H. Brooks and Major W. M. Brown, commonly known as "Buck Brown, the bushwhacker;" and, during the last two weeks of October, of fifteen thousand men under Sterling Price; then for nearly the whole month of November, the "Army of the Border," under command of Major General Curtis, caused a destitution among the people almost unknown in the annals of history. *On the return of Jennison's 15th Kansas Cavalry through Washington and Benton Counties, they plundered the citizens indiscriminately of the last restige of moveable property that had been spared by all previous gangs of thieves, and lighted their disgraceful march homeward, by the burning dwellings of the peaceful citizens, whom they had made outcasts and beggars in their own country.* And to-day, the blackened chimneys that mark the burial ground of all that was dear to hundreds of once happy families in Northwestern Arkansas, are appropriately termed 'Jennison's tombstones.'"

It is to be deplored that such acts should have tarnished a fame so fairly and honorably won on the field. But there are men who mistake passion for principle; who, animated by revenge, believe themselves the instruments of retributive justice; and whose mode of conducting war will always degenerate into pillage and cruelty, leading after them the baser mass who make no pretence whatever.

With the return of Colonel Jennison's command to their stations, the campaign was completely closed. After forty days in the saddle, making almost unequalled marches of over one thousand miles in all; fighting battles and winning victories against a foe outnumbering us largely; bringing about their complete and overwhelming defeat; following them through an impoverished and destitute country for several hundred miles; allowing them no time to recover or recuperate their exhausted strength: saving by these rapid and daring movements our exposed garrisons in Western Arkansas and the Indian Territory. This, as well as the earlier portion of the same extraordinary campaign, when an army was organized out of raw militia, presenting the spectacle of the business of a whole State being suspended, and every male person capable of doing so, flying to arms to defend their homes from invasion and spoilation. In whatever light we look at the campaign, to the history of which these pages have been devoted, its claim to be considered one of the more daring and vigorously executed of the war cannot be contested by any who may be cognizant of the extraordinary facts thereof.

Great and disastrous as was the rebel defeat, yet none can deny admiration to the rebel leader, for the splendid manner in which the earlier portion of his great raid was conducted, nor for the endurance and energy displayed by him in his hardly pressed retreat. The sufferings of his troops must have been frightful. Success gilds all mistakes; misfortunes and defeats dim the lustre of the most brilliant career. General Price was no exception to these rules. On arrival in Texas, the mortification and chagrin, natural to men so utterly defeated, broke out in crimination and recrimination against their commander. Portions of a very bitter correspondence between him and the perambulative rebel claimant for the governorship of Missouri, Tom Reynolds, found their way into Northern newspapers. It also appeared that at the time our officers were at Shreveport, La., discussing terms of surrender with Kirby Smith, that General Price was then in arrest and being tried by court martial for the issue of his campaign. So completely demoralized were portions of the rebel command, that it was found necessary to remove the Missouri cavalry into the interior of Texas to prevent their complete disbandment by desertion and mutiny.

CHAPTER XXIII.

GENERAL ORDERS AND CONGRATULATIONS.

Colonel Jennison, on his return, issued the following congratulatory general order. Its modesty is as remarkable as its length:

Head-Quarters, Jennison's Brigade,
In the Field, Fort Scott, Kansas, Nov. 23. 1864.

General Field Orders,
No. 3.

I. In obedience to orders from the Major-General Commanding, the First Brigade, Army of the Border, is hereby dissolved; and the different regiments, battalions, detachments or batteries thereof, will proceed to their respective stations as elsewhere specified. In dissolving the Brigade, however, and relinquishing his connection with it as a Brigade, the Colonel Commanding desires to express to one and all his thanks for the undivided support and cordial co-operation afforded him during the entire campaign recently closed—one of the most arduous and extensive yet undertaken since the opening of the war. Where all have sustained themselves so gallantly in the field, the Colonel Commanding feels that it would be injustice to particularize, and he can therefore only award the fullest meed of praise to all under his command.

Since the organization of the brigade at Hickman's Mills, Mo., on the 15th of October, you have marched over one thousand miles, suffering all the privations incidental to a soldier's life; many of you on foot, without adequate clothing, blankets or commissary supplies, and yet no complaints were uttered: and whether in bivouac on the summit of the Boston mountains, or encountering an enemy your superior in numbers ten fold, it can still be said that the First Brigade was the same hardy, uncomplaining organization.

On the 16th of October, we left Hickman's Mills, Mo., marching towards Warrensburg, west of which, however, our direction was changed to Lexington, where we arrived on the 18th. The succeeding day we were attacked by the full force of the enemy, estimated at 26,000. We held our position until the entire rebel army was developed, when, overwhelmed by rapidly advancing numbers, we were compelled to fall back toward Independence, which movement was executed without the least confusion. To the First Brigade, then, is due the credit of having first engaged the rebel army under General Price in Central Missouri.

On the 21st, the brigade again encountered the enemy at the Little Blue, in conjunction with the brigades of Colonels Ford and Moonlight, where was fought one of the most stubborn engagements of the campaign, as the list of casualties will show. Falling back from this position through Independence, we again met the enemy at Byrom's crossing of the Big Blue, felling timber and obstructing his crossing for one entire day, with the First Brigade alone. Being compelled by force of opposing numbers to abandon this position, and closely followed by the rebels, we retreated slowly in the direction of Westport; meeting Shelby's Division of the rebel army on the prairie at the State line, below Westport, where the First Brigade held in check, and finally routed, a force five times its number, driving them some four miles into the timber of the Blue. In this action, however, the brigade of Colonel Moonlight took part, as did a portion of the Kansas State Militia. This action, more than any other, established the reputation of the Brigade for cool and determined courage, as it was fought at short range and entirely with small arms, the howitzers not being brought into action. This check, so unexpected to the enemy, prevented, in the estimation of all, Shelby's raid into Kansas; as he was compelled to fall back to the main army for the night.

On the morning of the 23rd, the brigade, numbering scarcely six hundred men, was early aroused and prepared for the crowning battle of the campaign—the complete and total rout of Price at Westport—for which we owe so much to our gallant comrades of General Pleasanton's Division. Our prospects were gloomy, it must be owned, until the white smoke puffs at our left gave evidence that the expected assistance had arrived; and then, with a courage that had ennobled it throughout the campaign, the First Brigade charged down the slopes. But through a campaign so extensive—a march covering so many miles—it is impossible to remember details, or to recount individual acts of daring on the field; but the Colonel Commanding is proud to report that he will ever remember the officers and men of the First Brigade, with feelings of gratitude and affection.

Then followed the battles of Little Santa Fe and Newtonia, in the former of which only a portion of the brigade was engaged, and which may perhaps be termed a mere desultory skirmish, in comparison to others preceding and subsequent. On the 28th, we came up with the rear of the rebel force at Newtonia, the main command having pushed into the timber south and west of the town; but the entire force was within easy supporting distance. Then the First Brigade, supported by the 1st Colorado Battery, and Colonel Ford's Brigade, engaged a force at least 20,000, while the total opposing army did not number eight hundred! Newtonia! at the third battle fought on that almost storied ground, the twin Regiments of the West—Colorado and Kansas—acquitted themselves, as the General Commanding justly remarks, "with a courage and heroism unparalleled in the history of the war."

On the march thenceforth to the Arkansas River, and the return, it is needless to speak at length; but the result is before us all. We have assisted in the defeat and total rout of a rebel army, estimated at 30,000 strong, and we have been among those who stood on the Arkansas, across which had so recently passed the disorganized and demoralized remnant of the most formidable army that ever attempted the invasion of Kansas. The nation appreciates your courage, and rejoices in the result of your heroic labors. Many of our comrades have fallen—some amid the roar and crash of battle—and others by the steady and ambushed rifle of the licensed banditti, who infest the Southern country. The former have nobly fallen; the latter were brutally murdered by those who outrage all laws of civilized warfare, and transform the soldier into the assassin. Among the victims of the latter, are

Orloff Norton, Captain Commanding Company L, 15th K. V. C., Emmett Goss, 1st Lieutenant Company M, 15th K. V. C., and J. T. Smith, 1st Lieutenant Commanding Company E, K. V. C. The two former have never been heard from, and it is hardly to be supposed they have escaped. The latter lies dangerously wounded at Fayetteville, Arkansas. Thus three among the bravest officers of the regiment have been lost to it; and after having stood in the fore front of every action, are to be recorded as killed or wounded by bushwhackers.

II. To Captain J. F. Broadhead, of Mound City, and Dr. Dubois, of Leavenworth, Volunteer Aids on his staff, the Colonel Commanding is greatly indebted for their efficient action and fearless discharge of duties which devolved upon them. To Dr. Dubois, especially, at the battle on the State Line, the Colonel Commanding would accord particular praise for his coolness and determination on the field.

III. In compliance with General Field Orders No. 6, dated Head-quarters, 1st Division, Army of the Border, camp on Arkansas River, November 8th, 1864, the troops comprising the First Brigade, are authorized to inscribe upon their banners, *Lexington, Little Blue, Big Blue, Westport* and *Newtonia*.

IV. At the disbanding of the division, on the Arkansas River, the 16th Kansas Cavalry, commanded by Major Ketner, the 1st Colorado Independent Battery, commanded by Captain McLain, and the 9th Wisconsin Battery, commanded by Captain Dodge, were attached to the brigade for the return march. To each of these, the Colonel Commanding tenders his hearty thanks for the very able and soldierly manner in which they have sustained their commands during the tedious marches of the return.

V. The Colonel Commanding, deems it unnecessary in a general order to particularize, as the details of the campaign will be set forth in the Brigade reports to the Assistant Adjutant-General, as soon as the various reports from subordinate commanders are received.

By order of COLONEL JENNISON:

JOS. MACKLE,
Lieutenant and A. A. A. General, 1st Brigade, 1st Division, Army of the Border.

Colonel Moonlight, commanding the 2d Brigade, also issued a field order, in congratulation to his command, which is here inserted:

HEAD-QUARTERS, SECOND BRIGADE, FIRST DIVISION,
ARMY OF THE BORDER,
PAOLA, KANSAS, December 15, 1864.

GENERAL FIELD ORDER,
No. 2.

The brigade has been dissolved by your late Division Commander, Major-General James G. Blunt, now commanding District of South Kansas, and the companies will again resume the stations occupied by them prior to the late campaign.

When Price, with a well organized army, found his way into Missouri, and threatened the border of Kansas, the 2d Brigade was the first to rally to the "Battle Cry of Freedom," and beard the lion in his den. It was you that led the advance and captured Lexington on the 18th of October, by a dashing charge of eight miles, killing in the *very* streets several bushwhackers (then holding the town awaiting Price's advance) wounding a few and capturing a number of prisoners. It was you who bore the brunt of the battle of Lexington on the following day, and by your determined will and indomitable courage, was the enemy held at bay, until his entire force was developed, and the eyes of the blind opened to the danger then threatening your young State. To *you* was assigned the duty of covering the retreat— and nobly was it done. Long after dark did you contest every inch of ground. Stand after stand was made for miles, and while the cry was "still they come," your front remained unbroken and your courage unabated. The battle of the Little Blue on the 21st was certainly no less yours than that of Lexington. The 2d Brigade *began* the fight, having been left to meet the advancing enemy. The 2d Brigade *maintained* the fight and held their ground for several hours, part of the time with not twenty rounds of ammunition throughout, while cheer after cheer rent the air, for the purpose of blinding the enemy and bidding defiance to rebellion. The 2d Brigade *again* covered the retreat on the evening of *this* day, battling with the enemy in the very streets of Independence until darkness put an end to the strife.

You participated in the fight on Big Blue, and Kansas owes her safety to your gallantry and devotion, combined with that of the 1st Brigade, when you forced back the invading enemy on that memorable night, and compelled them to revere the *very* soil of Freedom and the institution against which they were fighting; nor were you found wanting on the morrow, for the dawn of day found you in the saddle prepared to renew the inequal contest. To you was assigned the right of the line of battle, and *could* you have been properly supported, when you drove the enemy back foot by foot, for over a mile, the battle field would assuredly *then* have been ours. When the enemy retreated, the 2d Brigade was on the right flank, and at Little Santa Fe compelled him to abandon his purpose of marching south through Kansas. At Cold Water Grove the enemy again felt your presence, and after a continuous march of sixty-five miles, you arrived in time to save Mound City from ruin and her inhabitants from destruction. While the enemy was being scattered "like chaff before the wind" by our pursuing forces at the Marias des Cygnes, you were whipping *in* the vandal flankers on the right, and while the battle of the Osage was raging, the 2d Brigade was forcing its way to Fort Scott. At Fort Lincoln, the enemy denied you a passage, and by sheer force of numbers you were compelled to march to Fort Scott by a circuitous route, having made thirty-five miles in five hours, including an hour's fight at Fort Lincoln. Fort Scott was saved. The enemy was whipped, and for the first time in ten days you were reluctantly permitted to refresh yourselves in a *sweet sleep of victory*. It was not your fault that you did not participate in the battle of Newtonia, as instructions had been received to await rations then forty-eight hours due. You participated in the pursuit of Price until he crossed the Arkansas River, returning to your present stations *via* Fort Smith.

In two months you have marched over twelve hundred miles, repeatedly engaged an enemy ten times your number with varied success. You have endured hardships of no ordinary magnitude; braved dangers in every shape, and still you are the same uncomplaining, devoted patriots; uniformly obedient, and consistently careful of the interests of the Government and her loyal supporters. To you the country is indebted; of you the State of Kansas feels proud; guard well her interest in your *new* yet *old* positions on the border. Many gallant comrades have fallen during the struggle, and "sleep the sleep that knows no waking;" and while we mourn the departed heroes, let us nerve ourselves to deeds of still greater daring, remembering that rebellion still lives, and that Freedom knows no conqueror.

To my Acting Assistant Adjutant-General, Lieutenant I. I. Taber, Regi mental Adjutant 11th Kansas Volunteer Cavalry, I cannot give too much praise. He was my only staff officer throughout the entire campaign, and performed the duties of three officers, never faltering, ever ready and devoted to the interests of the brigade. Other officers and men deserve special mention, which is carefully made in my report.

      THOS. MOONLIGHT,
      Colonel 11th Kansas Cavalry, Commanding.
IRA I. TABER, 1st Lieutenant and A. A. A. General.

Colonel James H. Ford, 2d Colorado Cavalry, with the modesty that marks his character and distinguishes the true soldier, did not indulge in this luxury. The Governor of Colorado, however, paid to the troops from that Territory, the following handsome and well-deserved compliment:

LETTER OF THANKS.

   EXECUTIVE DEPARTMENT, COLORADO TERRITORY,
    Denver, December 2, 1864.

To the Officers and Men of the Second Regiment of Colorado Cavalry, and the First Colorado Battery:

I thank you in behalf of our common country, and especially of your fellow-citizens of Colorado Territory, who have heard with pride and pleasure, the report of your gallant and heroic conduct in the late and bloody battles with the rebel hosts under Price.

While our citizens mourn the loss of friends fallen nobly contending for their country's honor, every patriotic heart rejoices that victory perched upon your banner.

The hopes, the prayers and benedictions of those you have left behind you will follow you, and when you return from the field, their gratitude will prove that the defenders of their country shall receive the honors of their countrymen.
      JOHN EVANS,
      Governor Colorado Territory.

At Department head-quarters, a special order was issued, relieving Sergeant Spencer P. Wade, Company "E," 11th K. V. C., who with a detachment had been placed on the steamers "Emile" and "U. S. Grant," while they were employed in the military service as patrol boats. The last paragraph thus honorably speaks of Sergeant Wade:

"In relieving Sergeant Wade from the important duty assigned him, the General Commanding takes pleasure in acknowledging the soldierly conduct and efficient manner in which he and the men under his control have discharged their trust, and sincerely hopes their example may actuate others to the discharge of their duties in the same laudable manner.

"By Command of Major-General Curtis:
"JOHN WILLANS, A. A. G."

The following deserved tribute to a member of the once "despised and rejected race," is worthy a place here:

> HEAD-QUARTERS, FORT SCOTT, KANSAS,
> November 18, 1864.
>
> *Lieutenant* W. D. MATTHEWS, *Colored Light Artillery, Fort Scott, Kansas:*
>
> SIR:—On leaving this post, pursuant to orders from Department Head-quarters, I desire to express to you my sincere thanks for the patient industry and skill, with which you have discharged your various duties since I placed you on duty, to assist in preparing the post for a vigorous defence against the probable attack of the enemy.
>
> You have been a model of proper discipline and subordination, strictly attentive to duty, promptly obedient to orders, and acting with a wise discretion in all matters requiring the exercise of your individual judgment.
>
> Trusting that you may be successful in the service, and in life, I am
>
> Very respectfully yours,
> CHAS. W. BLAIR,
> Colonel Commanding Post.

We close with the order of General Blunt, relieving the Volunteer Aides who served upon the Division Staff:

> HEAD-QUARTERS, FIRST DIVISION,
> ARMY OF THE BORDER,
> In the Field, Fort Scott, Nov. 22d, 1864.
>
> GENERAL ORDER,
> No. 7.
>
> I. The campaign against the rebel forces under General Price, having successfully terminated, the following named persons, Volunteer Aides on the Staff of the Commanding General, announced in General Field Orders, No. 5, are hereby relieved from further duty:
>
> Lieutenant-Colonel J. T. Burris, late of the 10th Regiment Kansas Volunteers.
> Major Thomas H. Penny, late of the 35th Missouri Volunteers.
> Major R. G. Ward, 1st Regiment Kansas Colored Volunteers.
> Captain A. J. Shannon, Provost Marshal District South Kansas.
> Captain T. E. Milhoan, late of the 10th Regiment Kansas Volunteers.
>
> II. In taking leave, the General Commanding desires to express his gratitude to these officers, for their valuable services and uniform gallant conduct.
>
> III. Company E, 14th Kansas Volunteers, under command of Lieutenant

W. B. Clark, detailed as escort to the Commanding General on the 22d of October, are deserving of especial mention for their gallantry in the battles of the 23rd and 28th. They will inscribe on their guidon " *Westport*" and " *Newtonia*."

BY COMMAND OF MAJOR-GENERAL BLUNT:

GEO. S. HAMPTON, A. A. General.

The returns from the medical officers of the army (which do not show the militia who fell, the large number who were but slightly wounded, and many who were allowed to proceed to their homes for attendance and care) give the following as our loss: Killed, seventy-five; wounded, one hundred and seventy-three; three died in hospital; total, two hundred and fifty-one. Missing (probably bushwhacked) six; prisoners, one hundred and twenty. The total loss with the militia will be about five hundred.

General Pleasanton reports, three hundred and sixty wounded in hospital, and about one hundred killed, in all four hundred and sixty. Our entire loss, resulting from casualties of battle, exposure, bushwhacking, &c., would thus not exceed one thousand men.

APPENDIX.

In Memoriam.

How sleep the brave who sink to rest,
By all their country's wishes blessed !
By fairy hands their knell is rung;
By forms unseen their dirge is sung;
There Honor comes a pilgrim gray,
To bless the turf that wraps their clay;
And Freedom shall awhile repair,
To dwell a weeping hermit there.
— *William Collins*, **1746.**

We live in deeds, not years; in thoughts, not breaths;
In feelings, not in figures on a dial.
We should count time by heart-throbs.   He most lives
Who thinks most, feels the noblest, acts the best.
—*Philip James Bailey.*

APPENDIX.

HORATIO KNOWLES, of Marmaton, Bourbon County, Kansas, was murdered October 23rd, by a gang of guerrillas, under command of Major S. Piercy, formerly of Missouri, who attacked the town.

Mr. Knowles had just resigned his commission as Lieutenant-Colonel of the 2d Regiment Kansas Colored Volunteer Infantry (Colonel S. J. Crawford) owing to ill health, and returned to his home in Kansas, and commenced business as a merchant. He was one of the best and most esteemed citizens of the county, and his loss was keenly felt. Coming to Kansas in 1857, he took a decided position as a Free State man, during all the troubles which, in '57, '8 and '9, disturbed South-Eastern Kansas, though never identified with the lawless element which the fierce agitation had produced.

He was elected in October, 1857, to the first Free State Territorial Legislature, and again to the first State Legislature, in 1861, in which as a representative, he ably discharged his duties. He was recognized as a man of sterling integrity, great worth, good business ability and sagacity. He was elected to the State Senate in the Fall of 1862. In the Spring of 1863, he received an appointment as Major in the Fourth Regiment, Indian Brigade. Two regiments were authorized by the Secretary of War, and provisional appointments issued to field officers and captains of companies. The parties were then ordered to report to Colonel William A. Phillips at Fort Gibson. Among them was Colonel Knowles. On reporting, Colonel Phillips assigned them regularly to various duties, so that they were precluded from recruiting, even if the presence of an active enemy had not rendered success almost impossible.

Major Knowles afterwards accepted the position of Lieutenant-Colonel, tendered him by Major-General James G. Blunt, in the colored regiment he was then raising. In this position he gained the esteem of his brother officers, and the confidence and regard of the men. Owing to ill-health, after six months' service, he was compelled to resign.

Colonel Knowles was a man of middle age and fine appearance. Universally esteemed while living, his sad and ill-starred fate woke a common regret. His name adds another to the long list of those who fell that the land might be free and the nation redeemed.

DANIEL M. BROWN, shot down in an attempt to escape, was formerly from Indiana, and settled in Kansas in 1860. He was an active citizen, having been Postmaster and Justice of the Peace. An old man, and esteemed by all, he was one of the most uncompromising foes to the rebellion by whose murderous hand he fell. He has three sons in the army.

DR. L. M. SHADWICK came from Missouri to Kansas in 1861. A Southern man by birth, he was devotedly attached to the Union, and in the same year gave proof thereof by joining as a private, Company "E," of the 10th Kansas Infantry Volunteers (formerly the 3rd and 4th Regiments, Lane Brigade). He served through the memorable campaign of the Lane Brigade at Drywood, Morristown, Osceola, and elsewhere on the Border. He was early appointed Hospital Steward, in which position he remained till his three years' service expired, and he was mustered out in August of 1864. Serving with his regiment throughout the campaign in the Indian Territory under Colonel William Weer; and with General Blunt, in that which put Northwestern Arkansas under our rule, he did his whole duty. Resuming his profession at Marmaton, he was rapidly gaining an extensive practice, when the bushwhacker's bullet finally mustered him out, and sent him to fill an untimely grave.

JOSEPH STOUT came to Kansas from Jasper County, Missouri, and had just completed a term of three years' service in Company "E" of the 10th Kansas Volunteers.

WARREN HAWKINS was a much respected citizen, an industrious farmer, and leaves a large family to mourn his loss.

ALBERT MCGONIGLE was a promising young man, not more than 17 years old; the son of Josiah McGonigle, of Bourbon County, a well known and much esteemed citizen.

WM. A. DeLong, First Lieutenant, Company "G," (Captain Bush) Second Regiment Kansas State Militia (Colonel G. W. Veale) resided at Auburn, Shawnee County, where his widow now lives. He came to Kansas in 1860.

Lieutenant DeLong was severely wounded in the right shoulder at the engagement between Jackman's and part of Dobbins' Brigades, and the 2d Regiment (Colonel Veale) Kansas State Militia, the Topeka Battery, and portions of other militia organizations, under Brigadier General Grant, Kansas State Militia, on the 22d of October.

The wound was not necessarily fatal, but disabled him so as to prevent an attempt to escape in the retreat of the remnant of the regiment. All concur in praise of Lieutenant DeLong's gallantry. He was shot *after* capture, by men detailed by the infamous Colonel Jackman himself, being wounded several times, one ball passing through the spinal column, paralyzing his lower limbs. That all our prisoners did not meet the same fate, was owing to the personal interference of General Shelby, to whom, as a gallant and generous foe, all praise is accorded.

Lieutenant DeLong was left on the field by the rebel assassins, and there found by our men. Being carried to the General Hospital at Kansas City, he lingered in great agony till the middle of November, when he calmly met a patriot's death.

Emmet Goss, First Lieutenant, Company "M," 15th Regiment, Kansas Cavalry Volunteers, was killed by bushwhackers while out with Captain Norton on a foraging expedition near Cane Hill, Arkansas, November 12th, it is believed, by the rebels under a notorious guerrilla, known as "Jencks" or "Tucks."

Lieutenant Goss was still a young man, but leaves a wife and children to mourn his loss. He was a native of North Carolina, but previous to the outbreak of the rebellion was living in Jackson County, Mo., where his avowed Union principles and active services soon made him a marked man. Always radical, he was uncompromising in his devotion to the national cause, and served in the militia regiments of that State. When the 15th Kansas was being recruited he assisted in the organization of Company "M." Lieutenant Goss was esteemed a valuable officer, especially in the scouting service, in which the exigencies of the border required the employment of cavalry.

Orloff Norton, Captain, Company "L," 15th Kansas Cavalry Volunteers, was killed by bushwhackers, while the regiment was on its homeward march from the Arkansas River. Colonel Charles R. Jennison, commanding the troops moving by way of Cane Hill and Fayetteville, Ark., thus speaks in his report of the circumstances under which Captain Norton fell: "He was undoubtedly killed (with Lieutenant Goss, Company "M") while in charge of foraging parties, in the vicinity of Cane Hill, on the 12th of November, as all search has proved useless, and when last heard from they were closely pursued by a large force of guerrillas, said to be under command of Lieutenant Jencks, C.S.A."

In "General Field Orders, No. 3," dissolving the 1st Brigade, the Colonel commanding says of Captain Norton and Lieutenant Emmet Goss, Company "M," 15th Regiment Kansas Cavalry: "The two former have never been heard from, and it is hardly to be supposed they have escaped." Nothing has since been heard of this gallant officer: there is no doubt remaining of his fate. Orloff Norton was a native of Delaware County, Ohio. Born in 1837, at the time of his death he was but 27 years of age. He came to Kansas in 1860, settling in the Neosho Valley. At the organization of the 12th Regiment Kansas Volunteer Infantry (Colonel C. W. Adams) he enlisted as a private, serving on the border, until, in the Fall of 1863, he received a commission as second lieutenant in the company whose captain he was at the time of his death. He participated through the whole of the campaign—his regiment forming part of the First Brigade in General James G. Blunt's Division. He was in the battles of Lexington, Little Blue, Byrom's Ford, Big Blue, State Line, Westport and Newtonia. His Brigade Commander, Colonel Jennison (15th Kansas Cavalry), speaks of Captain Norton and Lieutenant Goss, in his report to the General commanding First Division: "Their loss is one which can be illy sustained by the regiment; and their memory will be cherished by all whose good fortune it was to be associated with them."

CHARLES V. HYDE, Orderly Sergeant, Company "C," 11th Kansas Cavalry Volunteers, was killed at the engagement, Lexington, Missouri, while gallantly performing duty with his company in the extreme advance of our line.

He was a citizen of Lyon County, Kansas, where his parents still reside. A young man, twenty years of age, he served his country for over two years, participating with his regiment in the memorable campaign of the Army of the Frontier, under General James G. Blunt ; and distinguished himself as a soldier in the fatigues and trials incidental to a soldier's life, not less than by his courage at Newtonia. Cane Hill and Prairie. He was with the Company in its arduous services against guerrillas during General Ewing's administration of the Border District of Missouri and Kansas, in the Summer and Fall of '63.

Rev. Richard Vernon was murdered on the march of the rebels from West Point, Cass County, Missouri, to the Trading Post, Linn County, Kansas. Of the manner of his death the following incidents are told. Lieutenant Colonel Wheeler, 13th Kansas Volunteers, Assistant Field Officer of the day, and Captain Young of the 5th Kansas Cavalry, Acting Provost Marshal of the 2d Brigade, were the first officers of our army who reached the scene of desolation after the rebel marauders had passed. From their knowledge and our own observation the facts are gathered.

Mr. Vernon lived in Linn County, close to the State Line, having removed from Cass County, where for several years as a preacher of the Methodist Church North he had lived and labored. He was a faithful Anti-Slavery Unionist, and for these opinions had been much persecuted

At the time of the passing of the rebel army, Mr. Vernon, with a wagon and team, was standing in a neighbor's yard. A lot of the ruffianly bushwhackers who followed along the flanks and rear of the invading army, rode in and demanded the horses. This was the first house entered by the rebels after crossing the State line, and is about six miles north of the Trading Post, and about two miles from West Point. The trail had beaten the prairie like a long used road, and was as distinguishable in the night as a wagon road would have been in the daytime.

Mr. Vernon, expostulating with the invaders, told them he owned the ponies. The reply was a brutal order to unhitch them. The old man, still demurring, was instantly shot down. Death ensued immediately. This fiendish act occurred in sight of the inmates of the cabin, who were the wife and family of a settler, fortunately absent. After murdering the inoffensive old man of 60 years, they commenced a work of devastation which was as complete as our rapid approach would allow.

They burned the forage, set fire to the fences, attempting to do the same to the house. The poor woman, however, put out the fire. Every article of clothing or food was taken or destroyed. Among other things they found a pot of soap-grease, which they devoured like so many half famished wolves, and then, to exhibit their petty spite against the poor woman, they smashed the pot. A little way from the house was a splendid spring of pure cold water, which the family had excavated to the depth of ten or twelve feet and had walled it up, making a very wide and capacious well. After exhausting the water in supplying themselves and animals, these brave soldiers led one of their old broken down horses up to the mouth of the well, shot him and tumbled him in.

This was the condition of the dwelling when our advance came up. The murdered form of their venerable neighbor lay in the door yard, as it fell under the assassin's bullet. The cabin was a scene of devastation and ruin.

The poor woman and children were cowering in almost idiotic terror, while the fires lit by the marauders still smouldered. By direction of Captain Young, a portion of the provost guard were set to work, clearing out the spring, and otherwise aiding the poor people.

Mr. Vernon was a man universally respected. Originally from Pennsylvania, his life had been spent upon the frontier in discharge of the self-sacrificing duties incidental to the life of an itinerant preacher. A faithful upholder of the principles of Union and Liberty, he at last fell a victim to Slavery's treason. Mr. Vernon left a wife and five children, who removed to Media, Delaware County, Pennsylvania, where his brother, Mr. D. A. Vernon, edits the *American*, a Conuty Republican journal.

JOHN MILLER, an aged citizen sixty-five years old, was murdered at his home in the vicinity of the Trading Post.

ELDER WILLIAMS, living two miles north of the Post, with a son just discharged from the 6th Kansas Cavalry, were taken prisoners the night of the 24th. Both were probably murdered.

G. L. GOVE, Captain, Company "G," 11th Regiment Kansas Volunteer Cavalry (Colonel Thomas Moonlight) died at Olathe, Kansas, November 7th, 1864, of disease contracted through exposure in the field in the early part of the campaign.

Captain Gove was one of the most promising and efficient officers among those serving in the Kansas regiments. He was a citizen of Riley County, where his father, Hon. Moses Gove, Mayor of Manhattan, is highly esteemed. His gallant son was but 23 years of age when he died, and had, by his own merit and hard service, won the commission he then bore. Entering the service in August, 1861, as private in Company "F," 6th Regiment Kansas Volunteer Cavalry, he served in all the actions his regiment participated in, till August of the following year. He was in engagements on the Osage, and at Coon Creek, and in the pursuit after Shelby during the Spring of 1862, when General Blunt made his first campaign after assuming command of the Department of Kansas. He also served in the Indian Territory campaign, under Colonel William Weer, during the summer of the same year.

On the 13th of August he was appointed second lieutenant and recruiting officer in the 11th Kansas Volunteers. He, with Captain Adams, raised Company "G," among his neighbors and associates in Riley County, and was unanimously elected first lieutenant. With his regiment he served throughout the brilliant campaign of the Army of the Frontier, under the gallant General Blunt, participating in all the engagements. At Cane Hill and Prairie Grove, he was distinguished by his coolness and courage.

With his Company, he was stationed upon the border during the summer of 1863. At the time of reorganizing the regiment as cavalry, Captain Adams was promoted to a majority, and Lieutenant Gove being unanimously elected captain, was commissioned as such by the Governor. On the reorganization of the Department of Kansas, under General S. R. Curtis, Captain Gove's Company was selected to serve as his escort. This mark of confidence was due entirely to the soldierly qualities displayed by their young commander, and the high state of drill and discipline into which he had brought the company.

While serving in that capacity at Department Head-quarters, he was several times sent into Missouri, and during the continuance of the Paw Paw rebellion, was on duty in Platte County. He was with the General on his late Indian expeditions, and when the campaign against Price commenced, moved to the front to take part in the actions of the hour. This in spite of the fact that his health was precarious. He was in the heat of the engagement at the Little Blue, October 21st, being sent with Major Hunt, Chief of Artillery, to support the howitzers of his own command, and two under Sergeant Patterson, 14th Kansas Cavalry, attached to the First Brigade. In this position he was subjected to the heaviest fire from the enemy's lines. At the engagement on the afternoon of the 22d, when Colonel Jennison (after being driven from Byrom's Ford) assisted by Colonel Moonlight with the 2d Brigade, met and turned the leading rebel division under Shelby, which had already entered Kansas near the Shawnee Mission Manual Labor School, driving them for four miles. The body guard, under Captain Gove, was taken to the front by Major Hunt and placed to support the centre of our line, where it did gallant service.

The body guard with its gallant captain participated in the final charge south of Westport upon the eventful morning of the 23rd, and was active in the pursuit that followed. He remained in the field until sickness compelled him to leave. The result was fatal.

This gallant soldier died in the early dawn, with the flush of young manhood upon his brow. His military career was alike honorable and brilliant, and it is not to be doubted that a character so marked, as was that of Captain Gove's, would have won for him a proud place in life.

JAMES NELSON SMITH, Second Major of the Second Regiment Colorado Volunteer Cavalry (Colonel James Ford) fell while in command of the regiment at the Battle of the Little Blue, between Independence and the stream thus named, on the morning of the 21st of October, 1864.

At the time of his death he was leading the advance line of the 4th Brigade—Colonel Ford commanding; the Second Colorado having been ordered to the support of a battery of howitzers brought from Independence and placed in position by Major R. H. Hunt (15th Kansas Volunteer Cavalry) Chief of Artillery, upon the staff of Major-General Curtis. Major Smith was on the right, and in advance of a farm house two miles from the bridge, in which the howitzer battery had been placed. Before them was an open field skirted by timber, which was occupied by the rebels. It is generally believed that the command immediately in front was the bushwhacking force which had recently joined General Price, under the infamous George Todd; the same gang which, under Quantrell, Todd, Yeager, and others, participated in all the atrocities of Lawrence, Bater's Springs, the "Sam Gaty" massacre, and other affairs on the Border.

Major Smith's towering form and fine appearance attracted the rebels' attention, and the fusilade in his direction became marked and dangerous. While the line was in this position (Colonel Moonlight, with the 11th Kansas Volunteer Cavalry, having moved to the front again in support of the artillery, forming on the left) Major Smith was pierced to the heart with a rebel bullet. He never spoke, but fell from his saddle dead.

The deceased was a man of fine appearance, being over six feet tall, and well proportioned; with an open countenance which bespoke intelligence, energy and decision of character. He was formerly a citizen of Kansas, having resided at Elwood, Doniphan County, in 1859. His brother, Major Samuel D. Smith, Brigade Surgeon, was formerly surgeon of the famous First Kansas; and another brother, Ebenezer Smith, is a partner of Jerome B. Chaffee, of Colorado, who has since been so successful both in business and public affairs, in that flourishing Territory. All of them resided at one time in Elwood, and together (except the Doctor) moved to the mountains.

When the alarm was sounded at Fort Sumter, in '61, and Governor William Gilpin commenced the organization of the 1st Colorado Regiment, J. Nelson Smith was among the first to respond. At the time of the organization of the 3rd Regiment Colorado Volunteers, the Major was commissioned as such by Governor Evans; Colonel Dodd and Lieutenant-Colonel Samuel S. Curtis being the other field officers.

With six companies of this regiment (afterwards consolidated with the 2d under Colonel James Ford, thus forming the now famous Second Regiment) Major Smith marched from Fort Lyon to Fort Scott, and afterwards participated in the engagement at Cabin Creek, against the rebel Stand Waitie, with his mongrel force of Indians and Texans. On reaching Fort Gibson, General Blunt soon assumed command, and the campaign of '63, in the territory south of the Arkansas River, commenced. The regiment participated in the victory of Honey Springs, July 17th, 1863; in the march on and rout at Perryville, Choctaw Nation; and in the subsequent occupation of Fort Smith, Arkansas. Afterwards, when the regiment was ordered to Springfield, previous to consolidation, Major Smith was in command on the march.

After reorganization, the 2d Colorado was stationed upon the western border of Missouri, with head-quarters at Kansas City. For over a year its record has been of a most brilliant character, and the personal services of the gallant and lamented Major most untiring and valuable.

Throughout the entire term of its services in Jackson and the adjacent counties of Missouri, Major Smith had command of stations involving great activity and responsibility. During the continuance of what is known in Missouri and Kansas as "The Paw Paw Rebellion," Major Smith was vigorously employed under Colonel Ford, and in conjunction with troops from General Curtis' command in operations against Taylor, Thrailkill and others, in the counties of Platte and Clay, Missouri. He was foremost in the attack on and rout of the rebels at Camden Point, Platte County, and afterwards, in the same campaign, he had several sharp encounters with Thrail Kill near Liberty, Clay County. Throughout his service in this region, Major Smith made himself the dread of the treacherous bushwhackers and their allies, while at the same time he was always found opposed to the unlicensed spoliation and robbery which had been construed to mean living off the enemy, and was too often permitted as a "radical" method of warfare, to the utter demoralization of our troops, making marauders out of soldiers.

At the commencement of the Price Campaign, Major Smith, with the regiment, was under orders to report to General Curtis, preparatory to an expected removal to Colorado, where the continued hostilities of the Indians of the Plains rendered additional force necessary.

By request of General Rosecrans, they were detained until the growing emergencies rendered their presence imperative. Being then stationed at Pleasant Hill, the force under Colonel Ford thus became the advanced outpost of the Department of Kansas, and the forces of General Curtis. In this position Major Smith was constantly employed in command of scouts to feel the enemy's positions and watch their movements. He occupied Independence upon the 14th of October, only retiring before a superior rebel force. On the 15th he was sent on a reconnoissance towards Lexington, which city he occupied on the 16th, remaining till next day, then returning to Independence, which he left only to face the foe, and nobly met a soldier's death.

J. Nelson Smith was born in January, 1837, at Beaver Dam, Erie County, Pennsylvania. At the time of his death he was consequently not 28 years of age. He received a liberal education, graduating at the Meadville College in his native State.

One who knew him well thus speaks of his life in his adopted home: " The "career of the deceased in Colorado was that of an earnest, honest and "capable young man. He made friends wherever he went, not because he "sought them, but for the reason that he deserved them and they came to "him."

He was first buried with military honors at Kansas City by his mourning comrades, who, of all grades, regretted his loss as that of a tried, true and valued friend. Afterwards his remains were removed by his brother, Surgeon Smith, to Greenwood Cemetery, near Leavenworth, Kansas.

He fell battling for nationality, for liberty, for the broadest human opportunities, and the grandest development of the highest Christian civilization. Dying for America, young, honored and brave, his name shall be esteemed as one who deserved well of his country, and who gave all for that country's welfare.

> "Sleep, soldier! still in honored rest
>   Your truth and valor wearing;
> The bravest are the tenderest,
>   The loving are the daring."

H. C. COVIL, Company "B," Second Regiment Kansas State Millitia, was killed at the engagement near the Big Blue River, on the road from Kansas City to Hickman's Mills, on the 22d of October, 1864, in the fight between the regiment to which he belonged and the advance brigade (Jackman's) of Shelby's Division, which had just succeeded in forcing the passage of the stream at Byrom's Ford, about four miles from the one held by the militia.

Mr. Covil was a farmer, living three miles from the city of Topeka. He leaves a wife and one child. His age was about forty. He came to Kansas among the earliest settlers, locating in Shawnee County, and was always an active participant in the Free State troubles. A man much esteemed by his neighbors, he had twice been elected County Commissioner, and his loss is regretted as that of a good man and valuable citizen.

HARVEY G. YOUNG, Company "B," Second Regiment Kansas State Militia, was killed in the engagement near the Big Blue, at the Hickman's Mills Crossing. He was a citizen of Topeka, doing business there; a young man but little over 30 years of age, and settled in Kansas in 1854, passing through all the troublous Free State agitation, in which warfare he bore an active part.

DANIEL HANDLEY, of the Topeka Battery, fell at the engagement, October 22d, on the Blue, while most bravely attempting to defend the gun used by our militia, against a charge from Jackman's Brigade. He was an Irishman, a butcher by trade, and came to the State in 1858.

NICHOLAS BROWN, of the Independent Battery, was shot down while working the 24-pound howitzer captured by Shelby from General Grant, Kansas State Militia, October 22d. He was a young man but 33 years of age, Prussian by birth, and very generally esteemed by his associates.

GEORGE GRINOLD was a member of Battery, an industrious German carpenter, whose death is felt severely by his wife and children. He came to Kansas, settling in Topeka, in 1860. Like the large majority of Germans, he was an ardent Republican, and a sincere and loyal citizen.

MCCLURE MARTIN, of the Battery, was not only an active member of that organization, in which he fell, but a respected and esteemed citizen of Topeka. He was but a young man. Came to Kansas from Pennsylvania. His brother and family reside at Topeka. He was an active Free State man throughout the perilous hours of '54, '5 and '6, and at last gave his life in defence of the principles he had so long sustained, meeting death at the hands of Slavery's minions with the same courage that he had combatted it in life.

C. H. BUDD was a native of Maine, who came to Kansas in 1860. A brickmason by occupation, he was esteemed as a faithful and industrious workman. He fell with the Battery to which he belonged, on the 22d of October

LEO SELKIN, a German citizen of Topeka, was killed in the engagement upon the Big Blue, October 22d, while working the gun to which he was attached.

MERRICK D. RACE was born in North Ridgeville, Loraine County, Ohio, January 24th, 1842. At the time of his death he was then 22 years old. He received an excellent education. In August, 1861, he joined the 11th Regiment Ohio Volunteer Cavalry, and soon after came to Kansas with his command. He served through Kansas, on the Border and in the Indian Territory, until being taken sick, he was, after a long illness, mustered out for disability at Columbus, Ohio, in the Spring of '63.

He then entered the Commercial College at Oberlin, where he rapidly perfected in the studies, having the intention of becoming a teacher himself. Removing to Topeka, Kansas, August, 1864, he engaged in the starting of a Commercial College. This institution, known as Mills and Race's College, was in a flourishing condition when Price's invasion summoned all to arms.

Young Race immediately joined the battery and proceeded with it to the Border. In this he was very useful, having considerable practical knowledge of artillery drill and practice. At the fight near Russell's Ford, on the 22d, the gallant young soldier, after having actively aided the resistance by the small detachment with the gun before the arrival of Colonel Veale, passed amid the storm of bullets along the entire front of the rebel line for the purpose of reconnoitering, and returned to Colonel Veale with the information that they were several thousand in number. He was taken prisoner in the final charge, after being promised treatment as a prisoner of war, and immediately, on delivery of his arms, was shot twice, one ball passing through his leg and the other passing through his lungs.

Being left for dead he was, after the rebels moved off, succored by a member of the Auburn Company, who had also escaped. This young man brought water, and succeeded in removing him to a house near by. Here he remained until re-captured by our forces on Sunday. In the evening he was moved two miles for the purpose of better attendance. He remained, enduring his agony with cheerfulness, at times believing he would recover, until Monday morning, when at 2 A. M. his spirit left for the better land. He was buried on the field, but his body was afterwards removed, by an uncle, to Loraine County, Ohio.

He died regretted by all. Active, talented, generous, earnest, his cowardly murder, after surrender, is but another evidence of the hellish spirit engendered by slavery.

Besides those already given, we record the names of those of our dead, killed October 22d, of whom no particulars have reached us:

Company "B" (Topeka)—Private J. B. Alverson.

Company "C" (Tecumseh)—Privates Albert Chipman and Elias Roberts. R. B. Hoeback and Osborne Nayor, taken prisoners, escaped on the 4th day, died after return home, of the exposure.

Company "D" (Indianola)—Privates Robert McKown, Dennis Ray, and Moses Banks (colored).

Company "F" (Big Springs)—Privates David Rake, James Eagle and Robert Campbell.

Company "G" (Auburn)—Privates W. P. Roberts and Samuel Allen.

Company "I" (Monmouth)—Privates William Wann and Robert Rolls.

The Topeka Battery, Company "A"—Ben Hughes (colored).

JAMES MAYRERS, of Wyandotte, Wagon Master of the 23rd Kansas State Militia, was killed in the same engagement. As also a colored teamster, whose name is unknown.

AARON COOK, was a citizen of Jefferson County, Kansas, and a member of the 4th Regiment Kansas State Militia (Colonel McCain commanding). This regiment was ordered from Independence after the engagement near the Little Blue, October 21st, and during the night were directed to proceed to and hold Byrom's Ford, four miles above the old Independence and Kansas City Road. On arrival here, a party of twenty-one men were sent as scouts and messengers towards Hickman's Mills, where was stationed a militia force under Brigadier-General M. S. Grant, Kansas State Militia. On their return, and when within a mile or two of the Ford, the party were surprised and all but one taken prisoners—he escaping by the fleetness of his horse. Aaron Cook was shot down in cold blood after capture, and his body left in the road, where it was found shortly after. In all probability he was murdered by Jackman's Brigade.

Adjutant Dutton thus writes: "Aaron Cook, taken prisoner by Shelby's men, was one of the early settlers, and a bold, fearless, outspoken champion of the principles of freedom; always active and earnest in the good cause; generous to a fault, but uncompromising in his political faith; a kind husband and father, and left a large family to mourn his sad fate."

DAVID FULTS.—On Sunday, October 23rd, between 4 and 5 P.M., two gentlemen found a wounded man near Little Santa Fe, who gave his name as David Fults, Company "I," 2d Regiment Kansas State Militia. His statement was that having been separated from his regiment at the Big Blue the day before, he fell in with a body of our cavalry, which he believed to be Colonel Jennison's regiment. He told several soldiers who he was; also told the commander, whom he believed to be Colonel Jennison, the same story, but the officer declared him a rebel bushwhacker, and ordered him to be shot. The unfortunate man was wounded in the small of the back and in the leg. The first ball passed through his body. They left him where he was found. He died shortly afterwards.

This statement created much indignation, and by General Curtis' orders was investigated. Lieutenant J. M. Hubbard, Signal Officer, made an investigation which elicited the following facts:

David Fults resided some eleven miles southwest of Big Springs, Shawnee County. Another brother resides in Douglass County, and in the Campaign against Price was in the field with the 21st Kansas State Militia. Two other brothers are members of the 16th Kansas Volunteer Cavalry, and two more have been in the Federal service in Kentucky, from which State the family emigrated to Kansas eight years since.

David Fults leaves a widow and two children. He took with him on the campaign a horse and equipments, of which the family have never been able to find any trace.

Of the circumstances under which he was shot his family know nothing, except from the statement of parties who saw and conversed with him during the interval of time that he lived after being wounded.

Of these statements the one most circumstantial is that of John J. Ingalls, who seems to have been the first man that discovered him after those at whose hands he received his wounds had passed on and left him. To Mr. Ingalls, after stating his name, residence, and the company and regiment of K. S. M. to which he belonged, he said that he had been separated from his command in the fight of the preceding day, and while endeavoring to avoid the enemy, and rejoin it, at about noon of that day (Oct. 23rd) had fallen in with Jennison's command, then in pursuit of the retreating rebels. He told them his story, but Colonel Jennison refused to credit it, or give him time and opportunity to prove it; cursed him as a liar and a rebel, and ordered his men to shoot him, which they did, and taking his horse and equipments with them, left him where he fell.

Major E. G. Moon, Aide-de-Camp to General Deitzler, and Dr. S. E. Martin, Surgeon 2d Kansas State Militia, both of Topeka, and Mr. Silas Lyons, a neighbor and member of the same company with the deceased, also saw and conversed with him before his death, and to them he repeated the same statement in all essential particulars. He did not tell either of these parties upon what he relied to identify Colonel Jennison. His father and brother both stated in answer to inquiries, that as far as they know he had never seen Colonel Jennison, and could not therefore be able to identify him from personal knowledge. Other information bearing upon the question of identity, and also upon the circumstances of the shooting, is as follows:

Nathaniel D. Horton, Chief Bugler 11th Kansas Volunteer Cavalry, states that he accompanied Colonel Moonlight in the pursuit of the rebels from Shawnee Mission southward, on the 23rd of October last, and that when about five miles out, a young man dressed in homespun clothing, similar to that worn by the rebels, rode out of a field on the left of the road and joined the column. Colonel Moonlight called him to the head of the column, and demanded of him who he was, where he belonged, and what he was doing there. His answer was in substance that he belonged to the Kansas Militia, but that he had been compelled to join them against his will, and had left them the day previous with the intention of joining the rebels.

This last point seemed rather to be inferred by his hearers than explicitly stated by himself; and the inference rested, at least in part, upon an assumption that he had mistaken the character of the command he had joined, and supposed it to be rebel. Horton thinks his exact words were, "I've been wanting to get with you," though he would not speak positively in regard to the language used.

Proceeding apparently upon the assumption referred to above, Colonel Moonlight repeated once or twice, in form slightly varying, a question, the substance of which was, "Would you rather go with the Feds. or with us?" Each time the answer of the stranger was in substance, "I would rather go with you," upon which Colonel Moonlight declared himself satisfied, and ordered him to be shot. He turned to run, but was shot by Adjutant Tabor and Quartermaster-Sergeant Cowan before he had gone many steps, and was left by the road side still living, but judged to be mortally wounded.

The material portions of this statement are corroborated by 1st Lieutenant Wm. G. Drew, Company "I," 11th Kansas Volunteer Cavalry, who was at that time riding at the head of the column, and also by Quartermaster-Sergeant Wm. H. Cowan, who was one of the parties that did the shooting.

Lieutenant Drew says that the horse ridden by the stranger was seized by some one in the column, he thinks by Private E. G. Ham of Company "K." Lieutenant-Colonel Plumb, 11th Kansas Volunteer Cavalry, states that when this affair took place, he was riding sufficiently near the head of the column to notice the shooting, but not near enough to hear the words that preceded and led to it. He noticed the man was still living as he passed him, and saw the Assistant Surgeon of the regiment, Dr. D. J. Adams, and the Chaplain, J. S. Kline, dismount and hold some conversation with him.

All these parties unite in the statement that the affair occurred at a time of intense excitement, and that it occupied but a very few moments, occasioning no halt, and scarce any delay in the march of the column. Rev. J. S. Kline, Chaplain 11th Kansas Volunteer Cavalry, states that while accompanying his regiment in pursuit of the rebels on the 23rd of October, 1864, his attention was arrested by seeing the Assistant Surgeon of the regiment, Dr. Adams, dismounted and talking with a wounded man dressed in homespun butternut colored clothing.

When Mr. Kline came up the wounded man was insisting that he was a citizen of Kansas, and a member of the militia, which statement Dr. Adams refused to credit, and told him he was mortally wounded and had better tell the truth. He still adhered to his first statement, and in answer to questions from Mr. Kline, stated further that he lived in Shawnee County, and belonged to Colonel Veale's regiment of militia, and that his name was Fults. Mr. Kline tested him by a number of questions in regard to localities and persons in Shawnee County, all of which he answered correctly, evincing an amount of local information which none but a resident, would be likely to possess, and which fully satisfied Mr. Kline of the truth of his statements. He said further that he had become separated from his regiment the day previous, had remained secreted in the timber over night, and was trying to make his way back to his friends when he fell in with that column, and that the Colonel had ordered him to be shot without giving him an opportunity of proving his account of himself true.

All these parties agree in fixing the locality of this affair as the same where young Fults was found later in the same day by Messrs. Ingalls and Moon, and that the whole chain of evidence seems to establish beyond question the identity of the man shot by Colonel Moonlight's order, with the one found by Ingalls, and identified the next morning by Mr. Lyon as his acquaintance and neighbor David Fults.

Of course this conclusion absolves Colonel Jennison from all responsibility in the premises. In regard to the circumstances attending the shooting, a material difference will be noticed between the account given by Mr. Fults and that given by other witnesses. To account for this, it is not in my opinion necessary to impeach the veracity of either party. There seems to have been a fatal misunderstanding between them. It was very likely true in Fults' case, as in thousands of others, that he was compelled to come out with the militia, and he may have made the statement casually, and without a thought of the suspicion which it would fasten upon him. So too his statement of his separation from his command on the preceding day, and his

his efforts to rejoin it, may have been given in perfect innocence, and yet in such terms as to strengthen in the minds of those who heard him, the suspicion that he was at heart a rebel—a deserter from our flag, and that he supposed himself talking with rebels at that time.

So also, in answer to Colonel Moonlight's final questions, not understanding the suspicions with which he was regarded, he may have deemed it amply sufficient to declare his wish "to go with them."

On the other hand, it should be borne in mind that his personal appearance, dress, and the place, and manner of his joining the command, all combined to make him an object of suspicion, and that those who had stood in battle against the rebel foe for nearly a week, and then had just prevented the desolation of their homes, could hardly be expected at that time, and under such circumstances, to exercise a cool and deliberate judgment.

MAJOR-GENERAL S. R. CURTIS,
COMMANDER OF THE ARMY OF THE BORDER.

Major-General Samuel Ryan Curtis is a member of an old Connecticut family, which counts honored names of patriotic soldiers of the Revolution. He was born in 1806, while the family were moving into Ohio, and is now in his sixtieth year.

His career has been emphatically that of a western man, and his name is associated with the rapid progress of that section. He lived in Ohio, until being appointed Cadet, he went to West Point. There he graduated creditably, and was commissioned 2d Lieutenant of Infantry, in which capacity, and as 1st Lieutenant and Captain, we believe, he served for several years. He resigned and practised law in Ohio. When the Mexican war occurred he was Adjutant-General of the State, and was commissioned Colonel of the 2d Ohio Volunteers. Proceeding to Mexico, he was placed in positions where his large administrative abilities were brought into use. He was Military Governor of an important point, and while acting in that capacity, organized a column of troops and marched to the relief of General Taylor at Buena Vista, where he arrived at the termination of the engagement, but still in time to be of considerable service.

On his return to Ohio he embraced the profession of engineer, and was for several years thereafter engaged in building up the great railroad systems of the West. He was afterwards engineer of St. Louis, and materially aided in saving to that city its invaluable landing and levee. He was afterwards appointed engineer of the Des Moines Improvement, Iowa, and made his residence at Keokuk, where he still lives. He was one of the most active in inaugurating the Iowa system of railroads, and bringing the Pacific Railroad movement to success.

He was the first Republican elected to Congress from Iowa, and was reëlected to the House of Representatives in session when the rebellion began. He soon laid down the toga and took up the sword. We brief his latter military career, full of interest as it is, as follows :

Marched as Volunteer Aid with New York 7th Regiment to Washington City, April, 1861; elected and commissioned Colonel 2d Regiment Iowa Infantry Volunteers, June 1st. 1861; marched with his regiment, captured and occupied Hannibal and St. Joseph Railway in Missouri, from June 13th, 1861, to June 30th, 1861. While attending extra session of Congress was present at the Battle of Bull Run, Virginia, July 21st, 1861. Commissioned Brigadier-General United States Volunteers, to date from May 17th, 1861. Reported to General Fremont at St. Louis, Missouri, and assumed command of camp of instruction at Jefferson Barracks, August, 1861. Assumed command of camp of instruction at Benton Barracks, Missouri, September 12th, 1861. Assumed command of St. Louis District of Missouri, October, 1861. Assumed command of the Southwestern District of Missouri December 26th, 1861. Having marched from Rolla, Missouri, to Lebanon, Missouri, in January, 1862, organized "The Army of the Southwest," and assumed command of it, February, 1862. Marched from Lebanon to Pierson's Creek, Missouri. In command at the skirmish with Price at Pierson's Creek, February 13th, 1862. Marched into Springfield, Missouri, after its evacuation by Price, February 14th, 1862. In command of the Army of the Southwest on the ensuing march in pursuit of Price from Springfield, Missouri, to Fayetteville and Cross Hollows, Arkansas, February, 1862. Commanded at the skirmish with Price at Flat Creek, Missouri, February 15th, 1862, and during the skirmishing in Cross Timber Hollows, Arkansas, on February 16th, 1862, and at the engagement at Sugar Creek, Arkansas, February 17th, 1862. Occupied Cross Hollows, Arkansas, February 22d, 1862. Concentrated the army at Pea Ridge, Arkansas, March, 1862. Commanded at the battle of Pea Ridge March 6th, 7th and 8th, 1862. Camped at Cross Timber Hollows, Arkansas, March, 1862. Promoted Major-General of Volunteers, March, 1862. Commanded same army in the ensuing march through Missouri and Arkansas to Batesville, Arkansas, from April 5th to May 3rd, 1862. Commanded at Batesville May 3rd, 1862. Marched to Little Red River and Searcy Landing, Arkansas, back to Batesville, and thence to Jacksonport, Arkansas, May and June 1862. Commanded on march through Arkansas from Jacksonport, July 1st, to Clarendon, Arkansas, and thence to Helena, Arkansas, July 14th, 1862. Commanded at Round Hill, Arkansas, July 7th, 1862. Captured and occupied Helena, Arkansas, July 14th, 1862. Commanded United States forces at Helena, Ark., and vicinity from July 14th, '62, to August 29th, 1862. On leave of absence from August 29th, 1862, to September 24th, 1862. In command of the Department of the Missouri from September 24th, 1862, to May 24th, 1863, when being relieved from command, remained at home in Iowa until January. During his command of Department of Missouri, organized the Army of the Frontier, under General Schofield, and afterwards Generals Blunt and Herron. The latter officers won the battles of Cane Hill, Prairie Grove and Van Buren. Sent troops to Grenada, Mississippi, also drove out Shelby and Marmaduke, during their raids in South-East Missouri. In command of Department of Kansas, from January 16th, 1864, to February 7th, 1865. On a campaign against hostile Indians in Kansas and Nebraska, July, August and September, 1864. In command of Kansas troops, volunteer and militia, known as the "Army of the Border," in the pursuit of Price from the Missouri to the Arkansas river, on the Missouri and Arkansas border, October and November, 1864. Commanded at the following engagements in the pursuit of Price along the border: Little Blue, October 21st, '64; Big Blue, October 22d, '64; Westport, October 23rd, '64; Marias des Cygnes, Mine Creek, Osage, and Charlot, October 25th, '64; Newtonia, October 28th, '64. Terminated the pursuit of Price on the banks of the Arkansas River, thirty miles west of Fort Smith, November 8th, 1864, and returned to Fort Leavenworth. Relieved of the command of the Department of Kansas, February 7th, 1865. Assumed command of the Department of the North-West, February 16th, 1865, of which he was relieved July 26th.

No officer in the army deserves greater credit than General Curtis, for the uniform success and devotion he has won and shown. No citizen deserves more of his State or nation. Always faithful, earnest, judicious and energetic, the future will recognize him as one of the most sagacious and truest of the host who have gained immortal renown. General Curtis was a successful and influential politician, with admirable abilities for the post he held. He went into the war because the services of men with military education were needed. He has borne misrepresentation and slander without a murmur. The victim of a political cabal, while commanding in Missouri, he was not allowed to correct all wrong. Conscious of his own integrity, and certain that his acts would judge him rightfully, he leaves active service with the flattering certainty of having done his whole duty in the nation's hour of trial. Nor has he escaped affliction. His eldest son, Major H. Z. Curtis, was wounded by Quantrell's butchers, at Baxter's Springs, October 19th, 1863. His daughter fell a victim to disease and exposure in the hospitals at Rolla, Missouri, in early Summer of '62.

General Curtis is a man of noble presence. In stature about six feet, large and well proportioned. His head is a large and well balanced one; brow high and well developed; eyes that are dark, thoughtful, yet full of fire, while the expression of his countenance is that of a grave, dignified man of intellect. A thorough gentleman, always mindful of the courtesies of life, it is not alone as a public man, statesman, and soldier, that he has won the regards of the people. A warm and earnest friend, and a magnanimous, generous foe, General Curtis is universally respected and honored by all who know him.

HON. JAMES H. LANE,
UNITED STATES SENATOR FROM KANSAS.

James Henry Lane, was born in Lawrenceburgh, Indiana, June 22d, 1814, and is now 51 years of age. His father, Honorable Amos Lane, was one of the most active public men in Indiana. For a number of years he represented the Territory and State in Congress, and was a warm partizan and personal friend of President Jackson. His mother was a superior woman, possessed of high moral and fine intellectual character. She was a poetess of no mean order. Her memory is preserved by her sons, as only that of a good mother can be.

Senator Lane was carefully educated, his mother intending him for the ministry. His own taste turned for the law, for which he qualified himself, and was admitted to practice in 1840. During the Mexican war, Lane entered the service, enlisting as a private, in May, 1846. Immediately thereafter, he was elected Colonel of the 3rd Indiana Regiment, known as the "Steadfasts." In this capacity he served with distinguished honor throughout General Taylor's entire campaign. His services, and that of his regiment, at the battle of Buena Vista, have become matters of history. After their term of service had expired, he returned with it in June, 1847. The 5th Regiment was immediately organized by Colonel Lane. With it he returned to Mexico, and remained in the City of Mexico till peace was declared. On his return, he was, in 1849, elected Lieutenant Governor of Indiana. In October, 1852, elected to Congress from the 4th Congressional District. In November of the same year, was chosen Elector for the State at large on the Democratic ticket. Mr. Lane followed devotedly in his father's footsteps in this regard. He was in Congress during the memorable contest over the Douglas Kansas-Nebraska Bill, to which he was not at first favorable. Party influences succeeded in securing his vote for the repeal of the Missouri Compromise. In April, 1855, Colonel Lane removed to Lawrence, Kansas, settling on the farm where he now lives. In a short time he became an active Free State man, participating largely in all the movements inaugurated to resist the pro-slavery domination. He was one of the prominent leaders in inaugurating what is now known as the Topeka Free State Government, being appointed Chairman of the Executive Committee, organized at the Big Springs Convention, of which body he was the most active member. Colonel Lane was most untiring in the canvass, and when the Topeka Constitutional Convention assembled, was elected President of that body.

When the Missouri Border Ruffians invaded Kansas, besieging Lawrence, in the winter of '55-'6, Colonel Lane was elected commander of the Free State forces organized for defence. He contributed largely to that sagacious activity and policy which resulted in the departure and defeat of the pro-slavery forces, and yet did not embroil us with the General Government, then on the pro-slavery side. In March, 1856, with Governor Reeder, General Lane was elected to the United States Senate, and sent to Washington to secure the admission of Kansas as a free State. While on this mission, intelligence was received of the sacking of Lawrence, May 21st, 1856, by the Missouri Raiders, under Atchison and Stringfellow.

Lane at once threw himself into the work of defence, and aided in organizing that large Northern emigration, the presence and active aid of which, in August and September following, secured the freedom of Kansas. General Lane marched across Iowa with a number of companies, consolidated them in Nebraska, and early in August entered Kansas. Then rapidly followed, under the leadership of the Senator elect, a series of movements which resulted in the driving out of the Missouri invaders. His career then, as afterwards, is the history of Kansas. In 1857, General Lane, with a force, marched to the assistance of the Free State men of Linn and Bourbon counties, driving out and subduing the remnants of Border Ruffianism which had congregated at Fort Scott. During the same year, he was elected Delegate to, and subsequently President of, the Constitutional Convention, which met at Leavenworth. In 1858, the terrible misfortune occurred which resulted in the death of Gaius Jenkins at the hands of General Lane. The difficulty grew out of a dispute in relation to the claim, on which the Lane homestead is situated. The General was placed on his preliminary trial, and released on the ground of self-defence. Efforts were made to indict him before the Grand Jury, but each failed. The general impression made on the community was that of justifiable homicide.

Kansas was admitted in February, 1861, and shortly after, General Lane was elected to represent the State in the United States Senate. He was in Washington during all the earliest and darkest hours before the gun at Sumpter aroused the people to arms. As commander of the Frontier Guard,

General Lane did good service in guarding the President, and generally aiding the work of organization. He was then, as afterwards, till his lamented death, the confidential and trusted friend of President Lincoln. In July and August, 1861, he raised three regiments of volunteers. At the same time he was commissioned Brigadier-General, but did not muster in. He, however, assumed command of the brigade, and until November following, had command thereof in the field. Lane's Brigade, as it was called, did good service, defeating the rebels in several well contested fights; and by its activity and good management, protected the State of Kansas from invasion. In 1862, General Lane was confirmed Brigadier-General by the Senate. It was intended that he should have command of an expedition in the South-west, but owing to causes not necessary to name here, the idea was abandoned, and General Lane resumed his seat in the Senate. In '63, he was appointed by Mr. Stanton a Recruiting Commissioner for the Department of Kansas, and under this authority raised five regiments of infantry; one of them being the famous First Kansas Colored Regiment, now numbered in the Corps d'Afrique, as the 76th. This was the first regiment actually raised by the United States (the two regiments of Louisiana Home Guards, being State troops, first organized by the rebels, whose services were accepted by General Butler). It fought the first fight under the flag, at Island Mound, Bates County, Missouri, October 26th, 1862.

General Lane narrowly escaped from the Lawrence massacre in August, 1863. He was the leader of the pursuit which followed that wholesale butchery, and advocated measures which added bitterness to the quarrels that in Missouri had disrupted the Union men. He remained at his post, in discharge of his duties as Senator, till the Fall of '64, when the advance of General Price, and the events which the preceding pages have narrated, caused him to take the field again, as Volunteer Aid-de-Camp to General Curtis. In this capacity he served most gallantly, participating in the battles of Lexington, Little and Big Blue, Westport, Marias des Cygnes, Osage and Charlot.

In the Winter of '64-'5, General Lane was re-elected United States Senator for the term commencing the 4th of March, 1866.

Such is a brief outline of the career of General James H. Lane. He has had an extraordinary experience, is a man of great ability and possessed of wonderful energy, endurance and versatility. This his enemies acknowledge. Opinions differ very widely as to his character. No public man has had warmer partizans or bitterer foes. On the other hand, no State ever had a more indefatigable representative. He has linked his name to its history, and so interwoven his personal success into its interests, that the name of Kansas naturally calls up that of Senator Lane.

General Lane is tall, spare and sinewy. His frame is muscular and nervous. He has a high, long head, strong features, high cheek bones, square chin, firm, hard-lined mouth, deep-set eyes of grey and hazel combined, which are full of magnetic fire. His manner, socially, is pleasant and courteous. As a stump speaker—given an impassioned theme—he is unequalled in arousing his audience. As a managing politician, judged by success, he is without a peer. Whatever may be his faults, whatever may be said of his personal character, the struggle for freedom has had in him an invaluable ally, and the ruder contestants in that important strife, an able, vigilant and capable leader.

BRIGADIER-GENERAL JOHN McNEIL,
OF MISSOURI.

John McNeil, was born of American parents, in the British Provinces, and is now about 45 years of age. At an early age he moved to Boston, where he learned the hatter's trade. Shortly afterwards he commenced and failed in business in New York city. Afterwards moving to St. Louis, he entered into business. He was very successful, continuing therein for twenty-five years, making a large fortune, a large portion of which he lost by the Southern Rebellion. In politics McNeil always was a strong Democrat. The rebel leaders counted confidently on his support. But his patriotism was stronger than his partizanship, and when the lamented Lyon took command in St. Louis, McNeil was one among the first to place himself by his side. On the 8th of May, McNeil was first sworn into the service. He fought Harris, a rebel Brigadier, at Fulton, routing him utterly. He was then placed by General Fremont in command of St. Louis, and was afterwards made Provost-Marshal-General.

He was commissioned Colonel of the 19th Missouri Volunteers—known as the Lyon Regiment—August 3rd. For this position he was selected by General Lyon himself. At his own request he was afterwards transferred to the command of State troops and placed in command of Western Missouri, next to the Kansas line.

In the Spring of '62, he assumed command of a cavalry regiment, and of the District of North-East Missouri, containing the Hannibal and St. Joseph Railroad, a most important line of communication. The position was a very responsible one, the district being very disturbed and the rebels active. A rising took place in July, '62, under the lead of Porter, Cobb and Poindexter, who committed many gross outrages. Colonel McNeil moved against Porter, pursuing and fighting him until August 6th, when, at Kirksville, Adair

County, he defeated the rebels. McNeil had 1,034 men; Porter 3,000. The rebel leader had a narrow escape from capture, while his forces were completely routed. Our loss was five killed, thirty-five wounded; the enemy's was one hundred and fifty killed, four hundred wounded, and forty-seven prisoners. Among these were fifteen who had been previously paroled, and were now in arms in violation of its terms. Acting under the recognized laws of war, and by authority of orders from General Halleck, Colonel McNeil shot these fifteen men. For his success in the defeat of Porter, Colonel McNeil was made Brigadier in the State troops. At this time he inaugurated a system of active hostilities. The parole-breaker and bushwhacker met no mercy at his hands. He now established his camp in Munroe County. This was the worst section in Northern Missouri. Announcing that where Union men *could not* live, rebels *should not*, General McNeil proceeded to break up the guerrilla and recruiting camps. On the 14th of September, having destroyed the last, head-quarters were established at Palmyra, on the railroad, west of Hannibal.

Here occurred those events which first gave General McNeil a national reputation. Andrew Allsman, an old and respected Union citizen of the county, was taken prisoner from his home by the guerrilla Colonel Porter. General McNeil was appealed to by Allsman's friends. Having a number of prisoners, among whom were a score of parole-breakers, he selected ten of the worst, and notified Porter, that, unless Allsman was restored to his friends by noon, October 18th, these ten men should be hung in retaliation. They had all made themselves liable to this fate by their violation of the oath. Allsman was not returned to his friends, having been murdered. At the time named, the ten bushwhackers were hung.

This act, the first distinct carrying out of a retaliatory policy on our part, created great excitement throughout both sections. Rebel sympathizers in the North denounced McNeil. Abroad, capital was eagerly manufactured by distorted accounts. Jefferson Davis demanded the surrender of McNeil as a murderer and violator of the laws of war. The Government and the people sustained General McNeil, and he was rewarded by a commission as Brigadier-General, United States Volunteers.

He remained in command of North-East Missouri, when having effectually quieted it, he was relieved and put in command of South-East Missouri. He was in this command, when, in the Spring of '63, Marmaduke made one of his most famous raids. General McNeil was besieged in Cape Girardeau, which he gallantly defended, ultimately driving them away. In July of the same year, he was transferred to the command of South-West Missouri. In the following October, he was President of a Court-Martial at St. Louis. Shelby making his celebrated raid, General McNeil rapidly concentrated troops, joining them in St. Clair County. Instant pursuit was made and rapidly followed up. Shelby crossed the Osage in two columns. McNeil pursued him till near Huntsville, Arkansas, where he was joined by Colonel Brooks. He could not bring them to a fight, though outnumbering him four to one. The pursuit was continued till the enemy crossed the Arkansas. Their last gun was captured, as also much of their train, and many prisoners. At Clarksville, Arkansas, General McNeil received orders to take command at Fort Smith. He held this till January, '64.

Early in the Spring, he was ordered to the Department of the Gulf. He reported to General Banks at the close of the disastrous Red River Campaign, and was placed in command of the District of Lafourche, at the time New Orleans was seriously threatened in that direction by General Dick Taylor. The district was a very important one, requiring great vigilance on the part of commander and troops, to counteract the enemy's plans. He received the thanks of the commanding General, and at his own request, was placed in command of the "Corps d'Afrique," with head-quarters at Port Hudson.

In August he was ordered, by the War Department, to Missouri. The change was made by request of loyal Missourians. There he was placed in command of the District of Rolla. He was at this post when Price invaded Missouri. What he did therein, forms part of this history.

One correction is necessary. General McNeil was court-martialed under charges made by General Pleasanton. When the prosecution closed their case, General McNeil was informed that he need not call any witnesses, as the court was perfectly satisfied. Resting on this assurance, the General made no defence, when he could most completely have done so. The surprise of all was great when the findings of the court—three months' suspension of rank and pay—was announced. The case was referred to the Judge-Advocate-General, by whom the finding was revoked, and General McNeil was restored in honor to his rank and duty. This correction is necessary, as on page 177 it is stated that the court acquitted him.

After this, General McNeil was placed in command of the District of Central Missouri, which he held till after the surrender of Lee and Johnston, when he resigned.

He is now in St. Louis, engaged as actively in civil life as he has been in military.

General McNeil is a man of five feet ten inches, deep-chested, broad-shouldered, capable of withstanding great fatigue; martial in spirit, he is very soldierly in appearance. He is a strict disciplinarian, and vigorous fighter. His features are strongly moulded, nose Roman, forehead broad and compact, brain broad at the base, head well developed, mouth stern and firm, light hair and beard, sprinkled with grey, and flashing blue-grey eyes. His speech is like his acts—curt, brusque, yet weighty. His words are indeed bullets, full of force.

BATTLE OF THE LITTLE OSAGE.

The following letter of Major Hunt will be found of interest and value. It is published by permission of Colonel Benteen:

> OFFICE CHIEF OF ARTILLERY, DEPT. OF KANSAS,
> *Fort Leavenworth, January 9th,* 1865.

Lieutenant-Colonel T. W. BENTEEN, 10th Cavalry, Missouri Vols.

COLONEL,—In compliance with your request, for a statement of the facts of that charge on Mine Creek, October 25th, 1864, as to what brigade led it, made the attack, broke the rebel lines, continued the pursuit, &c., also as to whether the brigade you commanded "either faltered or fell back."

I take great pleasure in writing to you the following account of what occurred on the 25th October, 1864, in the engagement of that date, between the Union forces under Generals Curtis, Pleasanton and Blunt, against the enemy, so far as came under my observation. It would be necessary, for an intelligent statement, to give some account of matters preliminary to the charge on Mine Creek, to which, I take it, your letter asking information specially refers.

As will be remembered, on the evening of the 24th, the column under General Curtis in pursuit of Price was halted at West Point, Missouri, eight miles west of the trading post situated on the north side of the Marias des Cygnes, for the purpose of changing the order of march, which is the custom. General Blunt with the 1st Division was in front, General Pleasanton with his division of cavalry took the front or right of the army; General Sanborn's Brigade was then in advance; three companies of the 2d Colorado Cavalry, under Captain Kingsbury (forming the advance guard of General Blunt's Division) moved on towards the Trading Post. Having no knowledge of the change, and supposing themselves supported, they attacked and drove in the enemy's pickets. Captain R. J. Hinton, Aid-de-Camp to Major-General Blunt, had followed this battalion during the delay caused by the change of divisions. Finding that Captain Kingsbury was skirmishing with the enemy, he sent back word to General Sanborn and General Blunt to that effect. General Sanborn on reaching Elder Williams, about two miles from the Post, sent Colonel Gravelly with his regiment or brigade to relieve the Colorado Cavalry. He himself believing the enemy strongly posted on the mounds flanking the road through the timber on the Marias des Cygnes, withdrew his own lines half a mile north of where Kingsbury had skirmished. The night was dark, and General Sanborn pleaded this, and the want of topographical knowledge, as reasons for not feeling the enemy in force, and ascertaining his position more definitely. This is the statement made to Major Weed, Major McKenny, Captain Meeker and myself, when by order of General Curtis we were sent to find General Sanborn. A report was duly made to General Curtis, who immediately sent an order to General Sanborn to get a battery into position, shell the enemy, and under cover of this move upon him. General Sanborn complied; the other officers with the exception of Captain Hinton returned to head-quarters. I inviting the Captain to go along, we rode to our advanced line, aroused Captain Kingsbury's battalion from bivouac, and moved towards the rebel pickets on the mound east of the road. Informing Colonel Gravelly of my intention, and inviting him to accompany us, he did so, and by the aid of his advance, and the second Colorado, during the storm and rain the enemy's rear guard was driven and the mound carried. The hill west of the road was also carried after daylight, by a force which I afterwards learned was the 4th Iowa Cavalry, part of your command. The movement with which Captain Hinton and myself were associated commenced between three and four o'clock a.m., was carried out by my direction, acting in accordance with General Curtis' wishes, which were to press the enemy in order to save Southern Kansas.

It is not necessary to particularize the incidents which followed so rapidly after sunrise of the 25th. It is however necessary to state that when General Sanborn's artillery opened, I was compelled to go back and have the position of the guns changed, as our advance was in more danger from the shells than from the enemy. After the hills were carried and as the enemy got into motion, Generals Sanborn and Pleasanton rode up to the crest of the east mound, the former unattended save perhaps by some orderlies. General Sanborn complained of having no staff with him to communicate his orders. Our services were offered to General Pleasanton, who requested us to report to General Sanborn. We acted as Aids in the skirmish at the Ford and in the bottom beyond, where the 2d Arkansas Cavalry (Colonel Phelps' and Captain Kingsbury's Col. Battalion) charged the enemy's guns which were shelling our advance. They were routed after a most desperate effort to maintain their position. It was at this time I knew of your presence. Colonels Philips' and Gravelly's brigades, were advancing in column in pursuit of the enemy whose rear had rapidly fallen back towards Fort Scott, which it was evident was the goal of Price's efforts. With these troops I and other officers of General Curtis' staff moved for about three miles or more. Amongst these officers were Colonel S. J. Crawford, 2nd Colored

Volunteers, Colonel C. W. Blair, 14th Kansas Volunteer Cavalry, Major Weed of General Curtis' and Captain Hinton of General Blunt's staff, whose division was in the rear. Not a general officer nor one of the staff officers other than those named were with these advanced brigades. Both Philips' and Gravelly's brigades advanced as quick as possible, and in good order, until within one thousand yards or less of the enemy, who had massed their best troops—not less than 15,000 strong—from four to six lines deep in our front, north of Mine Creek, and then opened upon us with seven or eight guns, when they checked our further progress. A portion of our centre seemed to waver and become disorganized. Our artillery was in the rear. Colonel Crawford and other staff officers suggested that less disaster would occur to us by charging than by receiving the enemy's fire. You were coming up on the left of our line and facing the enemy's right. I rode towards you, and in the name of General Curtis ordered you to form and charge the enemy; this you promptly responded to, and though your brigade was the last of the three, it was the first to charge, the other brigades following in the right, breaking their lines completely, and pursuing them energetically across the creek. Your command neither faltered nor fell back, and only gave up pursuit when an order from General Pleasanton, directing a halt, was received, which order did not arrive until after our guns had shelled your troops. There was difficulty in getting some of the Missouri State Militia to charge, as they were exposed to a terrible fire of musketry and artillery, and it is my conviction had it not been for the presence of your veteran troops, and their cheers, which inspired the whole line, that we would at last have received a temporary check, whereas a brilliant and glorious victory was achieved. I do not say this in disparagement of Missouri troops (under other officers) who deserve great credit—whose courage and bravery cannot be doubted, especially those under Gravelly, who signally proved their heroism in the night attack on the mound. The battle at Mine Creek was participated in by an addition to your own and other brigades—the battalion of Colorado Volunteers, and one hundred and sixty men of Major Hopkins' 2d Kansas Cavalry, Captain Gove of the 11th Kansas Volunteer Cavalry, which were sent to the front by General Curtis immediately after the engagement near the Trading Post, under the command of Colonel Cloud, 2d Kansas Volunteer Cavalry, and Aid-de-Camp. The charge of Mine Creek was directed by Major-General Curtis through his staff officers, Colonels Crawford, Blair, Cloud, Volunteer Aid-de-Camp, Major Weed and Captain Hinton, Aid-de-Camp of General Blunt's staff, who charged with the extreme left of your brigade through the corn field, and endeavored to attack the enemy as he was emerging in disorder from the timber south of the corn field, which effort was defeated by the shell from our own guns. These officers personally assisted in executing the orders they gave. Neither General Pleasanton nor General Sanborn, nor were any of the proper staff there until after the gallant charge, and the successful breaking of the enemy's lines. In the subsequent operations of that day, so far as your brigade came under my observation, it was always with or in the advance, and doing as good work as in the morning. When, owing to General Pleasanton abandoning the pursuit—during the engagement at Charlot—General Curtis with a portion of his staff moved to Fort Scott, whither Sanborn, Philips and McFerren were marching by General Pleasanton's order, owing to which General McNeil was left alone to cope with the enemy, General Blunt's division having been unavoidably thrown to the rear, so far as to render it unavailable at the time, your command moved to General McNeil's assistance, and until after dark with him you fought the enemy. Here again it is stated by Colonel Crawford and Major McKenny, Inspector-General and Aid-de-Camp of General Curtis' staff, and Captain Hinton, who were at the front with General McNeil's brigade, that your command rendered essential service in checking the flanking movements of the enemy, and jointly advancing against their entire army. Throughout the remainder of the pursuit I can say that your command, officers and men alike, showed the same energy, courage, devotion and judgment which marked its conduct during October 25th. In saying what I have, I do not mean to cast any reflections upon the courage of any portion of the Missouri State Militia, or to criticise the action of any of its officers; on the contrary, they deserve the plaudits of their country.

The people of Kansas, soldiers and citizens alike, owe and acknowledge the gratitude due them, which will not be forgotten; but in compliance with your wish, I cannot refuse to state what I know as to the conduct of your brigade. I have sought to do this moderately and correctly, and believing the foregoing is the exact truth, as to what transpired and came under my observation, you are at liberty to use this as you desire.

Regretting most sincerely the unfortunate and unprofitable controversy which I fear will yet sully the fair fame and good repute won so hardly, and to be borne so proudly, by all who participated in the memorable campaign of the Army of the Border,

I am, much respected sir, yours,

(Signed) R. H. HUNT.

Major 15th K. V. C., and Chief of Artillery, Dept. of Kansas.

R.

www.ingramcontent.com/pod-product-compliance
Lightning Source LLC
Chambersburg PA
CBHW020239240426
43672CB00006B/580